Flexibilisation and Mod
the Turkish Labour Mark y

Flexibilisation and Modernisation of the Turkish Labour Market

Editor: Roger Blanpain

Guest Editors: Frans Pennings and Nurhan Süral

Contributors
Toker Dereli
Peter Donders
Frank Hendrickx
Frans Pennings
Karin Sengers
Nurhan Süral
Martijn van Velzen
Peter van der Valk
Ton Wilthagen

This project was financed within the framework of the Matra Pre-accession Projects Programme, financed by the Netherlands Ministry of Foreign Affairs.

KLUWER LAW
INTERNATIONAL

A C.I.P Catalogue record for this book is available from the Library of Congress.

ISBN 90-411-2490-X

Published by Kluwer Law International,
P.O. Box 316, 2400 AH Alphen aan den Rijn, The Netherlands
sales@kluwerlaw.com
http://www.kluwerlaw.com

Sold and distributed in North, Central and South America by
Aspen Publishers, Inc.,
7201 McKinney Circle, Frederick, MD 21704, USA

Sold and distributed in all other countries by
Turpin Distribution Services Ltd.,
Stratton Business Park,
Pegasus Drive, Biggleswade,
Bedfordshire SG18 8TQ, United Kingdom

CONTENTS

PREFACE

'Flexibilisation and Modernisation of the Turkish Labour Market' – many readers will be puzzled by this title. Isn't the Turkish labour market already very flexible? The confusion is understandable: Turkey has a large informal labour market and it is indeed very flexible. Labour law requirements which might interfere with the matching of supply and demand are simply evaded. This project is, however, concerned with the formal labour market, where – as in many Western countries – the issue of flexibility has become a key factor in the drive to increase competitiveness and employment.

Another dimension of the flexibibility discourse is the implementation of the *acquis communautaire*. The *acquis* requires Turkey to increase workforce adaptability, to reorient social security instruments in order to promote reintegration into work, and to promote employment. Several instruments give guidance on allowing flexible forms of work and for providing security for the affected workers. Consequently, Turkey has two reasons to be interested in flexibility: to increase national competitiveness and to implement the *acquis communautaire*.

The aim of this project is to provide support to the Turkish Ministry of Labour and Social Security in its efforts to implement the acquis and to consider whether further steps to increase the flexibilisation and modernisation of the labour market should be taken. To fully address this aim, the informal market has to be taken into account, along with the social protection of flexible workers, in order to prevent workers from becoming worse off as a result of flexibilisation.

Thus, before we could provide an adequate analysis and recommendations, the project required a thorough study of the formal and informal labour market as well as the role of labour market institutions, social partners and social protection. Our analyses and recommendations were presented in several reports which contained so much information, that we thought it worthwhile to present the contents to a wider audience. The result is this book. The texts underlying the various chapters were completed at different dates throughout the two-year term of the project. The information underlying the various chapters was revised only where developments had an substantial impact on the contents of the chapter concerned, with a final deadline of the end of October 2005.

This project was initiated within the framework of the Matra Pre-accession Projects Programme, financed by the Netherlands Ministry of Foreign Affairs. This programme aims to assist the candidate Member States in meeting the criteria for EU

Pennings, *Flexibilisation and Modernisation of the Turkish Labour Market*, xi–xii

membership, through bilateral co-operative projects focusing on the consequences of the implementation of European legislation. Furthermore, the programme aims to establish sustainable working relationships between governmental institutions in the Netherlands and in the recipient countries. This project was monitored by the Agency for International Business and Cooperation (EVD), part of the Dutch Ministry of Economic Affairs.

The fourteen experts participating in this project worked in three teams: Tilburg University (the Netherlands), BMT consultants (Utrecht, the Netherlands) and the Dutch Ministry of Social Affairs and Employment. The team was supplemented by two Dutch social partner representatives: Willem Plessen of Randstad Holding and Han Westerhof, of FNV Bondgenoten, who participated in a workshop in Ankara. Essential support was given by Professor Toker Dereli, of Işık University, Istanbul.

The Turkish Ministry of Labour Law and Social Security was the host for our many visits and workshops. Mr Cengiz Delibaş, Director General, and his team cooperated fully and were always prepared to take account of our suggestions and recommendations. We also would like to thank Mr Şahabettin Akşahin, who took care of all organisational matters and more than that, and Ms Nedret Durutan for her support. A number of affiliated institutions, including İş-Kur, SSK and SGK, were active in the project and participated in all discussions.

An essential role in the discussion on flexible work was played by the Turkish social partners. We would like to also thank them for their comments on our papers.

We are grateful to Audrey MacDougall from the University of Edinburgh who made an indispensable contribution to this book by editing the text and through her suggestions for clarifications and additions.

Tilburg/Ankara, December 2005

Frans Pennings
Nurhan Süral

f.j.l.pennings@uvt.nl
sural@metu.edu.tr

LIST OF CONTRIBUTORS

Toker Dereli	Professor at Işık University, Istanbul
Peter Donders	Director of BMT Consultants
Frank Hendrickx	Associate professor at Tilburg and Leuven University
Frans Pennings	Professor at Tilburg University and Utrecht University
Karin Sengers	Consultant at BMT Consultants
Nurhan Süral	Associate professor at Middle East Technical University, Ankara
Peter van der Valk	Self-employed consultant
Martijn van Velzen	Research fellow at Tilburg University
Ton Wilthagen	Professor at Tilburg University

LIST OF ABBREVIATIONS

Bağ-Kur	Social Insurances Institution for the Self-Employed
CEEP	European Centre of Enterprises with Public Participation and of Enterprises of General Economic Interest
DISK	Confederation of Progressive Trade Unions of Turkey
ECR	European Court Reports
EES	European Employment Strategy
ETUC	European Trade Union Confederation
EU	European Union
FNV	Federatie Nederlandse Vakverenigingen
FSWW	Foundation for the Support of Women
Hak-Iş	Confederation of Righteous Trade Unions
IIBK	Public Employment Services Organisation
ILO	International Labour Organisation
OJ	Official Journal of the EC
Iş–Kur	Employment Organisation of Turkey
MISK	Confederation of Nationalist Workers
NGO	Non-Governmental Organisation
SMEs	small and medium sized enterprises
SSK	Social Insurances Institution
TESK	Confederation of Turkish trades- and craftsmen
Tisk	Turkish Confederation of Employers Association
Türk-Iş	Confederation of Turkish Trade Unions
UNICE	Union of Industrial and Employers' Confederations of Europe.
YTL	new Turkish lira

1. INTRODUCTION

Frans Pennings and Nurhan Süral

1.1 GENERAL

Turkey is a young State which has experienced a fairly turbulent history so far. This history is narrowly connected with labour market and labour law developments. The country has now reached a new turning point, as it prepares itself for accession to the European Union. This means implementation of the *acquis communautaire*, requiring Turkey, to amongst other things increase the adaptability of the workforce, to reorient social security instruments in order to promote reintegration into work and to promote increasing employment. Apart from the adjustments required by accession, a modernisation of the labour market is necessary to be better equipped for competition with other countries, notably with EU Member States.[1]

In this chapter we will describe the context of the flexibility debate. In Section 1.2 we describe our approach towards flexibility, Section 1.3 is focused on the historical background of present Turkish labour law, while Section 1.4 provides an introduction to the main actors involved in the labour market in Turkey. The final section, Section 1.5, discusses this project's progress.

1.2 THE RELEVANCE OF THE FLEXIBILISATION PROCESS

Flexibility is a very broad term and anyone not familiar with the debate may fear that it means a total relaxation of employment rules and regulations in favour of employers. This interpretation of the term is, of course, not very productive and indeed is not used in any EU Member State. Flexibilisation refers to a process of examining employment rules and regulations to establish if they are overly restrictive and if their abolition would lead to a better adjustment of labour supply and demand. If employers can only employ full-time permanent workers, they may lack

---

1 We are aware that since the Labour Act has been modernised recently, some Turkish readers are sensitive to the term 'modernisation'. However, modernisation is a continuous process in all modern economies. The process of reforming the economy and the labour market will never be completed.

the flexibility to deal with the peaks and troughs of demand. However, they may also be unwilling to run the risk of overstaffing on a permanent basis.

Over the last ten years, flexible forms of work have become increasingly familiar in the Member States of the European Union. Behind it is an effort to increase the adaptability of the work force to the demands of the labour market. This is taking place with a view to increasing employment and thus reducing poverty and social exclusion by improving competitiveness. Flexible work is also known as atypical work. In a recent paper by the European Commission it is defined as follows: 'Atypical work is a type of work that is performed by what is often referred to as the flexible workforce. This is a large and growing group of workers, most of whom are women (over eighty per cent of the flexible workforce). Examples of atypical workers include part-timers (twenty-one million people in the EU), those on fixed-term contracts (fourteen million), home workers (ten million), and those in a large number of other arrangements, such as seasonal work, casual work, telework, family work, or self-employment. The main common characteristic of all such groups is that their working arrangements differ from those of the 'typical employee' (an imaginary person working full-time on an indefinite contract).'[2] In various official documents, the European Commission has outlined its view on flexibility within the wider context of adaptability,[3] stating that the use of atypical work or flexible work can contribute to employment policies.

The European Commission argues that the capacity of firms and their workers to manage change in a positive way is one of the keys to ensuring the success of future employment policies. It will depend on achieving a balance between flexibility and security in the labour market. In addition to the regulatory framework implemented by governments, negotiation between social partners has a key role to play in managing such change. Flexibility should continue to be encouraged, in particular where it involves the availability of different contractual or working time arrangements. At the same time, steps should be taken to prevent segmentation of the labour market into different types of workers and to facilitate the transition between different forms of work. The Commission encourages widespread encouragement of initiatives to modernise the organisation of work and improve internal flexibility within firms.[4]

The issue of flexibility is not simply a Member State matter. It has increasingly attracted the attention of the European Union, resulting in a number of policy initiatives. The regulation of flexible forms of work at the European level may

2 'Atypical Work in the EU'. Working Paper, SOCI 106 EN, 3–2000, p. 29.

3 Communication from the Commission to the Council, the European Parliament, the Economic and Social Committee and the Committee of the Regions, *Taking Stock of Five Years of the European Employment Strategy*, Brussels, 17 July 2002, COM(2002) 416 final, p. 15.

4 Communication from the Commission to the Council, the European Parliament, the Economic and Social Committee and the Committee of the Regions, *A Strategy for Full Employment and Better Jobs for All*, Brussels, 14.1.2003, COM(2003) 6 final, p. 15.

improve the position of flexible workers and introduce flexibility and a-typical work into European employment policies.

From this it follows that increasing flexibility is crucial to increasing employment. For this reason, the European Union is in favour of creating greater labour market flexibility. Although it is difficult to measure the impact of flexibility on the growth of employment – various other factors, such as the changes in the economy, also contribute – flexibility is an important factor. A very important indication of the effect of flexible work can be seen in the activities of agencies that provide temporary work: when an economy starts to improve these agencies experience an increased demand for temporary workers, since during the initial stage of economic recovery employers will not yet recruit permanent employees. For this reason, economists wishing to identify the early stages of economic recovery use the economic figures of temporary work agencies to provide initial information. As the recovery progresses employers often recruit temporary workers as their own permanent employees.

There are several dimensions to the process of flexibilisation. In a system with rigid labour laws, employers will always look for opportunities to evade the rules. The informal labour market will thus grow and/or new forms of employment will be created which avoid the statutory rules. Since such developments may lead to unfair competition this is an undesirable side effect. Moreover, workers in the informal market and those working in new and flexible forms of employment (such as self-employed persons or on-call workers) tend to have little legal protection. Overly rigid labour law may lead to such a division of labour markets, whereas flexibilisation can draw these informal workers into the formal market and improve their legal position although this may be offset by a slight reduction in the legal protection of permanent workers. In other words, flexibilisation may mean a redistribution of rights which may, within certain limits and under certain conditions, lead to greater fairness.

Regardless of the position of labour law, flexible workers exist in every economy. A strong legal distinction between permanent full-time workers and flexible workers often disadvantages women, who are more likely to work in the flexible jobs. The EU takes the view that if such labour legislation makes flexible jobs unattractive for women in particular, there is indirect discrimination on grounds of sex, which is forbidden unless an objective justification can be found.

In principle flexibilisation does not require specific forms of flexible work, but requires a review of the rigidity of existing labour law to ascertain if it is preventing the creation of employment. However, flexibilisation has to be subject to some restriction. For instance, employers should be forbidden to offer a worker a series of fixed-term contracts in order to avoid the legislation covering permanent workers.

Another dimension of the flexibility debate is that flexible workers should be socially protected. For example, they should be able to acquire adequate old age and disability pension rights. The EU adopts the principle of equal treatment of flexible workers and full-time workers in permanent employment.

Flexibilisation requires the establishment of a balance between the needs of employers and employees resulting in possible 'flexicurity' solutions. Achieving such a balance requires mutual trust between the social partners: hence social dialogue has been given considerable consideration in this project.

Alongside this more theoretical approach we will consider EU instruments which focus on specific aspects of the flexible labour market, such as employment contracts for a definite period. We will discuss these instruments in Chapter 5 and will compare them with Turkish labour law.

Given the importance of flexibilisation and in order to analyse whether the *acquis* on flexibilisation has been implemented correctly and whether further improvements can be made, Turkish labour law will have to be closely examined. This will be done in the subsequent chapters.

1.3 THE HISTORICAL BACKGROUND TO THE FLEXIBILITY DISCUSSION

1.3.1 A Very Short Overview of the Developments up to the 1990s

Shortly after the Turkish Republic was established in 1923, the Constitution of 1924 recognised the right of association, a right which formed the basis for trade unions. However, this freedom did not last very long: the Restoration of Peace Act of 1925 forbade the establishment of trade unions. The Associations Act of 1938 prohibited the formation of class-based organisations, a prohibition which was to continue until 1947. The new Republic adopted the 1926 Civil Code, which was largely based on the Swiss legal system. Hence the basis for the regulation of labour contracts lies in the Western tradition as the Swiss code is based on the French Napoleonic Code.

When peace returned, the one-party regime did not encourage the development of associations and particularly not labour unions, despite the liberal provisions of the Constitution and the Civil Code. In 1936, the Labour Act, whose coverage was limited to manual workers and establishments with ten or more workers, was adopted. In 1952, its coverage was extended to establishments employing four to nine workers in cities with at least 50,000 inhabitants. This Labour Act remained effective until the 1960s. As in the past, relations with white-collar employees were regulated by the provisions of the Obligations Act, which was an adjunct to the Civil Code of 1926.

Turkey became a member of the International Labour Organisation (ILO) in 1932. In 1951 it ratified ILO Convention 98 (1949) on the Right to Organise and Collective Bargaining, although until 1961 trade unions still did not have the right to collective bargaining or the right to strike. During the 1950s and 1960s the governing political parties encouraged the large-scale organisation of the working class through centralised trade unionism as a means of influencing the political orientation of the workers. The Confederation of Turkish Trade Unions (Türk-Iş) was founded in July 1952.

The military takeover of 27 May 1960 brought vital institutional changes. The 1961 Constitution, which set forth a legislative framework favourable to the growth of trade unions, was an important milestone in the history of labour relations. Among the social provisions introduced were the right to unionisation, to collective bargaining, and to strike. The 1961 Constitution led to a new Labour Act, Unions Act and the Collective Labour Agreements, Strikes and Lockouts Act. We could say that modern unionisation started with the 1961 Constitution.

A significant development occurred in 1967 with the foundation of DISK, the Confederation of Progressive Trade Unions. It was established by four major trade unions: the Metalworkers' Union, the Rubber Workers' Union, the Press Workers' Union and the Chemical Industries Workers' Union which broke away from Türk-Iş. MISK, the Confederation of Nationalist Workers, was founded in 1970 and Hak-Iş was founded in 1977. Türk-Iş and DISK remained the two major confederations until 1980.

The late 1970s were witness to a wave of terrorism, which created a climate unfavourable to the exercise of union rights. On 12 September 1980 a military takeover took place. For reasons of public order and general security, the military authorities suspended the activities of DISK, MISK, and their affiliated unions and froze their assets. In addition, the main trade union rights, including the right of collective bargaining and the right to strike, were suspended. MISK was reactivated in May 1984 and the Military Court of Appeals exonerated DISK in July 1991.

Subsequently, the Act respecting the Re-entry into Force of Expired Collective Labour Agreements in Cases of Social Necessity was issued in December 1982. This Act brought a system of compulsory arbitration for the renewal of expired collective agreements and the settlement of interpretation disputes. This system was not intended to replace a free collective bargaining system. The Act was designed as a form of appeal in exceptional circumstances defined as the suspension of union activities and/or the suspension or prohibition of industrial action. The duties conferred upon the Supreme Arbitration Board through this Act remained effective until 6 December 1983, the date on which the National Assembly met and assumed its duties following the first general elections after the military takeover.

Following adoption through a referendum on 7 November 1982, a new Constitution was published in the *Official Gazette* of 20 November 1982. Compared with the 1961 Constitution, the 1982 Constitution was relatively detailed, restrictive and prohibitive in character where it concerned the constitutional provisions on collective labour relations. The union-related provisions of the 1982 Constitution were amended in July 1995 and October 2001 together with some other provisions to achieve democratisation.[5] Article 52, which restricted the political activities of

5 *Official Gazette* 26 July 1995 and 17 October 2001.

unions, was abrogated and a paragraph was added to article 53 to clarify public officials' rights to unionise and collective bargaining.

1.3.2 Preparation for Accession

The Council Summit in Helsinki in December 1999 decided that Turkey could apply for accession to the EU on the basis of the same criteria applied to the other applicant countries and noted that it would also benefit from a pre-accession strategy. The general objective of such a strategy is to offer a coherent programme for preparing Turkey for membership of the European Union. The objective of the partnership for accession is to register the following within a single legal framework: the working priorities identified in the Commission's 2000 report on Turkey's progress towards accession, the financial resources available to implement these priorities and the conditions which apply to this aid. In accordance with the Conclusions of the Council on 16/17 December 2004, accession negotiations with Turkey started on 3 October 2005.

Turkey is currently adopting the Community *acquis* in stages. The implementation approach is set out in the following documents, some of which will be referred to further on in this book:

- The Association Agreement between the European Community and Turkey (1963) and the 1970 Additional Protocol
- The Commission's communication on a European strategy for Turkey (4 March 1998)
- The Commission's Regular Reports on Turkey's progress towards accession
- The Council Decision of 8 March 2001 on the principles, priorities, intermediate objectives and conditions contained in the Accession Partnership with Turkey
- The National Programme for the Adoption of the Community *acquis*,[6] the revised version of the National Programme for the Adoption of the *Acquis* (NPAA) and the Decision on the Implementation and Coordination and Monitoring of the NPAA.[7]

Attempts by Turkey to implement the EU *acquis* were the driving forces behind the evolution of labour issues in the 1990s and early 2000s.

In June 2001, the Ministry of Labour and Social Security formed a tripartite commission composed of nine university professors: three appointed by the Government, three by the Turkish Confederation of Employers Association (Tisk)

---

6 *Official Gazette* dated 24 March 2001, no. 24352 *bis*.
7 *Official Gazette* dated 24 July 2003, no. 25178 *bis*.

and one by each of the three labour confederations (Türk-Iş, Hak-Iş and DISK). This commission had the task of preparing a new Labour Act. The bill, completed in June 2002 constituted a drive towards flexibility in line with the Community *acquis*. The Commission adopted an active role by providing a degree of protection for atypical employment and looking favourably on the extension and relaxation of certain legal provisions[8] beyond that required by a minimalist interpretation of the rules to be implemented. Although the social partners initially promised to respect the resulting text, in practice they lobbied intensely for change throughout the period the bill was discussed in Parliament. As a result, the provisions on subcontracting and atypical types of employment, regarded as insecure and precarious, were revised in the unions' favour. At the same time increased job security was confined to workplaces employing thirty or more workers and the level of compensation in cases of unfair dismissal was lowered to the advantage of employers. As a result, the initially proposed degree of flexibility could not be maintained in the final bill. With regard to flexibilisation issues employers were left disappointed.

The resulting legislation became the Labour Act.[9] The main issues regulated by the Labour Act are as follows: form, types, content and termination of labour contracts including individual labour contracts, employment contracts and service contracts; the reciprocal rights and duties of the worker and the employer during the course of the labour relationship; and individual labour disputes and their settlement. The Act was introduced in order to promote the growth of employment. Flexitime and flexible modalities of employment regulated on the basis of relevant Community directives via this new Labour Act were envisaged as the means whereby this objective was to be realised.

The introduction of an unemployment insurance scheme in 1999, plus the revision of pensionable ages for men and women in the same year, the passage of Public Officials' Unions Act No. 4688 in 2001 and the adoption of Act No. 4904 in 2003 on the Employment Organisation of Turkey (İş-Kur) were some of the recent major legislative developments.

One of the main problems is that of unemployment. This is at the root of many industrial relation problems. The size of the informal economy (which has featured prominently in recent debates) stands out as another significant problem,

---

8 New provisions on flexibility and atypical types of employment largely drew on Council Directive 93/104/EC, of 23 November 1993, concerning certain aspects of the organisation of working time as amended by Directive 2000/34/EC of June 2000 of the European Parliament and of the Council, Council Directive 94/33/EC of June 1994 on the protection of young people at work, Council Directive 97/81/EC of 15 December 1997 concerning the Framework Agreement on part-time working concluded by UNICE, CEEP and the ETUC as amended by Council Directive 98/23/EC of 7 April 1998, and Council Directive 99/70/EC of 28 June 1999 concerning the framework agreement on fixed-term work concluded by ETUC, UNICE and CEEP. The ETUC-UNICE-CEEP framework agreements try to give priority to achieving a better balance between flexibility in working time and security for workers.

9 Law no. 4857 of 22 May 2003, *Official Gazette* 10 June 2003.

for though there is no legal impediment to unionisation in informal employment, union penetration is virtually impossible in this sector.

1.4 AN INTRODUCTION TO THE MAIN INSTRUMENTS AND ACTORS

1.4.1 The Main Statutory Instruments

At present, the major labour legislation in Turkey includes the following statutes: the Labour Act; the Maritime Labour Act; the Act concerning Labour-Management Relations in the Press (Press LA); the Unions Act; the Collective Agreements, Strikes and Lock-Outs Act; Public Officials' Unions Act; the Social Insurances Act; and the Labour Courts Act. There are also several Acts of a more general nature which are relevant to labour relations: the Associations Act of 2004, the Civil Code of 2001 and the Obligations Code of 1926,[10] and the Civil Procedural Act. Other laws concern specific issues, including the National Holiday and General Vacations Act, Weekly Rest Periods Act, the Act on Noon Rest Periods and the Act on the Employment Organisation of Turkey (İş-Kur). Although İş-Kur has been established as an independent entity with financial and administrative autonomy, the Act links it in general terms to the Ministry of Labour.

The Council of Ministers may issue regulations governing the mode of implementation of laws or designating matters ordered by law, provided that they do not conflict with existing laws and are examined by the Council of State (high administrative court). Regulations are signed by the President of the Republic and published in the *Official Gazette*. The Prime Ministry, the ministries, and public corporate bodies may issue by-laws to ensure the application of laws and regulations relating to their particular fields of operation, provided that they are not contrary to existing laws and regulations.

Labour legislation may require that by-laws be made to provide for detailed clarification of certain issues. For example, the Labour Act has general provisions on occupational health and safety on the basis of which the Health and Safety By-law of Workers with a Fixed Duration Employment Relationship or a Temporary Employment Relationship has been issued by the Ministry of Labour and Social Security.

10 The new Civil Code (Act no. 4721, *Official Gazette* of 8 December 2001) replaced and abrogated the 1926 Code. The Obligations Code of 1926 is still in effect but a bill has been introduced for a new Obligations Code.

1.4.2 The Organisation of the Actors within the Labour Market

The role of the Ministry of Labour and Social Security is to encourage co-ordination measures for maintaining industrial peace and settlement procedures for the benefit of the country, to improve the productivity of the work force and to and implement measures to provide for full employment and adequate social security. The Ministry is headed by a Minister and a Deputy Minister. In the central organisation of the Ministry there are various General Directorates with well-articulated functions including the General Directorate of Labour, the General Directorate of the Social Security Organisation, the General Directorate of Labour Affairs Abroad and the General Directorate of Workers' Health.

The Ministry of Labour and Social Security may set up regional directorates wherever it deems necessary within budgetary constraints. Each regional directorate is in charge of fulfilling the tasks assigned to it in a certain province or several provinces. The tasks of the regional directorate include those functions prescribed by other pieces of labour legislation, as well as the functions directly imputed to the Ministry by Act No. 3146. Regional directorates are not autonomous units; they are merely adjuncts of the Ministry, subject to its orders and supervision.

The Social Security Institution (*Sosyal Güvenlik Kurumu*), established on 6 August 2003, has financial autonomy. It is an affiliated institution of the Ministry of Labour and Social Security.[11] Other institutions attached to the Social Security Institution are:

- the Social Insurances Institution (SSK)
- the Social Insurances Institution for the Self-Employed (Bağ-Kur)
- the Turkish Employment Organisation (İş-Kur).

The Social Insurance Institution is in charge of the application of social security legislation to insured employees.

Because the inspection of working conditions concerns public order and the nation's health, the State has the obligation and the right to undertake supervision and inspection in establishments to ensure that labour legislation is properly enforced.[12] ILO Convention 81 which was ratified by Turkey by Act No. 5690 requires the fulfilment of the inspection function by a central organ. This function has been assigned to the Ministry of Labour, amongst others. The actual inspection of workplaces is performed by labour inspectors who are officials attached to the regional directorates of labour. Labour inspectors supervise and inspect not only the workplaces subject to the general Labour Act, but also those undertakings covered by the Maritime Labour Act (article 49) and the Press Labour Act (article 24). In order to supervise the implementation of by-laws and regulations, the Ministry of

---

11 Art. 1, Social Security Institution Organisational Act, Act no. 4947, *Official Gazette* 24 July 2003.

12 Art. 91, Labour Act.

Labour and Social Security may also employ experts such as engineers, medical doctors and chemists acting as labour inspectors. Alongside the inspectors employed by other public bodies, these experts must report to the Ministry of Labour and Social Security on the results of their inspections and any remedial measures.

In Turkey, the employment service was organised as a state monopoly until 2003. Despite the variety of functions conferred on the previous Public Employment Services Organisation (IIBK), most IIBK activities had centred on providing jobs for the unemployed within the country and on regulating the flow of Turkish workers to foreign countries. Special regulations required the public sector to recruit workers through the IIBK, and employers in both the private and public sectors were under an obligation to hire a certain number of disabled persons and ex-convicts.

With the expansion of the Turkish economy in the early 1980s and coupled with the growing demand for more efficient utilisation of human resources and flexible work arrangements, it became obvious in Turkey that employment services had to be overhauled. As temporary and part-time work and subcontracted labour has become more commonplace in Turkey in recent years, it has become clear that employment services have to be liberalised and the operation of fee-charging private placement agencies permitted. Some private consulting firms had already circumvented the existing legal restrictions, particularly where the search for and placement of executives and skilled employees were concerned. The IIBK, whose activities were centred mainly on the public sector, appeared ill-equipped to tackle the problems of today's markets, particularly in respect of the trends towards privatisation which would eventually lead to the contraction of employment in the public sector. Efforts were undertaken by the IIBK to restructure and reorganise its activities while also permitting the operation of private employment agencies under its supervision and licensing. Having various labour market mediators was believed to function better than having one monopolised solely by the State. New legislation to improve the structure and functions of the organisation under the new name İş-Kur and to amend the relevant articles of the Labour Act while also issuing a new by-law on the licensing and inspection requirements of the private employment agencies became an urgent matter. However, due to procedural difficulties, enactment of the İş-Kur Act was delayed until 2003.

In addition to its employment services, İş-Kur is also in charge of administering the unemployment insurance scheme and as such is linked to the Social Security Organisation of the Ministry of Labour and Social Security.

1.5 THE PROJECT'S PROGRESS

In this project we investigated ways of assisting the Turkish government to introduce greater flexibility to the labour market and to modernise the labour market. Our research was undertaken during 2004 and 2005 at the request of the Turkish Government, whose stated aim was to increase the flexibilisation of the formal labour market. This project was made possible by a MATRA subsidy.

Each of the reports were presented to workshops during the two years the project lasted and were discussed with Government officials, civil servants, social partners and representatives of the labour market and social security institutions. These discussions and the feedback received were used to finalise the report.

In addition we made extensive use of local experts who through a series of very useful reports helped us understand the local context.

The project started by analysing the flexibility clauses of the new Turkish Labour Act with a view to assessing its consistency with the *acquis* as described in Chapter 5. In order to come up with alternative solutions we did not restrict our analysis to EU law, but compared Turkish solutions with those of EU Member States. This also offers an important comparative dimension, which is important as the role and speed of the flexibilisation process may differ from country to country and could impact on the decisions of the Turkish Government in relation to flexibilisation.

We did not limit ourselves to a study of labour law, but also considered its context: the labour market. For this purpose we undertook an analysis of the labour market, focusing on the relationship between the formal and informal labour market as set out in Chapter 2. The informal labour market is, of course, extremely relevant to the topic of flexibilisation, since in that market flexibility is at an optimum. However, since the informal market leads to unfair competition (not only with enterprises working in the formal labour market in Turkey, but also those within the EU Member States), the scale of the informal market must shrink, whereas the formal market has to become more flexible.

The attitude of the relevant labour market actors (employers, employees, government, public institutions) is very important for flexibilisation to be instigated. For this reason we examined the public institutions (to be dealt with in Chapter 3), and the social partners (to be dealt with in Chapter 4) and their attitude towards the flexibility debate.

Flexibility without adequate social protection will lead to unacceptable results and will hinder the implementation of the flexibility rules; therefore the link between flexibility and social security is of the utmost importance. We analyse this link in Chapter 6.

Chapter 7 outlines models of flexibilisation and the relationship between flexibility and security ('flexicurity') adopted by other countries. This chapter demonstrates that the debate surrounding flexibility and how to implement it are ongoing issues subject to further development.

Under the impact of transition dynamics and the EU integration process, the potential of Turkey's labour market became a much debated issue. This study tries to provide a factual and descriptive analysis of the flexibilisation of the formal labour markets with a view to helping to elucidate the current period of transitional change. Moreover, the authors try to make the reader aware of the considerable gaps in our understanding of working life in Turkey by addressing the impact of important interacting issues.

2. FLEXIBILISATION AND THE FORMAL AND INFORMAL LABOUR MARKETS

Toker Dereli, Karin Sengers and Peter Donders

2.1 INTRODUCTION

In this chapter we describe the present situation of the Turkish labour market from the perspective of flexibilisation. It will, therefore, not be a complete picture of the labour market. We based our work on EU reports,[1] an İş-Kur report[2] and on interviews with institutions, social partners and NGOs in Ankara and Istanbul.

Before describing the labour market, we will give (in Section 2.2) a description of European policy with regard to employment. This is relevant since the flexibilisation and reform processes in Turkey have generally been instigated by preparation for accession to the EU.

In Section 2.3 the Turkish labour market situation is described. Facts and figures are given and then a reflection on the main topics relating to the flexibilisation of the labour market:

- the informal labour market
- the position of women
- sectoral differences and subcontracting
- flexibilisation measures

The situation of the Turkish labour market will be described in relation to each of these topics and analysed against the background of the current Employment Guidelines set by the European Union. The chapter ends with conclusions and recommendations.

---

1 *2003 Regular Report on Turkey's Progress towards Accession*, November 2003.

2 Insan Tunali, *Background Study on the Labour Market and Employment in Turkey*, June 2003.

2.2 THE TURKISH LABOUR MARKET AND THE *ACQUIS COMUNAUTAIRE*

2.2.1 A View on the *Acquis*: the Employment Guidelines

As stated in the EC Treaty, one of the objectives of the Union is to reach a high level of employment.[3] In order to achieve this objective, Title VIII of the Treaty commits the Member States to a coordinated employment strategy. This strategy cannot be seen separately from the guidelines of the Economic and Monetary Union. Articles 126 and 128(3) require the Employment Guidelines to be in line with the global guidelines of the Economic and Monetary Union mentioned in Article 99 of the Treaty. Article 128 mentions that each year the Council evaluates the employment situation in the Union on the basis of annual reports from each Member State. In this report each Member State has to describe the measures it has taken in order to implement the guidelines. These national reports are first discussed in the Permanent Committee on Employment of the EU. This Committee asks advice from the social partners and advises the European Commission and the Council. Subsequently, the guidelines are adapted on the basis of the results of the national reports and the debates in the Council. The final result is presented to the European Council.

While the Employment Guidelines are not legislation in the strict sense of the word, they exert considerable pressure on the Member States, as they are linked to the criteria of the Economic Monetary Union. Many Member States, for instance, have had to take measures to prevent social assistance schemes interfering negatively with employment policies.

In line with the Lisbon strategy, the new European Employment Guidelines adopted by the Council in 2003 have set three objectives:

- Full employment
- Quality and productivity at work
- Strengthened social cohesion and inclusion.

These three main objectives are elaborated in ten specific guidelines on employment policies, including improvement in the governance of employment policies. Several reports make it clear, however, that, although progress on the European labour market has been made, this growth will not be enough to reach the Lisbon objective of an overall employment rate of seventy per cent.[4]

The proposal of the European Commission for the Employment Guidelines of 2004 includes for the first time the employment policies of an enlarged EU. The Commission states that changing the Employment Guidelines as presented in 2003

3 Article 2.

4 *Communication from the Commission on Guidelines for the Employment Policies of the Member States*, Com(2004)239 final.

is not helpful as implementation of the guidelines via Member State policies and intensive monitoring of the reforms undertaken by the Member States needs to be given further emphasis. The European Commission consequently confirmed in its proposals for the 2004 Employment Guidelines the four key areas for action which were previously identified by the Employment Taskforce chaired by the former Prime Minister of the Netherlands, Wim Kok:[5]

- increasing adaptability of workers and enterprises
- attracting more people to the labour market and making work a real option for all
- investing more effectively in human capital
- ensuring effective implementation of reforms through better governance.

This was tantamount to the Commission proposing to maintain the guidelines of 2003.

In the Council Decision of 22 July 2003 the Council presented ten guidelines,[6] of which five directly refer to flexibility of the labour market and combating undeclared work, i.e.:

- Guideline 2: promoting job creation and entrepreneurship. Member States have to encourage the creation of more and better jobs by fostering entrepreneurship, innovation, investment capacity and a favourable business environment for all enterprises.
- Guideline 3: addressing change and promoting adaptability in the labour market. Member States have to facilitate the adaptability of workers and firms to change, taking account of the need for both flexibility and security and emphasising the key role of social partners in this respect.
- Guideline 6: by using an integrated approach combining gender mainstreaming and specific policy actions, Member States must encourage female labour market participation and achieve a substantial reduction in gender gaps in employment rates, unemployment rates and pay by 2010.
- Guideline 8: make work pay through incentives to enhance work attractiveness. Member States will reform financial incentives with a view to making work attractive and encouraging men and women to seek, take up and remain in work.
- Guideline 9: transform undeclared work into regular employment. Member States should develop and implement broad actions and measures to eliminate undeclared work. These should combine simplification of the business environment, removing disincentives and providing appropriate incentives

---

5 *Jobs, Jobs, Jobs – Creating More Employment in Europe*, Report of the Employment Task force chaired by Wim Kok.

6 Council Decision of 22 July 2003 on guidelines for the employment policies of the Member States OJ L197/13 of 5 August 2003.

in the tax and benefits system, improved law enforcement and the application of sanctions. They should undertake the necessary efforts at national and EU level to measure the extent of the problem and progress achieved at national level.

2.2.2 Turkey and the *Acquis* on the Employment Guidelines

Given the objective of increasing employment in the Treaty it is not surprising that the employment situation in Turkey attracted the attention of the European Commission when it drafted the Regular Reports on Turkey's progress towards accession. All these reports contain chapters on the Economic and Monetary Union and Social Policy and Employment. The contents of these reports are also reflected in Decision 2003/398/ EC concerning the accession of Turkey to the EU.[7] In the annex to this decision the Commission drew important conclusions concerning the improvement of employment in Turkey:

- Measures are necessary to tackle the informal economy including the informal labour market.
- Measures are necessary to improve social policy and employment including improving the social dialogue, implementation of the *acquis* (regarding labour law, equal treatment health and safety etc[8]) and a yearly plan for public investments.
- The drafting of a national employment strategy to be able to participate in the discussion on the employment guidelines (see also Section 2.1).

In the latest regular report on Turkey's progress towards accession the European Commission drew the following conclusions with regard to the employment situation in Turkey:[9]

- In respect of the field of labour law the European Commission believes that further efforts to align with the relevant *acquis* are needed. Turkey has to adopt more detailed legislation with regard to transfers of undertakings, posting of workers, young people at work, health and safety, temporary employment, European Works Councils, the involvement of workers in European companies, information and consultation of workers, and the obligation to inform employees on the conditions of their contract or their employment relationship.

---

7 Decision 2003/398/EC: Decision of the Council of 19 May 2003 concerning the principles, priorities, intermediate objectives and conditions contained in the Accession Partnership with Turkey.

8 See also Ch. 5 of this book.

9 *2003 Regular Report on Turkey's Progress towards Accession*, November 2003.

- Furthermore, the European Commission added that Turkey should accelerate its reform efforts concerning child labour and should take the necessary steps to enhance the administrative capacity of the Ministry of Labour and Social Security, the Turkish Employment Organisation and the Child Bureau.
- In relation to health and safety at work Turkey should enact the framework directive and the relevant implementing Turkish legislation in order to bring the Turkish legislation in line with the *acquis* in this area.
- The European Commission further said that Turkey should progress towards establishing full trade union rights including the elimination of the requirement of a 10 per cent threshold for a trade union to be eligible for collective bargaining at company level. Notably, at this moment there are restrictive provisions relating to the right to strike and to collective bargaining, in particular for public sector employees. The percentage of the labour force covered by collective agreements is extremely low (below 15 per cent).
- There is no social dialogue in most private enterprises. The absence of such a dialogue limits the proper implementation of the *acquis* at enterprise level. 'A social dialogue should be encouraged in private enterprises', according to the European Commission.
- At national level, the Economic and Social Council still shows insufficient functioning of the consultation of social partners at national level. Its structural deficiencies, such as the predominant position of the government, undermine the value of the Council and should be reviewed in conjunction with all the social partners. Private sector, public authorities and social partners need to show their commitment to social dialogue and take necessary measures to remove obstacles.
- The Commission points out that Turkey should accelerate its efforts to develop a national employment policy in line with the European Employment Strategy. Turkey has to strive for higher employment rates and low levels of youth and female unemployment as a beginning. In addition to the problem of official unemployment, the extent of the informal economy also remains a concern. Nevertheless, Turkey has adopted the Act on the Employment Organisation of Turkey (İş–Kur)[10] but this institutional law is not capable of creating adequate human and financial resources. Its capacity to elaborate active labour market initiatives and to combat the high level of unemployment in the country should be strengthened as a matter of priority.
- A national integrated strategy on promoting social inclusion should be created as well. This strategy should be developed fully in line with the objectives of the European Union. As poverty and social exclusion are multi-dimensional by nature, it is important to promote an integrated approach mobilising various governmental bodies. It is also necessary to develop systems for collecting social statistics on poverty and social exclusion in line with the commonly

10 Adopted by Turkish Parliament on 26 June 2003.

agreed EU indicators. In addition, the situation of disabled people needs to be improved further.

Within the field of social protection, most problems confronting the social security system are based on the lack of financial stability. This lack of stability is due to general macroeconomic imbalances, the presence of an informal sector and administrative and management problems. The EU encourages Turkey to take all necessary measures to ensure the financial stability of the social security system and effective coordination among the different social security institutions. The administrative capacity of the social security institutions should be enhanced.

The above mentioned conclusions of the European Commission are drawn in a broad and general way. They touch on many topics which indeed are related to each other. An inadequate social dialogue, failing health and safety policies, a fragmented approach to social inclusion and so on all influence labour market policies. Some of these topics will also be dealt with in other chapters. In this chapter we will concentrate on issues surrounding the flexibilisation of the Turkish labour market.

2.3 THE CURRENT TURKISH SITUATION

2.3.1 Employment and Unemployment: Facts and Figures

The Turkish economy has suffered from several major shocks in the past decade, which have resulted in fluctuations in the living standard of the Turkish people. These shocks fall under the following headings:

- The start of the first Gulf War in January 1991. This affected Turkey's trade with Iraq and other countries negatively.
- The devaluing lira. The lira lost seventy percent of its value against the US dollar during the first three months of 1994 because of governmental and public problems.
- Earthquakes. In 1999, two earthquakes devastated the Eastern part of the Marmara region. This area accounted for five percent of establishments, more than 6 percent of the workforce, and about 15 percent of the value added in Turkish manufacturing in 1997.
- The greatest economic crisis in Turkey since the 1950s. This took place in 2001.

Because of these major events Turkey has had to deal with low employment rates and a high level of unemployment.

In the fourth quarter of 2003, there was an estimated total employment in Turkey of 20,811,000 individuals, i.e. a decrease of 847,000 individuals compared to the results for the same quarter of the previous year. The employment rate, which is an important indicator for explaining improvement in employment, decreased from 44.8 per cent to 42.3 per cent (from 38.1 to 37.7 per cent for urban areas and from 55.3 per cent to 49.5 per cent for rural areas) compared with the results for the same quarter in 2002.

The following special characteristics can be noted of the Turkish labour market:

- In the fourth quarter of 2003, 27.2 per cent (5,000,652 individuals) of the total working population was female. Female employment decreased by 11.3 per cent (721,000 individuals), measured against the results for the same quarter of the previous year. In general this trend was caused by a decrease in the number of women working in the agricultural sector. When compared with the same quarter of the previous year, the number of women in the agricultural sector decreased by 600,000. While the proportion of women in the total employment was 19.9 per cent in urban areas, this rate was 35.9 per cent in rural areas. 57.1 per cent of employed women were working in the agriculture sector and 80.7 per cent of them were unpaid family workers.
- In Turkey many children between 12 and 17 are working. According to the statistics for the fourth quarter of 2003 there are 654,000 children working. However child labour decreased by 22.4 per cent (189,000 children) according to the same quarter of the previous year. 46.7 per cent of the child labour takes place in the agriculture sector, 27.3 per cent in the services sector and 23.6 per cent in the industry sector. 43.4 per cent of the employed children (284,000 individuals) were working in urban areas.
- According to the results for the fourth quarter of 2003, 3,000,245 individuals were estimated to be employed in the public sector, a decrease of 2.8 per cent compared with the results of the previous year. 73.1 per cent of the employed persons in public sector were residing in urban areas. Of the total number of individuals in employment 15.6 per cent were employed in the public sector in the fourth quarter of 2003 compared to 15.4 per cent in the same quarter of previous year. [11]
- As of 2000, a little more than thirty-four per cent of the workforce was still in agriculture. Services have emerged as the new leader, at over forty per cent. Industry accounted for around eighteen per cent and construction for six per cent. It is striking that employment is increasing in all sectors except for the construction sector.

As the employment rates decrease, unemployment rises. This process is ongoing. In the second quarter of 2003 it reached 10.0 per cent compared to 9.3 per cent a year before. Unemployment rates vary strongly between 13.2 per cent in urban and

11 Employment rates are based on data received from the Dutch Embassy in Ankara, Turkey.

6.3 per cent in agricultural areas and youth unemployment has increased to more than twenty per cent. Unemployment among young people was higher in urban areas. In the fourth quarter of 2003 the total unemployment rate of educated young people in urban areas was 26.3 per cent, of which 23.8 per cent was male and 29.8 per cent female. In rural areas the total unemployment figures are at 22.8 per cent, of which 22.5 per cent was male and 23.5 per cent female. [12]

When assessing these figures one has to bear in mind that Turkey has a large informal labour market. Despite economic growth in recent years, the unemployment rates have not declined. This is a strange phenomenon. It may be related to an increase in working hours and the absorption capacity of the informal market. Real unemployment must therefore be higher then the official rates, probably around 20 per cent. An official unemployment rate of ten per cent cannot explain the large informal labour market.

2.3.2 Specific Problems with Regard to the Flexibility of the Turkish Labour Market

In this section we will describe specific problems with regard to flexibilisation of the Turkish labour market. First, the informal labour market will be described and subsequently the position of women. In Sections 2.3.2.3 and 2.3.2.4 sectoral differences and the use of flexibilisation measures will be discussed.

2.3.2.1 The Informal Labour Market

As was stressed by the European Commission in its progress reports on the accession of Turkey, the existence of an informal labour market is a considerable problem. It will hamper accession to the EU because the magnitude of the informal market makes participation of Turkey in the internal market very difficult. Research by Istanbul University estimates the scale of the informal market to be about 52 per cent of the 2003 Turkish GDP.[13] However, it is virtually impossible to determine its size in exact terms. The figures available on this issue are derived from information on the employment status of individuals and social security coverage.

The informal market received a boost as a result of the post 1980s political agreements. In this period the Turkish government decided to increase exports. As a result, subcontracting firms within the informal market were used to reduce production costs considerably. These developments increased the competitiveness

---

12 Insan Tunali, *Background Study on the Labour Market and Employment in Turkey*, 27 June 2003.

13 Observations by Gülten Katal, professor at Istanbul University.

of Turkey on the export market. In addition, the wage growth amongst skilled and unskilled workers led to growth of the informal market. From 1971 on, the wage gap between skilled and unskilled workers narrowed, resulting in expensive labour. By subcontracting within the informal market the wage costs associated with unskilled work were reduced. Increasingly, skilled work is also tending to be subcontracted to the informal market.[14]

Another reason for the growth of the informal market is migration from rural to urban areas. The informal labour market creates flexibility and absorbs the surplus of labour in the urban areas created by migration.

The informal sector is, in fact, a natural phenomenon, one associated with humans promoting their own interests. They improve their standards of living by not sharing their income with the State. However, working within the informal market entails the risk of exploitation because of bad labour conditions, bankruptcy of the social security system, increasing budgetary deficits and unfair competition. It is obvious that the considerable size of the informal market is having negative effects on the Turkish economy as a whole. Therefore it is vital that informal labour be transformed into formal labour.

One way of doing so is by stimulating entrepreneurship in line with Guideline 2 of the Employment Guidelines. In most cases, entrepreneurship begins within small and medium-sized enterprises (SMEs). This is also the case in Turkey. However, although they have links with the formal market, a considerable number of SMEs in Turkey belong to the informal market, since the formal and informal sectors are inseparably intertwined. The Confederation of Turkish trades- and craftsmen (TESK) informed us that SMEs face several problems which are preventing them from becoming part of the formal market. This confederation regards the financial burden caused by tax payments and social security contributions as the major problem. The levels of taxes and social contributions are considered to be too high. Tax rates in Turkey start at twenty-five per cent and reach fifty-five per cent. These rates are tempting entrepreneurs to move into the informal sector. The temptation to avoid paying taxes is clearly being increased by the frequent changes of complicated tax legislation, the inefficiency of auditing and tax inspections, amnesty tax packages and insufficient penal sanctions. The same goes for social contributions.

There is also a lack of support for vocational and occupational training. The effect of this lack of support is a raising of the threshold for the formal market. Lower educational levels which render workers unemployable in the formal sector push them into the easily accessible informal sector, where activities which do not require training or capital – such as home-based work, street vendoring, and pretzel selling – are prevalent. A survey of the Turkish State Institute of Statistics shows that approximately 13 per cent of workers within the informal market (of which 72.6 per cent are female) are illiterate. 60.8 per cent of workers within the informal market have had some elementary schooling. Perhaps the basic underlying

14 See previous note.

factor is the predominance of employment with low added value. The value added created by a person minus deductions (taxes and social premiums) from his wage must be sufficient to maintain that worker at least at the minimum level possible. Therefore there is a need for more productive and qualified employment to deal with this problem. The added value is low in an environment where the average length of education is only six to seven years. Moving a workforce with such a low educational level into the formal labour market is, of course, very difficult. Employment Guideline number 3 is very relevant to the current educational situation in Turkey as it prescribes that Member States should create access for workers, in particular low-skilled workers, to training.

According to TESK, the government is overly focused on stimulating large enterprises. Measures for SMEs such as tax incentives (for companies with ten employees or more) and payment of social security contributions when hiring one or two more employees are difficult to implement and do not work in practice. The fact that in Turkish law thirty-two different definitions are used for SMEs is unhelpful. The adoption of more commonly used definitions of SMEs within the EU and by the European Commission could be useful.

Another element that could help shrink the informal market is to increase the enforcement capacity of the Turkish Labour Inspectorate. At present this department, being understaffed and poorly equipped, reacts only on the basis of complaints. Trade unions can assist the Inspectorate in this respect. Indeed, in some cases they have taken the initiative to cooperate with the Labour Inspectorate by reporting unregistered workplaces to the Labour Inspectorate. However, this is not particularly effective, since for the total working population of Turkey, eighty-seven labour inspectors for the Istanbul region are simply not enough. There is, however, no expectation that this situation will improve in the near future.

At present Turkish law already contains a framework of measures in the field of health and safety. These measures are meant to protect workers, but are regarded by employers as social costs. This has resulted in the problem that law-abiding employers are in unfavourable position vis-á-vis employers who operate in the informal market. This is especially the case in vulnerable sectors such as the service and construction sector (see also Section 2.2.3).

Guideline 9 prescribes the development and implementation of broad actions and measures to eliminate undeclared work. To reach this objective, the Turkish government will have to make a greater effort.

2.3.2.2 The Position of Women

The position of women in the Turkish labour market is closely connected to the informal market. Though reliable figures are not available, many women are working in the informal market. Most women work in the service and textile sectors. In the textile sector most of the work is home work traditionally undertaken by women. In the service sector (mainly in the hotel and catering business), work is part-time or on-call; whether this work is formal or informal is difficult to say. İş–Kur [15] stated that most on-call or part-time contracts are not in line with Turkish legislation.

As can be seen from migration figures, women in particular suffer from migration to urban areas. The agricultural sector has been a major employer of women. This sector is now decreasing because of migration to the cities. The EU has initiated many projects to improve the situation of women, as have other organisations such as the UN and American charities. These projects are run by Turkish NGOs. There are a number of interesting projects aimed at increasing entrepreneurship under women. TESK has operated a programme in five regions aimed at stimulating female enterprises in the metal, drivers and shoe making sectors. This programme includes training and education in amongst other things marketing, legal procedures and finance. The results demonstrate that stimulating female entrepreneurship is mainly working in the western and urban parts of the country and not in conservative rural areas. Early child care is not widespread in Turkey and is very expensive as it is not supported by the government. Employees often cannot afford childcare. Some NGOs such as the Foundation for the Support of Women (FSWW) try to fill this gap by operating an early child care and education programme. By founding day care centres which are also accessible for poor women these programmes can help combat the social exclusion of women. Child care provides women with an opportunity to become active in the labour market. FSWW also has programmes aimed at stimulating female entrepreneurship by providing training to increase the self confidence of women and offering micro-credit for starting a small firm.

Although these initiatives are very valuable, the Turkish Government has not developed an integrated approach that meets the requirement of Employment Guideline 6: to realise gender equality. The situation of women in the Turkish labour market clearly shows how the Turkish labour market is leading to female social exclusion. Consequently an integrated labour market approach in line with Guideline 6 should be formulated, including the following:

- Combating the informal market by implementing Guideline 9, as women suffer considerably from the informal market
- Providing an active policy with regard to child care
- Supporting programmes stimulating active participation and the entrepreneurship of women.

2.3.2.3 Sectoral Differences and Subcontracting

The study on labour market and employment by İş-Kur made it clear that growth of employment has taken place in nearly all sectors except the agriculture and the

15 We held interviews at the headquarters of İş–Kur (labour market organisation) in Ankara and a branch office in Istanbul.

construction sector. The lack of growth of employment in agriculture has led to migration to the cities. It is more difficult to explain why employment in the construction sector has stayed stable at around five to six per cent despite the economic growth of recent years. In all Member States, the construction sector has a bigger share of employment than five to six per cent. For the whole EU the share is 7.8 per cent, varying from 11.8 per cent in Portugal to 5.6 per cent in Sweden. Most Member States have a proportion of between 7.5 and ten per cent, even though economic growth has been low in Member States.[16] In the İş-Kur report it was concluded that better understanding is needed of where jobs are being created, in which sectors, for whom, by whom and where jobs are being destroyed.[17] A comparison of Turkey to the rest of the EU shows that the recorded proportion of employment within the construction sector in Turkey is too low.

Though not the largest industrial sector, construction is a key sector in Europe, with some eleven million workers directly employed. Compared with other industries, construction is by far the most labour-intensive industry. About fifty per cent of turnover in this sector is achieved through direct labour.[18] This means that the construction industry is contributing in a major way to employment within individual economies. This could also be the case for Turkey but the figures presented suggest that a considerable proportion of employment in construction takes place within the informal economy. Taking measures to prevent construction activities becoming unregistered will therefore directly contribute to an increase in employment in the formal market. As public expenditure is of great importance for this sector, the government has the instruments necessary to prevent fraud, illegal work and extensive uncontrolled subcontracting.

Recently the Turkish government introduced a statutory liability regime for social contributions and taxes with regard to public works. The introduction of transparent public tender procedures may also reduce the influence of the informal market in construction activities. The effects of these measures cannot yet be measured, as they have only recently been implemented.

According to the İş-Kur Report the growth of the service sector in Turkey seems to be following a similar pattern to that within EU Member States.[19] Growth specifications within the service sector are, however, not available. According to İş-Kur the growth mainly concerns work in the hotel and catering branches. In comparison service sector growth in the new Member States is mainly in real estate, renting and business activities. In these areas employment has grown by over thirty-five per cent, which is significantly higher than the average for the EU

---

16 Eurostat, 'Spring Results 2004', *Panorama of the European Labour Markets*, Ch. 1 part 5; European Commission, *Sectoral Employment Structures in the* EU *25 in 2003*, 2004.

17 Insan Tunali, *Background Study on the Labour Market and Employment in Turkey*, p. 93, not published, 27 June 2003.

18 L. Clarke, J. Cremers and J. Janssen, *EU Enlargement*. CLR studies, The Hague, 2003.

19 Insan Tunali, *Background Study on the Labour Market and Employment in Turkey*, p. 93, not published, 27 June 2003.

15. In the new Member States employment has also increased in health and social work, while employment in the hotel and catering industries has declined.[20] In the light of these statistics, it appears that Turkey is not following the same pattern with regard to services as the rest of the EU.

A sectoral policy, focused in particular on the construction and service sectors, could lead to more formal employment in Turkey. In addition, more control and legislative measures are needed to keep construction activities out of the informal economy. The creation of jobs in the service sector is a positive development. However attention should be paid to the quality of these jobs. Finally, to help the position of women, measures in line with Guideline 9 are needed.

2.3.2.4 Flexibilisation Measures

We will now discuss two issues: the prohibition on temporary work agencies and flexible work contracts. In 2003 greater flexibility was introduced into the Turkish Labour Act, despite resistance from, in particular, the trade unions. It is too early to draw conclusions about the impact of flexibility on the Turkish labour market. However, in their operations within the Turkish market, temporary work agencies such as Adecco and Manpower make use of the new Labour Act, in particular Article 7, which concerns the leasing of staff. This article stipulates that 'A temporary employment relationship is established when, in order to have work performed similar to what the employee was doing, the employer transfers the employee, upon written consent at the time of the transfer, to another establishment within the structure of the same holding company or the same group of companies, or to another employer'. Employment agencies make use of this article for their activities. The activities pursued by the employee are crucial in deciding the issue of whether temporary labour is legitimate. Agencies that want to 'lease staff' need a license provided by İş-Kur. İş-Kur is charged with verifying whether the activities of the workers provided remain the same so that there really is leasing of staff. These agencies are not called temporary work agencies but private employment agencies. In practice this provision in the Labour Act is very difficult to enforce as a detailed check of the activities of temporary employees is needed. Moreover the activities undertaken by the employee need to be the same as the ones carried out before the employee was posted to another company. As a result, there is a grey zone between the posting of workers and real temporary work.

Flexible work contracts are still at an early stage in Turkey. The provisions of the Turkish Labour Act concerning part-time work are defined in a minimalist way.[21] No active measures have been taken to stimulate part-time work and other possibilities

---

20 Eurostat, 'Spring Results 2004', *Panorama of the European Labour Markets*, Ch. 1 part 5; European Commission, *Sectoral Employment Structures in the EU25 in 2003*, 2004.

21 See Ch. 5.

for flexible work contracts. As a result the new flexible working arrangements have yet to have an impact on the creation of formal employment. Trade unions and workers have so far emphasised the job security dimension of the new Labour Act, while remaining reluctant to accept flexible changes in employment contracts and working time. This has especially negative consequences for women, as also recognised by the FSWW.

Employment Guideline 3 concerns adaptability and mobility in the labour market. According to this guideline Member States have to review, and where appropriate, reduce overly restrictive elements in employment legislation that affect labour market dynamics and the employment of those groups facing difficulties accessing the labour market. Member States should promote:

- diversity of contractual and working arrangements, including working time rules, favouring career progression, a better balance between work and private life and between flexibility and security
- the design and dissemination of innovative and sustainable forms of work organisation which support labour productivity and quality of work.

Within the Employment Taskforce of the EU, temporary work agencies are seen as useful instrument for assisting workers to enter the labour market and gain working experience, in particular at the beginning of their career. Although in the Employment Guidelines temporary work agencies are not mentioned as such, the Employment Taskforce calls them an instrument which can contribute to the fulfilment of Employment Guideline 1: active and preventive measures for the unemployed and inactive. The discussion on temporary work agencies focuses not on their value for the labour market but on the labour conditions which apply for temporary workers and their equal treatment with other workers.[22]

2.4 CONCLUSIONS AND RECOMMENDATIONS

In this chapter we have described and analysed the Turkish labour market from the perspective of flexibilisation. To become a member of the EU Turkey must be able to compete within the internal market. The progress reports of the European Commission make it clear that the functioning of the Turkish labour market is a major hindrance to accession. Improving Turkish labour legislation and social dialogue, combating the informal economy and increasing the administrative capacity to implement the rules are elements necessary to ensuring better functioning of the Turkish labour market.

Although exact figures on the Turkish labour market are difficult to obtain it can be concluded that despite economic growth unemployment has risen. The

22 Ibid.

unemployment has partly been absorbed within the informal economy and labour market. Recent studies estimate that the informal labour market is bigger then the formal one, a situation which cannot remain if Turkey wants to join the EU. A positive development is that government, social partners and other parties involved now wish to find ways to resolve the problem.

In this report four topics relating to flexibilisation have been analysed against the background of the Employment Guidelines of the EU. Although the Employment Guidelines cannot be considered as hard *acquis*, they show the expectations of the EU in relation to the labour markets of the Member States. Moreover, the European Commission judges the employment policy of Turkey using the Employment Guidelines as an analytical framework. Pressure to adopt the guidelines is consequently considerable. The Commission has pointed out that Turkey has to develop a national employment strategy in line with the European Employment Strategy.

In our analyses we referred only to the Employment Guidelines relating to flexibility. The informal labour market is one of the biggest challenges Turkey has to meet on its way towards accession. In line with Employment Guideline 2 Turkey should stimulate entrepreneurship especially among small and medium-sized enterprises. Simplifying the legal definitions of SMEs is necessary. Furthermore measures should be taken to develop a more stable tax and social security policy. Although it is reported as such by many parties, it is impossible to say whether the tax and social security burden is too high. Apart from the levels of contributions, simplification of legislation, more efficient tax and social security auditing and avoiding amnesty tax packages are measures which could be useful.

One of the main reasons for the growth of the informal market is the low rate of vocational education. Low educational levels make workers unemployable in the formal sector. It is obvious that Turkey has not fulfilled the obligations of Employment Guideline 3 in this respect. The development of easily accessible training and schooling programmes is necessary. Such programmes exist in Turkey, but they are too few, do not reach the target groups and could be better coordinated. The average length of education is an estimated six to seven years, which is too short. A policy to raise the average length of education has to be developed and implemented by the Ministry of Education.

Another important measure to be taken is to increase the enforcement capacity of the Turkish Labour Inspectorate. An extensive inspection system which can take immediate action upon receiving complaints of alleged violations must be promoted as a deterrent to work in informal employment. The number and pay of inspection officials who make on site visits must be increased to raise the effectiveness and respectability of labour inspectors.

In respect of the informal labour market it can be concluded that Turkey is not in line with Employment Guideline 9, which prescribes the development and implementation of broad action and measures to eliminate undeclared work. Greater effort on the part of the Turkish government is necessary. The provincial employment boards must be assigned special tasks in the struggle against informal employment and clandestine foreign labour. Coordination among provinces as well as work at the local level must be provided by the provincial employment boards, and the outcome of their activities should be monitored centrally by the Ministry of Labour and Social Security.

The position of women in the Turkish labour market is closely connected to the informal market. Measures taken to suppress the informal market will also increase the position of women in general. Increasing the support of the Turkish government for NGO initiatives for better education, child care and stimulating entrepreneurship is necessary. The current situation in the Turkish labour market promotes social exclusion with regard to women and therefore is not in line with Employment Guideline 6.

The development of a sectoral policy especially concerning the construction and service sectors could contribute to increasing formal employment. Recent measures taken by the Turkish government, including the introduction of a legislative liability regime for social contributions and taxes and more transparent tendering procedures with regard to public works, are positive steps. The growth of jobs in the service sector is also a positive development. However attention should be paid to the quality of these jobs and the position of women within the sector. The implementation of Employment Guidelines 6 and 9 are appropriate in this respect.

Employment Guideline 3 concerns adaptability and mobility in the labour market. Although one could consider the informal labour market as an example of adaptability and mobility the negative effects are too obvious to ignore. The formal market must develop greater adaptability and mobility. It will then also contribute to decreasing the informal market. The way temporary work agencies use Article 7 of the Labour Act should be reconsidered. Temporary work agencies can be a very useful instrument for labour market policies as they can create an entrance route to the formal labour market. The government could consider changing the Labour Act, introducing a licence system for temporary work agencies and agreeing on the development of vocational training programmes for employees working for temporary work agencies. In this way temporary work agencies can contribute to the obligations of Employment Guideline 1: active and preventive measures for the unemployed and inactive.

Turkish policies with regard to flexible work contracts are not in line with Employment Guideline 3: adaptility and mobility. Legislative provisions referring to flexible work contracts are relatively minimalistic. The Turkish government is not active in stimulating opportunities for flexible work contracts, which it should according to Guideline 3. This is having particularly negative consequences for women in the labour market. Further consultations with the social partners are necessary at this point. The unions must be convinced of the need to suppress the informal market by creating greater flexibility in the formal market. Better unionisation could contribute to the infiltration of union members within workplaces, thereby creating monitoring possibilities. Changing the law with regard to thresholds for collective bargaining could be helpful as well increasing the position of unions in the workplace.

3. LABOUR MARKET INSTITUTIONS IN TURKEY

Peter Donders, Nurhan Süral and Karin Sengers

3.1 INTRODUCTION

In this chapter we will discuss the institutional capacity of the Turkish institutions responsible for implementing legislation and policies relating to flexible work, labour market policies and social security. This chapter will focus on the main institutions involved, which include the Social Insurances Institution SSK; the Labour Market Institution İş-Kur and the Labour Inspectorate.

All these institutions fall under the competence of the Ministry of Labour and Social Security. They are firmly attached to the Ministry by legislation, including the Labour Act, the Social Insurances Act and the Employment Organisation Act. We will also discuss related topics including enforcement of the existing legislation, implementation of policy, exchange of information and cooperation between the various institutions.

These topics are also of major importance in the light of accession to the European Union. In its analysis of the administrative capacity of Turkey, the European Commission produced the following recommendations concerning the Ministry of Labour and Social Security:[1]

- The legislative programme relating to the *acquis* must be implemented.
- A new institutional structure for administering and coordinating social security, social assistance and social services is required.
- The legislative position of the Turkish tripartite Council needs to be improved in order to stimulate social dialogue.
- A tripartite authority needs to be established in the field of mutual recognition of professional qualifications and diplomas.
- İş-Kur needs to be reformed.
- A special Social Fund unit should be established within the Ministry.

In addition, the Commission's recommendations mention reform of the social security system and İş-Kur, the Turkish labour market institution.

---

1 European Commission, *Analysis of the Administrative Capacity in Turkey,* Brussels 2004.

Pennings, *Flexibilisation and Modernisation of the Turkish Labour Market*, 29–40

A thorough analysis of the institutional capacity of the Turkish government is, therefore, necessary if the requested reforms are to be implemented. Our analysis is based on interviews and documentation. We will discuss the SSK, İş-Kur and the Labour Inspectorate in turn and complete this chapter with conclusions and recommendations.

3.2 SSK

The Social Security Institution (Sosyal Güvenlik Kurumu) is an institution affiliated to the Ministry of Labour and Social Security.[2] It can be divided into three other institutions involved in social security namely:[3]

1. The Social Insurances Institution (Sosyal Sigortalar Kurumu – SSK), which includes a Directorate General of Insurance Services (Sigorta İşleri Genel Müdürlüğü) and a Directorate General of Health Services (Sağlık İşleri Genel Müdürlüğü)
2. The Social Insurances Institution for the Self-Employed (Bağ-Kur)
3. The Turkish Employment Institution (Türkiye İş Kurumu – İş-Kur).

The Social Insurances Institution is charged with the activities envisaged by the Social Insurances Act (SIA, Act no. 506) and the Agricultural Workers' Social Insurances Act (Act no. 2925).

The SSK is the body responsible for the insurance of workers who are in the possession of a contract of employment. The self-employed, who are registered at the Chamber of Commerce and in the possession of a tax registration number, are covered by the Bağ-Kur. The SSK and Bağ-Kur do not maintain any connect with each other as there is no overlap or confusion regarding the relative status of such workers.

For an organisation chart of the SSK, see the Appendix. The relationship between SSK and the Ministry of Labour and Social Security is defined by law. SSK falls within the sphere of competence of the Ministry. The SSK and the Ministry have regular consultation meetings.

The SSK is governed by a Board of Directors, a tripartite body. The Ministry is kept informed of the agenda of the Board. The Board is composed of a chair (General Director of the Social Insurances Institution) and seven members:[4]

– A member proposed by the Minister and appointed through a joint decree

---

2 Art. 1, Social Security Institution Organisational Act, Act no. 4947, *Official Gazette* 24 July 2003.
3 Ibid. art 3.
4 Act no. 4958, art. 6/1

- A member proposed by the Minister to whom the State Treasury is attached and appointed through a joint decree
- A member from the most representative workers' confederation
- A member from the most representative employers' confederation
- A member representing the pensioners' organisation
- The General Director of the Insurances Services as an ex-officio member
- The General Director of the Health Services as an ex-officio member.

Amongst other things, the Board of Directors of the SSK is authorised to analyse and to submit to the Ministry law proposals, statutory decrees, regulations and by-laws of interest to the Institution.[5] The contribution for insurance against industrial accidents and occupational diseases is determined according to the risks and hardships which occur in the sector concerned. The categories and degrees of risk and corresponding rates are prescribed by a tariff decreed by the Council of Ministers.[6] The SSK determines the category and degree of risk of the work performed and the corresponding contribution rates according to the tariff and communicates these in writing to the employer.[7] Higher contribution rates may be fixed by the SSK for activities that do not conform to the legal provisions on preventive measures for industrial accidents and occupational diseases. The SSK may modify its own initiative if an inquiry suggests this is necessary or modify the risk category and degree of risk at the request of the employer.

Approximately 10,000 SSK employees, of whom 3,000 are based in Ankara and 7,000 spread throughout Turkey, are charged with the administration of the Social Insurances Act (Act No 506). The head office and regional offices meet regularly to discuss key issues such as problems relating to interpreting the law and the implementation of regulations. An SSK policy management unit identifies gaps in policy implementation and evaluates the effect of laws. This unit provides valuable input for improving the implementation of law and regulations.

In total the SSK employs about 40,000 individuals. The SSK produces circulars and provides training activities to keep its staff informed and up to date.

The SSK is responsible for ensuring that employers fulfil their obligations in the field of social security. However Turkey is faced with major problems to do with undeclared work. In order to implement the law and to punish infringements, the SSK has set up an inspection board which has its head office in Ankara and seven or eight offices at provincial level, all of which report to the head office. The Inspection Board develops annual inspection programmes in conjunction with the Labour Inspectorate. The Inspection Board also deals with complaints relating to social security issues. Cooperation between SSK (Inspection Board) and the Labour Inspectorate is good. Both institutions notify each other of illegal practices and abuses. At the time of our study, about 350 social inspectors were working at the

5 Act no. 4958, art. 7/10.
6 SIA, art. 74/3.
7 SIA, art. 75.

SSK and it was planned to increase this number to 400 in May 2005. However not all inspectors undertake investigation activities; some work in different areas. The following table shows the inspection results for the period 2001–2004.

Table 3.1 Inspection Results

	2001	*2002*	*2003*	*2004*
Inspected work places	30,853	29,498	34,962	29,901
Unregistered work places	1,819	1,442	2,108	3,020
Inspection per inspector	93	92	112	110
Inspected workers	185,219	126,593	324,772	226,662
Unregistered workers	10,500	7,452	22,201	21,900
Inspector numbers	333	321	311	272

Source: ssk.gov.tr

This table demonstrates that that the number of inspected workplaces dropped in 2004 compared with 2003 though inspector productivity grew. This increased productivity is a positive development, strengthening the case for increasing the number of inspectors. However, a closer study of the figures reveals that in 2004 only 10 per cent of the workers checked by the Inspection Service of the SSK appeared to be unregistered. This raises the question of whether the SSK Inspection Service is focussing its efforts in the most problematic areas, i.e. in the informal labour market. Although statistics relating to undeclared work are not readily available, the number of undeclared workers found by the Inspectorate does not seem to correspond to the estimates produced by Istanbul University, which estimated the scale of the informal market at about 52–53 per cent of the Turkish GDP in 2003.[8] Consequently the number of undeclared workers found during inspections should be substantially higher than indicated in Table 3.1.

To combat undeclared work the SSK inspection service uses the minimum labour costs application method (quantity surveying).[9] On the basis of set standards, the SSK estimates the costs associated with a work place (for example, a construction site) and the number of workers needed for this work. This calculation results in a standard amount. The employer is charged the difference between the actual contributions paid and the standard amount. To be entitled to an occupancy permit, when the construction work is complete, the employer needs a clearance statement from the SSK: a declaration that all social contributions have been paid. Both employers and employees are obliged to inform the SSK of the commencement

8 See Ch. 2.

9 SIA, art. 83/1 as amended by Act no. 3395, *Official Gazette* dated 9 July 1987.

of the employment relationship. Neglect of this obligation can result in financial penalties. However, according to the SSK, these penalties are not discouraging evasion. Candidate workers are finding information about the level of social security contributions on the SSK website and are deciding to work for more attractive net wages in the informal labour market.

In practice, it is very difficult for the SSK to prevent fraud. Providing information to the public and holding inspections are important instruments of prevention, but some benefit schemes, including unemployment benefits, appear to be very sensitive to fraud. In particular, working in the informal market (even for a low salary) while also receiving unemployment benefits seem to be proving attractive. Orphans' and widows' benefits are also sensitive to fraud. In order to fight fraud, orphans, widows and unemployed persons have to prove that they do not receive any other income before they are eligible for benefits. Computers facilitate the cross checking of data, which helps to combat fraud.

The SSK uses a number of methods to inform the public about social security. The SSK website, which appears to be visited frequently, contains comprehensive information about employees' social security insurance benefits including information about contributions. The SSK also attends appropriate exhibitions and congresses. At the end of their military service, the SSK informs conscripts about their social security rights. In the future, there are plans to organise classes on social security in primary schools.

Other sources of information include the trade unions, which play an important role in providing information to certain categories of employee and financial consultants who are the main source of advice for employers.

As a first step, those who disagree with a decision taken by the SSK can make a complaint to the SSK. The next level of complaint involves lodging an appeal at court. Data about the number and kind of complaints that have been made is kept at provincial level but not collated centrally.

In order to increase the efficiency and effectiveness of the social security system as a whole, a new bill replacing the current one on the Social Security Institution has been prepared. The main objective is to establish a new Social Security Institution as an 'umbrella institution'. This umbrella institution will develop and implement the Social Insurances and General Health Insurance Act, and Non-Contributory Benefits Act. The three General Directorates of Social Insurances, General Health Insurance, and Non-Contributory Benefits will be affiliated to this new Social Security Institution. Civil servants, workers, self-employed, self-employed in agriculture, and agricultural workers employed on a temporary basis in the private sector who have been within the scope of various pieces of legislation will all be brought under the coverage of the Social Insurances and General Health Insurance Act.

3.3 İŞ-KUR

İş-Kur was established on the basis of the Turkish Employment Organisation Act.[10] It replaced the Labour Placement Organisation which was considered to have failed in its response to developments within the labour market. The general congress and the managing committee of İş-Kur have a tripartite composition. The same goes for the Unemployment Insurance Fund Management Board and the Occupational Standards Commission, which are part of İş-Kur.

İş-Kur is responsible for developing and increasing employment, undertaking and participating in activities to prevent unemployment, and implementing the unemployment insurance scheme (see also Section 3.2 on the SSK).

İş-Kur has relatively limited scope for introducing initiatives in the area of labour market policies. This is partly due to the limited budget available for labour market policies and partly to the somewhat centralistic approach adopted by the Ministry. İş-Kur cannot, for instance, make decisions on subsidised labour. An example of such subsidised work is a temporary work experience scheme in the public sector (with activities which benefit society) for the unemployed. İş-Kur is charged with paying at least minimum wages to the participants. The effect of these programmes is limited, partly because of budget restrictions.

İş-Kur is the main organisation charged with responsibility for providing jobseekers with vocational guidance and training in order to complement skills acquired within the education system. Furthermore, İş-Kur has to meet the needs of special target groups including the disabled, ex-convicts and the poor. However, the implementation of active vocational training activities is being hampered by strict public procurement rules. While these rules were adopted to avoid fraud, the result is that it is extremely difficult to run vocational training programmes. Vocational training programmes are funded on a year-by-year basis while tendering procedures may take several months. As a result, despite the importance of vocational training, İş-Kur has not implemented any vocational training programmes since 2003, when the new public procurement law was introduced. This problem could be overcome by using EU public procurement rules as an example and allowing financial planning for periods longer than one year.

İş-Kur also organises programmes to stimulate entrepreneurship. These include special training programmes, guidance and counselling services for those who want to become self employed.

İş-Kur employs 1,800 staff and it is planned to extend this number to 3,000. This envisaged increase of staff is a positive sign, but, given the size of the Turkish labour market, the number of İş-Kur employees, already too limited, will continue to be so. The overall quality of the staff seems to be good.

Most of the working capacity of İş-Kur is spent on the administration of the unemployment benefit scheme. It is questionable whether this division of tasks

10 Act No. 4904, *Official Gazette* dated 5 July 2003.

between labour market policies and implementing a social insurance scheme is really appropriate, as active labour market policies need more emphasis, given the Employment Guidelines of the European Commission. There are two ways to make more staff available for the various parts of the employment schemes: increasing the number of staff and setting clear priorities in the tasks to be carried out by İş-Kur. In the present circumstances, the second option is probably the most suitable. Provided that the quality of the administration remains the same, the administration of the unemployment benefit scheme could be transferred to SSK, thus enabling İş-Kur to concentrate fully on labour market policies. This is the most important task as İş-Kur is almost the only institution undertaking placement activities for those unemployed with limited opportunities within the labour market. This group constitutes about 19 per cent of the formal labour market. Despite the fact that the Employment Organisation Act has paved the way for the establishment of private employment agencies, their ability to assist this group is still unclear. In any case, İş-Kur is responsible for granting licences to these organisations and for monitoring these organisations.

As part of its placement activities, İş-Kur regularly visits individual employers and obtains information on job vacancies and possibilities for placing the unemployed. The Internet is also used to provide the unemployed with information on job vacancies and to notify employers of any unemployed people looking for work. In addition, it holds regular meetings with the social partners. İş-Kur places advertisements in the media to encourage the unemployed to register with İş-Kur and to discourage them from looking for jobs in the informal labour market. So far these advertisements have been rarely shown on TV, even though this medium reaches many more of the target groups than newspapers. There is therefore a lot more work to be done in this area.

İş-Kur cooperates with other institutions, including the Labour Inspectorate, but it has its own Inspection Board of Labour tasked with combating unemployment benefit fraud. The action taken following the discovery of fraud depends on the extent of the fraud.

Monitoring the effects of labour market policies is very important. For this purpose İş-Kur produces and publishes statistical data on the labour market situation. It also establishes and coordinates the studies of the Labour Market Information Consultation Board.

To keep the expertise of İş-Kur employees up to date, in-service training is frequently used, particularly in order to familiarise employees with new legislation and interpreting it. It is recommended that such training be supplemented by courses on comparable issues in EU Member States. Training to prevent fraud and to implement measures to avoid undeclared work could also be useful.

3.4 THE LABOUR INSPECTORATE

The Labour Inspectorate is also under the competence of the Ministry of Labour and Social Security. This is expressly stated in article 91 of the Labour Act, which provides that supervision and inspection of working conditions must be performed by officials of the Ministry of Labour and Social Security. Labour As such, inspectors are officials of the Ministry. Their main tasks are to follow up, supervise and inspect working conditions. The term 'working conditions' should be interpreted in a broad sense, and includes working arrangements, equipment, tools, apparatus and other facilities relating to the health and safety of workers.[11] A special Labour Inspection Regulation, issued under article 92 of the previous Labour Act,[12] is concerned with the functioning and tasks of the Labour Inspectorate. A new by-law on labour inspection is to be prepared under article 91 of the new Labour Act.

The new Labour Act puts the Labour Inspectorate in a relatively strong position, since its powers to check and verify situations are well defined. The Labour Act also describes the responsibilities of employees and the relationship between employees and employers, since the law obliges the social partners to cooperate with the Labour Inspectorate. One remarkable provision is that concerning the conduct of employees when informing Labour Inspectors about labour conditions: employees may not provide the authorities or officials with information contrary to the facts which could give rise to unnecessary action, false accusations or unlawful actions.[13] Even though the same provision protects workers against discrimination or measures by employers acting against the law, the strong wording of this provision may make workers reluctant to inform labour inspectors of unlawful behaviour. This is problematic since the Inspectorate relies on employees to report problems relating to bad labour conditions and poor health and safety measures. If necessary, labour inspectors can ask for police assistance in their work.[14]

In the event of unlawful activities or circumstances, the Labour Inspectorate can, as a first step, impose a financial penalty or can temporarily close down the workplace. In criminal cases the Inspectorate can ask for assistance from the Office of Public Prosecution.

In total there are 619 labour inspectors. These are split into two categories: social inspectors supervising the implementation and compliance with the working condition provisions of the Labour Act, and technical inspectors who conduct technical supervisions, thereby ensuring compliance with official occupational health and safety requirements.

---

11 Art. 92 Turkish Labour Act.

12 *Official Gazette* dated 28 August 1979.

13 Art. 96 Labour Act.

14 Art. 97 Labour Act.

The quality and expertise of the labour inspectors is regarded as good,[15] although their number is too low. Their work is performed on a project basis and the results are reported in well documented reports. In 2004, 5256 inspections were held in total. The problem is, however, that inspections cover many provisions of the Labour Act. As a result inspections are time-consuming and may include detecting trivial offences. This situation is demotivating for those enterprises and employers who wish to improve, since the labour inspectors will probably always detect minor offences. At the same time the situation prevents the Labour Inspectorate from carrying out more inspections. To increase the likelihood of individual enterprises of being inspected and given the limited capacity of the Labour Inspectorate a more efficient approach to inspection is necessary,. This would increase the pressure on employers to abide by the law: better maintenance of the law is an urgent issue in Turkey.

There are a number of other problems associated with the inspection system. These are partially caused by the low number of inspectors. Labour inspections tend to follow reports of problems rather than occurring spontaneously and on a random basis. In addition, the social partners are informed of inspections in advance. Although social partner involvement is important for the improvement of working conditions, giving advance notice of inspections can lead to concealment of poor working conditions. It is therefore recommended that the Labour Inspectorate undertake a greater number of random and spontaneous visits.

The Labour Inspectorate is also responsible for the maintenance of the flexibility provisions of the Labour Act.[16] However, as these provisions have yet to be fully implemented, we have no reports of the Inspectorate's experience in this area.

Besides project inspection reports the Labour Inspectorate produces a yearly report containing the results of their inspections and statistics associated with them. As the Labour Inspectorate is a state agency it is in regular contact with other state agencies such as SSK and İş-Kur and exchanges information and inspection reports, although such contact is not formalised. Where problems exist, interagency communication is required by law. Co-operation in terms of combined inspections could be improved. In addition, an increase in expertise in European legislation on health and safety legislation could improve the work of the Labour Inspectorate.

3.5 LAW ENFORCEMENT

As described in the previous sections, all three institutions have their own procedures for appeal and for the protection of citizens against unlawful decisions. There are

---

15 On labour inspection see the MATRA report by the Dutch Labour Inspection (www.minszw.nl).

16 Ibid. arts 10–13

71 labour courts which deal with cases relating to the Labour Act. These courts are specialised first instance courts.

Since the new Labour Act came into force, most cases have related to interpretation problems or accusations of violation of workers rights under the Act.

3.6 CONCLUSIONS

All the institutions discussed in this chapter are closely related to the Ministry of Labour and Social Security. The relationship of these institutions can be analysed in the light of the policy life cycle. The following diagram illustrates this cycle:

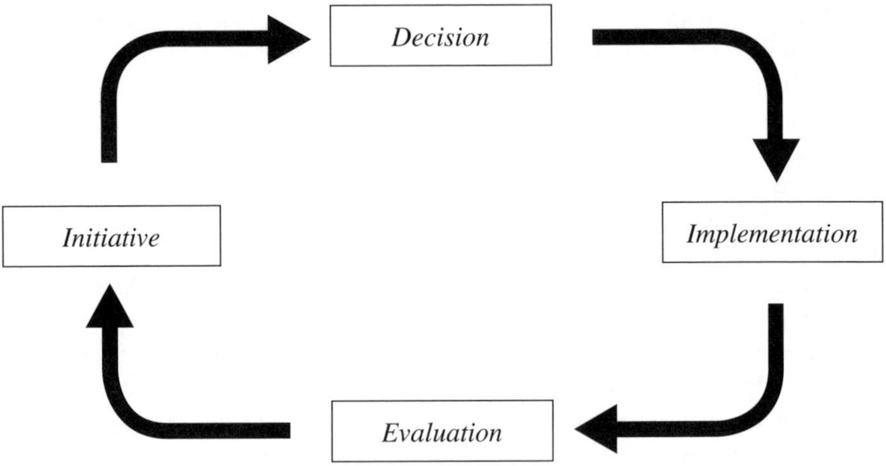

To develop policies that can be successfully implemented, all three institutions need to be involved in the implementation and evaluation of policies. Our analyses make it clear that the monitoring of policy effects is largely an internal affair. Institutions monitor their own policies. They publish the results every year, but they depend too much on the input from, for instance, the social partners. Of course, this information can be very useful, but the evaluation and monitoring of social policy should be done in a more structured, independent and inclusive manner. At the moment, (and in line with common EU practice) the State Institute of Statistics is being reformed in order to make it more independent of the Government. This is a positive development. In addition, a greater amount of independent research initiated by the Ministry but also by other involved parties may help to improve assessment of the policy concerned: is it a good policy? The present situation is unsatisfactory, as evidenced by the fact that the SSK could give no explanation for its inspections not coming up with the percentage of undeclared work cases expected by the informal labour market estimates. Effective implementation and evaluation also requires more distance between the ministry and the involved institutions. In the Netherlands similar institutions have a more independent role; the Ministry's role is to define and decide on policies.

We understand that the relationship between the institutions and Government is largely influenced by cultural and historical circumstances and that this relationship is under discussion. The problems which İş-Kur met when implementing vocational training programmes – a problem caused by the public procurement and budget rules imposed by the Ministry – illustrate the necessity for this discussion. It is recommended that in general a distinction be made between policy making and implementation. The Ministry should concentrate on policy making and leave implementation to those agencies that can be held to account for their performance. Furthermore, adequate policy making requires good evaluation instruments. It is recommended that the Ministry develop or obtain such instruments.

Regarding the institutions the following remarks can be made:

- In general, staff quality can be considered as good. The main problem is the availability of a sufficient number of qualified staff. In order to optimise use of the limited capacity it is recommended that İş-Kur concentrate on implementing labour market schemes instead of administering the unemployment benefit scheme.
- The inspection service of SSK must be strengthened in order to build upon recent improvements in efficiency. In particular, an increase in the number of inspections in the informal labour market is required.
- The Labour Inspectorate has a highly qualified team. It is recommended that the efficiency of inspection visits be increased by limiting the scope of inspections. Setting priorities will increase the pressure on employers to abide by the law, an urgent requirement in Turkey. An increase in the number of inspectors to enable a greater number of random inspections to be undertaken is also recommended.
- The mutual exchange of information and cooperation between the institutions is good and is assisted by the institutions' position within the Ministry of Labour and Social Security. However, the initiation of common inspection visits would improve efficiency further.
- All three institutions have regular institutionalised contacts with the social partners. During these meetings valuable information is reportedly exchanged. However the institutions should seek to develop independent sources of information. Structured and independent monitoring of their activities should also take place.
- Article 96 of the Labour Act provides for a relatively severe warning to employees if they report incorrect information. This could prevent employees from informing the authorities of infringements and abuses of laws.
- The public should receive better information about disadvantages of doing undeclared work. The SSK website is a very good example of how adequate information can be provided.

APPENDIX

The present SSK is organised in the following way:[17]

General Congress

Managing Board (Board of Directors)

General Director

Directorate-General of Insurances Services	Directorate-General of Health Services	Advisory, supervisory and supporting units
Main service departments: ❑ Insurance Services Directorate ❑ Allocations Directorate ❑ Short-term Insurances Directorate ❑ Services for Workers Abroad Directorate Auxiliary departments	Main service departments: ❑ Medical Services and Disability Directorate ❑ Health Services Purchasing Directorate ❑ Medicine and Pharmacy Directorate Auxiliary departments	❑ Inspection Board Directorate ❑ Insurances Inspection Directorate ❑ Legal Counsellors Unit ❑ Finance, Actuarial and Planning Directorate ❑ Accounting and Financial Works Directorate ❑ Data Processing Department

17 ssk.gov.tr.

4. TURKISH SOCIAL DIALOGUE: STRUCTURE, PRACTICE AND ATTITUDES

Peter van der Valk and Nurhan Süral

4.1 INTRODUCTION

A well-functioning social dialogue system (essential if the labour market is to develop consensually) depends on active and regular bilateral interaction between the social partners. The labour market is easier to restructure if there is adequate social dialogue. Any weaknesses in how dialogue takes place (weakness arising from a lack of responsibility, solidarity or participation, or from an unwillingness to accept responsibility) can have adverse effects. A strong social dialogue system is very useful, particularly in overcoming problems to do with implementing flexibility provisions. Consequently, dialogue between management and labour at national and enterprise levels has to be an essential part of the Turkish industrial relations system.

In this chapter we start (in Section 4.2) with a description of employer and employee organisations. In Section 4.3 we describe the evolution of the statutory framework which governs such organisations. In Section 4.4 we describe the context of the collective bargaining process. Section 4.5 examines the institutional framework within which social dialogue takes place, while Section 4.6 will deal with social dialogue as it functions in practice. The chapter ends with recommendations for better social dialogue.

4.2 THE TURKISH SOCIAL PARTNERS

Turkish labour relations are asymmetrical in the sense that there is only one confederation of employer organisations, while the unions are organised into three confederations. Tisk (Turkish Confederation of Employers' Associations) is the employers' confederation: 21 employers' associations comprising 8,300 enterprises and 1,200,000 employees and operating in various sectors of the economy are affiliated to Tisk. The public employers' associations (affiliates of Tisk) are Kamu-Is, Tuhis and Miksen.

Pennings, *Flexibilisation and Modernisation of the Turkish Labour Market*, 41–80

Of the trade unions, Türk-Iş (Confederation of Trade Unions of Turkey) is the largest confederation. It is situated to the centre left of the political spectrum. Disk is the Confederation of Progressive Trade Unions of Turkey and is situated politically more towards the left wing. Hak-Iş is the Confederation of Righteous Trade Unions and has an Islamic stance and leanings. However, under the pressures of globalisation and European integration, Turkish Islamists are embracing democracy and Hak-Iş is starting to incorporate democratic goals.[1]

On the basis of recent labour statistics issued by the Ministry of Labour and Social Security, it appears that there are 96 industrial unions established in 28 industries. Of the five million workers with a contract of employment, the unionisation rate is more than 58 per cent.[2] Appendix 2, Table 1, gives an overview of trade union membership.

Civil servant union organisations are also fragmented: there are fifty-four industrial unions established within eleven industries and six civil servants' confederations.[3] For further details, see Appendix 2, Table 2.

4.3 THE STATUTORY FRAMEWORK OF THE EMPLOYERS' AND EMPLOYEES' ORGANISATIONS

4.3.1 Principles Governing the Foundation of Trade Unions and Employers' Associations

The principle of freedom of association is laid down in Article 51 of the 1982 Constitution. On the basis of this article, workers and employers have the right to form unions and organisations without prior authorisation in order to safeguard and develop their economic and social rights and the interests of their members. Freedom of association means that practices which make the employment of a worker conditional on membership (either before or after recruitment) such as closed shop (pre-entry closed shop), union shop (post-entry closed shop) and agency

1 For a detailed analysis of Hak-Iş, see B. Duran and S. Sugur, 'Islamism, Trade Unionism and Civil Society: the Case of Hak-Iş Labour Confederation in Turkey', *Middle Eastern Studies,* Vol. 41 (2005), pp. 227–248.

2 Of 5,022,584 workers 2,945,929 are members of the union. The exact unionisation rate is therefore 58.65 per cent (*Official Gazette*, 17 July 2005). These 5 million workers work under a contract of employment. In addition there are 1.5 million individuals working as civil servants or in an assimilated legal position with their own unions, a huge military sector, and the self-employed. Note also that these numbers are relatively low compared to the total population of 70 million.

3 KESK, TURKIYE KAMU-SEN, MEMUR-SEN, BASK, HURRIYETCI KAMUSEN, ANADOLU KAMU-SEN.

shop, are forbidden. In other words, all workers are free to become a member or to end membership of a union.

The current Unions Act of 1983 provides more specific rules for employer and employee organisations. This Law has the following main principles: voluntary unionism, industrial unionism and union pluralism. Industrial unionism denotes unionisation at the industry level (work branches, branches of activity): under Article 3 of the Unions Act, trade unions have to be constituted on an industry basis by workers employed in the same branch of activity with the objective of undertaking activities throughout Turkey.

Confederations, the only form of higher organisations of trade unions or employers' associations, have corporate status and must be formed by at least five unions active in various industries.[4]

Employers' associations have to be constituted on an industrial basis by employers in the same industry and must have national scope. As an exception, public employers' associations are not subject to the principle of industrial unionism. Thus the social partners are generally expected to operate nationwide and to organise workers on a national basis, although they may actually only be active in a certain area.

4.3.2 A Historical Background to the Statutory Framework for Employees' and Employers' Organisations

Industrial unionism is motivated by the situation that all industrial unions which were formed before the Unions Act 1983 were in fact just local unions. Under the Unions Act of 1963, there was absolute freedom to found a local or industrial union and to define the geographical working area of the union. No legal measures to prevent unions from operating on an exclusively local basis were permitted. The legislation allowed union pluralism with more than one trade union present in the same industry or a single establishment. Although the exact number of trade unions which existed at the time is unknown, the result was a large number of unions.

The fragmentation of the unions was accompanied by aggressive organisational campaigns and hostility among workers of the same establishment. Such rivalry was detrimental not only to any joint action, but also to the growth of sound labour-management relations, since they caused outbreaks of violence which ultimately had to be controlled by the police. The trade unions took an intransigent and uncompromising attitude and contract negotiations used to be terminated by means of strikes. Moreover, their leaders were very keen to retain and consolidate their firmly entrenched leadership posts since they were rewarding both in terms of income and of prestige. They were, therefore, reluctant to convert their autonomous

4 Unions Act, art. 2, final section.

local organisations into branch offices of an industrial union as they would then be subject to the dictates of a central head office.

The fierce competition amongst unions had a detrimental effect on industrial output and severe damage was done to a number of establishments. Local unionism was therefore seen as one of the main causes of a total breakdown in industrial relations and a serious fragmentation of unions.

The Unions Act of 1983 consequently introduced measures to rectify the situation, including a requirement that an industrial union be 'genuinely' industrial. This was achieved by specifying twenty-eight industries in which unions may be constituted.[5] Another instrument aimed at changing the former situation is the Collective Labour Agreements, Strikes and Lockouts Act, which requires that a union represent at least ten per cent of the workers employed in a particular industry before it can be designated as an 'authorised union'. Moreover, the union has to represent more than half the number of total employees in the place of work concerned. It is the exclusive right of the authorised union to bargain with an employer or employers' association with the purpose of reaching a collective labour agreement. If this leads to a collective agreement, the authorised union, now called a signatory party, is entitled to receive its funds through the automatic deduction of union fees and solidarity ducs (contributions paid by workers who are not a member of the signatory union but who want to benefit from the collective agreement) by the employer, a system known as the check-off system.

Up to 1983, a union only had to represent one-fourth of the workforce of the establishment to benefit from this system. While creating financially strong unions with desirable leadership posts,[6] this situation led to a proliferation of trade unions and great rivalry. Following the Unions Act 1983, Article 61,[7] the situation was modified so that only the signatory union, and if there were no signatory union, the authorised union was entitled to benefit from the automatic (and statutory) check-off system.

5 Unions Act, art. 60: agriculture, forestry, hunting and fishing; mining; petroleum, chemical and rubber; food; sugar; textile; leather; woodwork; paper; press, publishing and broadcasting; banking and insurance; cement, ceramic and glass; metal; shipbuilding; construction; energy; commercial, clerical, education and fine arts; inland transportation; rail transportation; sea transportation; air transportation; warehouse and storage; communication; health; accommodation and entertainment places; national defence; journalism; and general services.

6 A lot more than half the total number of members would most probably refrain from paying dues without this system. The unions would not be able to expel them from membership due to the danger of falling below the authorised union threshold.

7 We cannot of course describe all changes in detail, but some major changes were as follows: a ceiling on the amount of monthly union dues was introduced, there were no other dues allowed than union dues, and prohibition of simultaneous membership (multiple membership). Simultaneous membership caused problems in determining which was the authorised union, sometimes leading to the designation of more than one union as the one authorised for the same establishment.

It is not difficult to see why the present system is also leading to financially strong unions and to a lot of competition and rivalry amongst unions. Unions are competing with each other in order to become the authorised trade union. This situation has lead to unions adopting a confrontational attitude simply to avoid being criticised by other competing unions for cowardice. This has resulted in a complex and emotional process of bargaining or consultation with a reluctance to compromise and a tendency to strike even if the results of bargaining are satisfactory.

The prohibition on locals unions and the ten per cent threshold are inconsistent with the right of free association as laid down in ILO Convention 87 (Freedom of Association and Protection of the Right to Organise Convention, 1948). For this reason Turkey has been criticised on a regular basis by both the ILO and the EU.

4.4 THE CHARACTERISTICS OF LABOUR RELATIONS IN TURKEY

4.4.1 An Emphasis on Conflict

An important characteristic of Turkish labour relations is the emphasis on differences and conflicts and not on common interests and consensus. An important explanatory factor is that for a long period of time trade unions and employer associations have regarded each other as rivals with totally conflicting interests. During negotiation and consultation by the Government the differences and conflicts are usually emphasised: the aim is not to look for common interests. There is constant and excessive win-lose confrontation and not enough win-win strategies at the bargaining and consultation table. Collective bargaining – as the most widespread form of social dialogue in Turkey – is characterised as distributive bargaining and not integrative bargaining. However, there is an increasing though gradual tendency to try and identify common interests (see Section 4.6.3 for more details).

A second characteristic is that the various unions, divided and inclined to conflict as they are (as discussed in the previous sections), have created a context within which 'the winner takes it all'. In other words, the industrial relations context can be described as a win-lose context: the other party must 'surrender'. That has been the traditional context for unions and employers, but it is also evident among unions themselves, as we saw in the previous section. It can be explained in terms of the rivalry between union representatives and executives being personally rewarding. Moreover, such representatives often use the unions as agencies for gaining personal and political power by encouraging aggressive organisational campaigns, strikes or militant activities. A reason for this situation is the high number (twenty-eight) of industries due to the principle of industrial unionism (see Section 4.3). Although an important goal of the introduction of industrial unionism was to diminish the number of unions, the high number of identified industries is still leading to partition on the part of the unions.

A third characteristic is that unions are focused more on government and labour legislation than on the employers or other unions or on consultation and negotiation. Labour legislation has always been the major means of establishing labour standards. In general, the social partners tend to expect more from laws than from negotiation or consultation between the social partners. As a result, legislation covers a broad spectrum of issues in Turkey, issues which in other countries are the subject of social dialogue. For instance, job security, fair treatment, training in occupational health and safety issues and paid leave are regulated in great detail by the law. Likewise, legislation rather than not collective bargaining plays the main role in transfers of undertakings and in collective dismissals. Collective bargaining mainly concerns wages.

4.4.2 The Collective Bargaining Process

Collective bargaining is the most widespread form of social dialogue. Although social bargaining is formally bipartite, the State, although not a participant, is responsible for creating a suitable environment and for providing the necessary legal and institutional framework for the activities of the partners.

4.4.2.1 Levels of Bargaining

Only a competent and authorised industrial union is allowed to bargain with employers and to conclude a collective labour agreement. This can be at three different levels: at the level of the workplace (establishment), at the level of groups of workplaces and at the level of the undertaking (enterprise). Consequently, there are local (workplace) collective agreements, group (workplaces) collective agreements and collective agreement undertakings. Workplaces belonging to the same employer and functioning in the same industry constitute an undertaking for the purposes of the Collective Labour Agreements, Strikes and Lockouts Act.

Where a single workplace is involved, the parties are statutorily obliged to conclude a local collective labour agreement. If a single undertaking is involved, an undertaking collective labour agreement has to be made. Parties do not have a legal obligation to conclude a collective labour agreement for a group of workplaces. If there is no such agreement, separate collective labour agreements at the level of each workplace or undertaking will have to be made.

A trade union can only be party to a group collective labour agreement if it is the authorised union for each grouped workplace and/or undertakings to be covered. Only employers' organisations can conclude a group agreement: unaffiliated employers cannot do so.

4.4.2.2 Parties to Collective Bargaining

A confederation is not competent to conclude a collective agreement. Workers' and employers' confederations may, however, meet and reach a 'common understanding' on labour issues. If they come to such an agreement, it serves as a guideline for developing collective labour agreements. It is the exclusive right of the competent and authorised union to bargain with an employer or employers' association with the purpose of reaching a collective labour agreement. As we have seen, there are two numerical requirements to be fulfilled to qualify as the authorised trade union: the industrial union has to represent at least ten per cent of the total employees in the industry concerned[8] and to represent more than half of the total employees in the place of work concerned.[9] For the conclusion of a group collective labour agreement, there can be only one trade union on the side of the workers and one association at the side of the employers. The Ministry of Labour and Social Security publishes statistics twice a year that serve as a basis for the designation of the authorised union.

As we explained in Section 4.3.2, the signatory union benefits from the automatic check-off system. As a general principle, only the member workers of the signatory trade union may benefit from the concluded collective labour agreement. Workers who are not a member of the signatory union can benefit from the collective agreement if they pay so-called solidarity dues. The consent of the signatory union is not required for non-member workers to benefit from the agreement via the payment of solidarity dues (otherwise the principle of voluntary unionism would be infringed). Workers who are not members of the signatory trade union may benefit from the agreement if they pay 'solidarity dues' to the signatory union. This applies also for those who are subsequently recruited but do not join the signatory union and those who have resigned or were expelled from the signatory union after the conclusion date. Solidarity dues amount to two-thirds of the union dues. Thus it is very important to be a signatory union. The solidarity dues are also collected by means of the automatic check-off system.[10]

---

8 An exception applies for agriculture, forestry, hunting and fishing (industry no. 1) where organisation is relatively difficult.

9 There may be a majority union, even one having the total employed as its members but if this trade union has failed to fulfil the other prerequisite (to represent at least ten per cent of the total employed in the industry to which the place of work concerned belongs) there can be no collective labour agreement.

10 As a rule, a very great percentage of the member workers of the non-signatory unions do not pay their union dues. Solidarity dues were imposed in the first place because the unions were very afraid of losing their paying members if the rest could benefit without having to pay dues. If the same result (benefiting from the collective labour agreement) could be acquired without any expense (dues), then the member workers would feel fooled and would prefer to resign once the collective agreement was signed, or at least for the term of the collective agreement (one to three years to be decided by the parties).

4.4.2.3 Collective Bargaining Issues

As we saw in Section 4.4.1, in Turkey labour legislation has been the major means of establishing absolutely and relatively binding labour standards. It may be claimed that power relations come to tangible expression in legislation and governmental regulations. Legislation covers a broad spectrum of issues that might otherwise have been the subject of collective bargaining. The unions tend to demand most laws and law amendments from the State rather than trying to make such gains through bargaining procedures. The relatively binding provisions of labour legislation do offer a starting point for collective bargaining. Any subsequent collective bargaining usually aims at increasing minimum standards (relatively binding provisions), but because many issues are regulated in great detail in the law, the parties tend to focus on remuneration issues.

The original purpose of labour legislation was the regulation of social powers aimed at establishing and maintaining equilibrium between the social partners. More recently, new debates have taken place, including the creation of employment via greater flexibility, corporate governance, socially responsible restructuring and alternative dispute resolution. The promotion of employment and enterprise efficiency is now expected to form part of labour legislation and collective bargaining. Collective bargaining as a dynamic process will undergo major changes with these new tendencies. In the near future, collective bargaining as the basic form of social dialogue may serve as a platform for the social partners to reach a common understanding on flexibility.

4.5 THE INSTITUTIONAL FRAMEWORK FOR SOCIAL DIALOGUE

In this section we discuss the social dialogue between the social partners themselves (bipartite) and between social partners and the government (tripartite) as well as consultation on national and other levels. Both formal and informal consultation will be described.

4.5.1 The Formal Tripartite Structures

The main platforms for the formal tripartite structure are described below.

Together with the then Ministry of Labour, the *Work Assembly* was already established by 1945. The Ninth Work Assembly (September 2004) is of particular importance. During this meeting three central subjects – employment creation, combating undeclared work and severance pay fund – were discussed. The discussion was on the basis of technical background reports prepared by the Ministry of Labour and Social Security. The Ninth Work Assembly Final Declaration became the first official document to use the term 'social partners'.[11] Its Final Declaration emphasised that a National Employment Plan consistent with the European Employment Strategy has to be developed and implemented via the joint efforts of the Government, labour and management.

The *Economic and Social Council* was established in 1995 following the issue by the Prime Minister of a circular whose subject was the addressing of economic and social issues at the highest level. It was regulated by a law in 2001.[12] The Council's main objective is to promote consensus building and democratic involvement among the main actors.[13] The Council consists of Government,[14] worker and employer representation. It has a 'tripartite-plus' composition. This means that it also consists of other relevant societal actors, including the Union of Chambers of Commerce and Commodity Exchanges, the Confederation of Tradesmen and Small Artisans, and the Association of Agricultural Chambers and NGOs. This is in order to gain a wider perspective, to incorporate the views of other social actors and to build wider consensus. The last convention of the Council was in March 2005, when it mainly discussed Council restructuring. The Council is not yet an effective institution. In an EC Progress Report, the Council was criticised by the EC for its poor functioning and structural deficiencies such as the dominant position of the Government.[15] A draft law was made to restructure the Council through a reduction in Government representation and to increase the representation of the social partners. It has not yet been adopted.

---

11 The notion of 'social partners' implies a significant shift from divergent objectives to shared objectives and a cooperative mode of engagement. The role of partnership has been envisaged for the social partners. In Turkey, the term 'social parties' tend to suggest adverseness rather than cooperation.

12 Act on Organisation and Functioning of the Economic and Social Council (no. 4641, *Official Gazette* dated 21 April 2001).

13 Among the duties of the Council is the election of the members to the EU–Turkey Economic and Social Consultative Committee that was established on the basis of article 27 of the Ankara Treaty in 1995. In doing so, the Council has to consider the structure and specialties of the EC Economic and Social Committee (art. 3d).

14 The Government is or may be represented by Prime Minister (chair), deputies to the Prime Minister, the State Minister responsible for the State Treasury, the State Minister responsible for the Under secretariat for External Trade, the State Minister responsible for the State Personnel Directorate, the Minister of Finance, the Minister of Agriculture and Village Affairs, the Minister of Labour and Social Security, the Minister of Industry and Commerce, the Minister of Energy and Natural Resources, the Undersecretary of State Planning Organisation, the Undersecretary of Customs, the Director of State Personnel, and other Government representatives and public servants to be determined by the Prime Minister.

15 The new Government Party declared an Urgent Action Plan on 11 November 2002 according to which the Council would be restructured and utilised efficiently. The Plan also confirmed the political will and commitment to engage in social dialogue on the part of the Government Party.

The *Tripartite Consultation Board* brings together the government, employers, workers and public officials, all of whom are represented on an equal footing, as provided by the new Labour Act (Article 114).[16] The main objective of this Board is to promote effective consultation at the national level between public authorities and social partners. The unit directors of the Ministry (or its affiliated bodies, depending on the particulars of the agenda), three representatives designated by the three representative workers' confederations, three designated by the representative employers' confederation and three designated by the three representative public officials' confederations have to meet three times a year under the chairmanship of the Minister of Labour and Social Security or his undersecretary. The Board must contribute to the development of labour policies, conduct studies to strengthen co-operation and compromise between the social partners, follow and express views on the amendments, preparation and implementation of labour laws, and promote efficient consultation, information and dialogue between the social partners on the harmonisation of Turkish legislation with the community *acquis*. The Board convened twice in 2004 and mainly discussed implementation problems under the new Labour Act. Its decisions aim at closer cooperation by the social partners.[17]

İş-Kur[18] was established by the Turkish Employment Organisation Act in 2003.[19] İş-Kur is an incorporated public body which is administratively and financially autonomous. Its main task is to maintain, develop, and increase employment, to engage in activities to prevent unemployment and to conduct unemployment insurance services.[20] The general congress and the managing committee of İş-Kur

16 Appropriate arrangements on Board composition, functions and working procedures were made through a by-law (*Official Gazette*, 4 April 2004).

17 For instance, the social partners must inform the Ministry of any implementation problems confronted under the new Labour Act, prepare a social policies package with the Ministry, and forward to the Ministry their concerns and recommendations on issues of employment and undeclared work following which a report is to be sent to the consideration of the Council of Ministers.

18 The Turkish Employment Organisation.

19 In that year a comprehensive organisational reform took place and the Social Security Organisation was established as a central body under which three administratively and financially independent State agencies were brought together: SSK, Bağ-Kur (Organisation for the self-employed, including those in agriculture) and İş-Kur.

20 The main responsibilities of İş-Kur as defined by law are:

- to become involved in activities relating to the development of a national employment program, to the maintenance and improvement of employability, to the prevention of unemployment, to labour placement and to the facilitation of worker mobility
- to administer the unemployment insurance scheme which became operational in April 2002. The system covers insured workers who lose their jobs.
- to compile, analyse, interpret, and publish national and local labour data, to support statistical databases measuring progress in its activities and to establish and coordinate the studies of the Labour Market Information Consultation Board.

have tripartite compositions. The Unemployment Insurance Fund Management Board functioning under İş-Kur and the Occupational Standards Commission of which İş-Kur is a member, also have a tripartite composition.

Other formal tripartite platforms for social dialogue at the national level are as follows:

- The Minimum Wage Board, which is charged with the determination of the minimum wage for industrial and agricultural workers[21]
- The Supreme Arbitration Board[22]
- The Commission on cessation of work in workplaces or disclosure of workplaces[23]
- The Board empowered to expend fines imposed upon workers' wages[24]
- The Board empowered to determine how to expend fines imposed upon employers who do not recruit the required number of disabled people and ex-convicts[25]
- The Vocational Training Council, the Provincial Vocational Training Boards, autonomous bodies such as KOSGEB and METARGEM which play important roles in vocational education and training, and general congresses and the managing boards of public social security organisations

To be successful, social dialogue depends on full participation by labour confederations. As a rule, newly established consultation bodies have the three labour confederations represented, whereas older consultation platforms limit participation to the representative labour confederation, Türk-Iş. The other two confederations,

---

- training, retraining and other employability measures including vocational guidance and counselling. İş–Kur is the main body for providing jobseekers with vocational guidance and training as a complement to the learning systems by which work knowledge and skills are traditionally acquired.
- to license and supervise private employment organisations
- to follow up the decisions made by the EU and other international organisations in respect of labour force, employment and work environment and to implement those relevant bilateral or multilateral international treaties to which Turkey is a party
- to carry out duties entrusted upon it in respect of foreign nationals in Turkey. The Act on Foreigners' Work Permits was enacted in March 2003. This Act is in line with international laws and regulations, especially the Community *acquis*. It came into force on 6 September 2003 and there is a heavy fine for those employing foreigners illegally.

21 Labour Act, art. 39.

22 Collective Labour Agreements, Strikes and Lockouts Act, art. 53.

23 Labour Act, art. 79.

24 Labour Act, art. 38.

25 Labour Act, art. 30/11.

Disk and Hak-Iş, have constantly challenged their exclusion, while Türk-Iş does not want to have the rule changed.

4.5.2 The Formal Bipartite Structures

On the national level there is no real formal bipartite structure for meetings exclusively between the representatives of the confederations of workers and employers. Of course, there are informal contacts between the social partners, but a more formalised platform where social partners meet regularly for discussing and developing common points of view is absent. Such contacts would be useful, amongst other things in order to have a stronger position in tripartite platforms including the Economic and Social Council. The labour confederations themselves do not even have a formal structure within which they meet to prepare for dialogue with employers or for their own contributions to tripartite platforms. This does, of course, have a lot to do with the serious nature of the rivalry between unions (see Section 4.3.2).

The trade unions and the employers' associations operate at the industrial (sectoral) level, although there is no collective bargaining at this level[26] (as was discussed in Section 4.4.2.1). Apart from collective bargaining, the social partners have some consulting obligations at the establishment level. These concern topics such as the election of trade union representatives and the exchange of information as well as consultation in relation to collective redundancies and short-time work. There are no works councils governed or required by statutory rules in Turkey.[27] Other formal platforms at the level of the establishment for social dialogue are based on the Labour Act:

- There must be occupational health and safety boards in workplaces with at least 50 workers where work of a permanent nature (lasting longer than six months) is performed.[28]
- There must be Paid Annual Leave Boards in workplaces with at least 100 workers.[29]

26 Although some people regard group collective agreements as 'something between company and sectoral level', they are actually no more than a collection of local collective agreements concluded at the same time. So far, group collective agreements have been concluded only in the metal sector.

27 Work councils are not prohibited: an establishment can therefore elect to have a work council. To our knowledge there are no such councils.

28 Labour Act, art. 80.

29 By the By-law on annual leave, art. 10.

– In addition, laws give a right to information such as the right of the worker to be informed and trained by the employer on issues relating to occupational health and safety (Article 77), the obligation of the employer to inform workers of the conditions applicable to the labour contract (Article 8/3), and the safeguarding of workers' rights in the event of transfers of undertakings or businesses or parts thereof (Article 6).

The formal consultation structure on the tripartite and bipartite level is summarised in Table 4.1.

Table 4.1: Formal Consultative Structure in Turkey

Partners:	*Tripartite (Employers, Unions, Government and Others)*	*Bipartite (Employers and Unions)*
National level: (level of confederations; corporate status formed by at least 5 unions active in different industries)	Work Assembly *Issues**: employment creation, combating undeclared work, severance pay funding	No formal bipartite consultation structure No collective bargaining for confederations is allowed. Confederations may reach a 'common understanding' on labour issues to serve as a guideline for collective labour agreements to be concluded by their affiliates.
	Tripartite Consultation Board *Issues**: implementation problems under the new Labour Act	
	Economic and Social Council (= tripartite+) *Issues**: restructuring the Council	
	Turkish Employment Organisation (Is-Kur) *Issues**: Employment activities, training, administering unemployment insurance, compiling labour data etc.	
	Other platforms: Minimum Wage Board, Supreme Arbitration Board, Vocational Training Council, Provincial Vocational Training Boards, Commissions etc.	
Sectoral level: (level of 28 industries)	Not applicable	Level for establishing trade unions and employers' associations

Partners:	*Tripartite (Employers, Unions, Government and Others)*	*Bipartite (Employers and Unions)*
Company level	Not applicable	Collective bargaining** Institutional framework (for selecting trade union representatives, information sharing during collective redundancies, and short-time work) Other platforms: occupational health and safety boards; Paid Annual Leave Boards

* = The term 'issues' refers here to the issues discussed in the latest conventions. Other issues may also have been discussed within these platforms.

** = collective bargaining is only allowed for an authorised union that fulfils the 2 conditions.

4.5.3 Informal (Non-institutionalised) Consultation

During our interviews, trade union and employers' organisation representatives stated that they have many informal contacts. Despite this, constructive informal consultation in Turkey seems to be rare and is much more dependent on individuals and personal capacities than elsewhere. An important reason for this is the rivalry between trade unions. Another reason is that trade unions and employers have long regarded each other as rivals with completely conflicting interests. Consequently the social partners are not familiar with constructive informal consultation.

4.5.4 The Attitudes of the Social Partners towards Flexibility

As a result of a long history in which the State has been the main employer and a guarantee of life-long employment especially for public sector workers, the trade unions are still staunch defenders of the status quo. The unions still insist on detailed legislation containing rigid provisions as their 'protection wall'. Job security is the highest priority for the trade unions,[30] whereas employers are inclined to make

30 For a detailed study of this topic, see A.N. Süral, 'Employment Termination and Job Security Under New Turkish Labour Act', *Middle Eastern Studies,* Vol. 41 (2005), pp. 249–268.

use of favourably changing patterns of work. For this reason employers have been taking the initiative in promoting flexibility.[31]

The trade unions have been contented with defending the existing levels of protection and institutional arrangements. These stand in the way of decentralisation and destandardisation of employment relations and there are no alternatives available for generating new employment. The renunciation of a set normal working time and atypical employment were regarded as heralding the end of trade unionism.

4.6 SOCIAL DIALOGUE IN PRACTICE: OBSTACLES, THE ROLE OF THE GOVERNMENT, STYLE AND OUTCOMES

4.6.1 Introduction

In order to explore social dialogue in practice we interviewed the representatives of the various confederations of trade unions and the employers' association in Turkey. In addition a questionnaire was sent by e-mail to the same representatives of the confederations of trade unions and the employers' association. This questionnaire made use of more or less standardised questions and answers. The results are shown summarised in Appendix 1. Below we will discuss the main findings.

4.6.2 Obstacles to the Success of Social Dialogue

The major causes hindering the enhancement and facilitation of social dialogue were identified as follows:

Different perceptions. The respective parties have different views on what social dialogue is or should be. Naturally, this affects how the institutions function and the consultation platforms. In particular, the unions and employers have been critical of the role of the Government, which takes a position of 'non-listening and not looking for an agreement' (see further Section 4.6.3).

The representativity problem. A main problem, mentioned by the unions, is that of full participation (in other words the problem of representativity). This problem particularly affects tripartite social dialogue, in which the 'persistence of a monopolist structure or attitude' has been identified as an important obstacle. According to the two other union confederations, Türk-Iş – the confederation with the highest number of members – acts like a monopolist. This confederation has the

31 See also A.N. Süral, 'Reorganization of Working Time and Modalities of Employment under the New Turkish Labour Act', *Middle Eastern Studies,* Vol. 41 (2005), pp. 407–420.

power to oppose amendments proposed to the Unions Act 1983 and the Collective Labour Agreements, Strikes and Lockouts Act.

Hak-Iş and Disk share the view that for the sake of genuine Turkish social dialogue, the full participation principle should be applied consistently, but that Türk-Iş has never been in favour of any involvement by the other confederations in the consultation bodies.

As a confederation, Türk-Iş benefits the most from the threshold determining the existence of an authorised trade union. As we have seen, this threshold requires that a union represent at least ten per cent of the workers employed in a particular industry. Türk-Iş has more than three times as many members as Disk and Hak-Iş put together. Of the affiliated unions that reach the threshold, 31 unions are affiliated with Türk-Iş, nine with Disk and five with Hak-Iş (Appendix 2, Table A).

Hak-Iş and Disk want to have the threshold lifted, while Türk-Iş insists on maintaining it. The Turkish Ministry has asked the social partners to reach an agreement on the issue after which legislation will be enacted. Tisk, the employers' organisation, has stated that it will accept the decision made by the workers' confederations, but no agreement has been reached so far.

Tisk mentioned two main obstacles. Like the union confederations, this organisation is critical of the role of the government within the social dialogue (see further Section 4.6.3), though the union confederations and the employers' confederation are critical of different aspects of this role. The employers' confederation claims that the government is too dominant in protecting workers' rights and interests, while the labour confederations complain that the government is too dominant in *not wanting* to protect these rights and interests.

The second obstacle mentioned by Tisk is the issue of the informal market or the undeclared sector. The informal market – estimated to be bigger than the formal market – and the workers and employers involved are not represented within the social dialogue.

4.6.3 The Role of Government within the System

The social partners describe the role of the Turkish government within the social dialogue as a problematic one. For this reason the opinion of a number of social partners on the role of the government is interesting. For some specific answers from the various social partners see Appendix 1, Table A.

The Turkish government asserts that social dialogue is the main tool for addressing new challenges. The Ministry, for instance, gives priority to social dialogue and has made repeated calls on the social partners to reach a common understanding and mutual agreement on controversial issues, declaring that such agreements will be respected and implemented.

The social partners, however, consider the present role of the government within social dialogue as insufficient and not productive. They are all of the opinion that the role of the government is too dominant. Simply put: the government should listen more to social partners and not always act on its own behalf.

The social partners claim that the government should take social dialogue more seriously. In our interviews and in answer to the questionnaire they criticise the government for not consulting them, claiming that all it does is give explanations, instructions and presentations. As an illustration, the social partners refer to instances in which the government has constantly claimed that there is no room to manoeuvre within the government's proposal because institutions such as the ILO or World Bank impose certain obligations. Social partners are of the opinion that the government is using these kinds of arguments too often as an excuse for sticking to its initial proposal. Another instance of not taking social dialogue seriously is, according to social partners, that they have not received necessary drafts of bills since sending all those drafts would make no difference in a situation in which Turkey has to conform to the law, come what may.

According to the social partners, the government should make a greater effort to ensure the success of the social dialogue. All social partners would prefer the government to develop the role of a mediator towards reaching agreement. They are also of the opinion that the government should facilitate social dialogue more (for instance, by organising more meetings and workshops) and thereby ensure its success. Some social partners, including Disk and Türk-Iş, favour the creation by the government of a code of conduct for social dialogue that all parties must respect. Tisk does not think such a code of conduct is a good idea.

It is obvious that all social partners disagree with the statement that 'the government should be going more its own way because social partners can never agree'. They differ, however, in their views on the way the Government can best reach agreement or make progress. The union confederations have in fact conceded that the government can only feel obliged to take the viewpoints of the social partners into consideration if the social partners themselves have first reached agreement. Even if it is agreed that the government can do more to promote social dialogue, the need for agreement between social partners themselves is very strong. This is the best way to get results within a system of tripartite consultation.

4.6.4 The Style of Turkish Social Dialogue

All the organisations underline the importance of social dialogue. They agree with the statement that good social dialogue is important. They differ, however, on whether to characterise the Turkish social dialogue as looking for common interests (as Türk-Iş and Hak-Iş have stated) or as looking for conflicting interests (as Disk has stated). The employers take an in-between position in this discussion.

Organisations agree that within the Turkish social dialogue bargaining is primarily 'distributive' and not 'integrative'. This means that the Turkish social partners see dialogue as being characterised by one side losing while the other wins (win-lose confrontation): adverseness and competition are prevalent. The only dissenting voice is that of Türk-Iş.[32]

4.6.5 The Outcomes of Social Dialogue

The importance of social dialogue is also underlined by the fact that all social partners – except for Hak-Iş – share the view that it leads to results. However, a number of the partners, including Disk and Türk-Iş, also agree with the conclusion that social dialogue is not successful at this moment. Tisk takes an in-between position; it thinks that the bipartite social dialogue is working well at confederation level, but the dialogue at the level of the trade unions and the employer is a problem and is the result of a pattern of behaviour displayed by the trade unions.

The social partners find it difficult to mention even one successful example of Turkish social dialogue. The example that comes closest to success concerns the enactment of the new Labour Act. They mention this as a success since the government did actually consult the social partners on this occasion and really wanted to have consensus on the final text. A tripartite commission of nine professors was formed to prepare the new Labour Act: three appointed by the government, three by Tisk and one by each of the three labour confederations (Türk-Iş, Hak-Iş, Disk). In the commission a balance had to be found between the objectives of the employers and the employees. The employers wanted to make companies more productive and competitive through improvement of flexitime and flexible forms of employment. The labour confederations wanted to protect the job security of its workers. In this minefield, the commission tried to find a balance by following the relevant EC directives. The social partners eventually agreed to respect the resulting text. However, they appeared not to do so in practice. The Ministry consulted the social partners before the text of the Commission was sent to Parliament. The social partners lobbied intensively throughout the period that the text was being discussed by the legislature. Partly due to misunderstandings and misinterpretations, the issues of flexibility were loudly contested by some union confederations and the opposition party. As a result, the provisions of the proposed act on subcontracting and atypical types of employment (regarded as insecure and precarious) were revised in the unions' favour. At the same time increased job security was confined to workplaces employing thirty or more workers and the level of compensation in the event of unfair dismissal was lowered to the advantage of the employers. As

32 For some specific answers from the various social partners, see Appendix 1, table B.

a result, the initially proposed degree of flexibility could not be maintained in the final bill. The employers were left behind disappointed.

Although the social partners are of the opinion that Turkish social dialogue is not successful and the outcomes are limited at this moment, they are modestly optimistic about the future.[33] This optimism has much to do with the growing importance of social dialogue. According to Hak-Iş social dialogue will be much more important in the future due to preparations for integration with the EU. Tripartite consultation will be extremely important in the implementation of new regulations on working life. Issues such as work councils have to be integrated into Turkish legislation in the future, and workers' right to information and consultation, as well as sectoral collective labour agreements, indicate the necessity of institutionalising social dialogue.

The optimism has also much to do with the expectations of all the social partners that the three tripartite platforms (Work Assembly, Tripartite Consultation Board and the Economic and Social Council) will function better in the near future.[34] According to Disk, these three bodies give social parties the chance of declaring, sharing and discussing their views and proposals and that will have a positive impact. For Türk-Iş it is important that they have a legal basis.

In general, the optimism has its roots in the fact that some of these platforms are constructed or are under construction in such a way that the position of the government is or will be less dominant and the position of social partners will be improved. However, if their own bipartite social dialogue is no better developed than it is today the social partners may well be too optimistic in this regard. They may have a better position in the new structure, but the outcome may remain poor if social dialogue is still too much based on conflicting interests and attitudes.

4.6.6 Social and Economic Factors Influencing Social Dialogue

In this section, social dialogue will be discussed against the background of some important Turkish social and economic aspects. Table 4.2 contains several key social economic figures. From these figures the following brief conclusions in relation to the current labour market in Turkey can be drawn:

- The population increases every year by about 1.55 per cent; it now consists of more than seventy million people.
- Civilian employment has decreased slightly since 2001. In 2004 civilian employment was on the way to 22 million persons.

33 For some specific answers from the various social partners, see Appendix 1, Table B.

34 For some specific answers from the various social partners, see Appendix 1, Table C.

– Unemployment (in total numbers and as a percentage) has increased since 2001. In 2004 more than 2¼ million people were unemployed (official figures).

Table 4.2: Important Turkish Social Economic Facts and Figures (2001–2004; where known)

Population	*2001*	*2002*	*2003*	*2004*
Total population (in thousands)	68,529	69,626	70,712	
Rate of increase (percentage)	1.63	1.59	1.55	
Employment*				
Civilian employment (in thousands)	21,524	21,354	21,147	21,791
Unemployment (in thousands)	1,967	2,464	2,493	2,269
Unemployment rate (percentage)	8.4	10.3	10.5	9.3
Employment* status (in thousands)				
Total	21,524	21,354	21,147	21,791
Paid workers	10,155	10,625	10,707	11,079
Self employed and employers	6,504	6,274	6,302	6,408
Unpaid family workers	4,865	4,455	4,138	4,303

* = 15+ age: annual average

Recent figures (February 2005) show that total employment is – compared to the average total employment of 2004 – again diminishing (20,838,000 persons are employed).

Table 4.3 shows that in 2004 more than ten million people were registered at the three social security organisations, SSK, Emekli Sandigi and Bağ-Kur, while at the same time employment was more than twenty-two million. Consequently less than half of those in employment were registered in social security, meaning that more than half were not registered and were doing undeclared work. This figure is striking and changing undeclared work into declared work is and should remain an important topic for Turkish social dialogue.

Table 4.3 Registered and Not Registered Social Security

	thousands	*percentage*
Registered by social security organisations:	10,246	
SSK (workers)	5,733	
Emekli Sandigi (social security organisation for civil servants)	1,916	
Bağ-Kur (self-employed)	2,487	
Total employment registered in social security	22,188	100%
Total unregistered	11,942	54%
Total registered	10,246	46%

Based on *Household Labour Force Survey Results 2004, 2nd quarter*

Table 4.4 shows the total employment by status and the percentage of 'un-registered in social security system' for 2004 and the statistics for February 2005. It is no surprise that the 'unpaid family workers' (95 per cent), the 'self-employed' (64.5 per cent) and the 'casual paid workers' (91.3 per cent) are not registered as recipients of social security in 2005.

Table 4.4: Total Employment and Unregistered Social Security by Employment Status

	Average 2004		*February 2005*	
	Total employment	*Unregistered*	*Total employment*	*Unregistered*
	thousands	*percentage*	*thousands*	*percentage*
Paid workers (regular)	9,279	21.2	9,713	21.5
Paid workers (casual)	1,800	91.7	1,233	91.3
Employer	1,020	24.2	1,062	25.2
Self-employed	5,388	65.5	5,458	64.5
Unpaid family workers	4,303	96.5	3,371	95.0
Total	21,791	53.0	20,838	49.0

The effects of these figures on social dialogue will be described in the following section.

4.7 TURKISH LABOUR MARKETS, SOCIAL DIALOGUE AND THE ISSUE OF FLEXIBILITY

In order to become a member of the EU Turkey must be able to compete within the common market. The progress reports by the European Commission demonstrate that the way the Turkish labour market functions constitutes a major hindrance towards accession. Improving Turkish labour legislation and social dialogue, combating the informal economy and increasing the administrative capacity for implementation are elements which are necessary to ensure better functioning of the Turkish labour market.

Recent studies estimate that the informal labour market is bigger than the formal market (see also Tables 4.2–4.4). This situation cannot continue to exist if Turkey wants to join the EU. In our interviews with Hak-Iş, Türk-Iş, Disk and Tisk, the organisations all shared the view that the large informal market is a major problem in Turkey. They differ in how this problem can be solved.

The central issue is how to change informal (undeclared) labour into formal (declared) labour. How can at the very least parts of the informal labour market be incorporated in the formal Turkish labour market? Many courses of action and measures have been proposed in the other reports that the current project has given rise to and which are included as chapters in this book. It was therefore interesting to ask the social partners to give their opinion on the importance and urgency of the recommendations which have been made so far.[35]

The urgency of the recommendations accepted by the social partners may be a good indicator of consensus on this topic.

In this section only significant conclusions are presented. Table D in Appendix 1 shows the following:

- The social partners agree on measures formulated for the following three issues: the informal labour market, the position of women, and sectoral policy; they disagree (in particular) on the topic of flexibility and flexicurity.
- The social partners agree on the following measures which they see as urgent to very urgent:
  - (In relation to the issue of the informal labour market) measures such as the development of a more stable tax and social security policy and the development of easy accessible training and schooling programmes

35 For an overview of these improvements, their contribution to specific Employment Guidelines and the specific scores given by the various social partners see Appendix 1, table D. See, in particular, Chapter 2. The representatives of Tisk, Disk, Türk-Iş and Hak-Iş have given their opinion ('yes', 'no', 'don't know') on these measures in a small standardised questionnaire and also expressed the sense of urgency they attach to the measures. The coding is as follows: – (= not urgent), + (= urgent) and ++ = very urgent.

- (In relation to the issue of the position of women) measures to combat the social exclusion of women such as more programmes for child care and educational programmes

– The social partners concur wholeheartedly with the following:
  - An *integrated* approach for changing informal (undeclared) labour into formal labour is missing. There is a need to coordinate the various measures within the various fields.
  - There is little *monitoring of progress* within this field (changing undeclared labour into formal labour). The little that is done is not done well.
– The social partners more or less agree (but certainly do not *dis*agree) on some of the following measure and topics as:
  - Greater effort and more measures are necessary in the region (for instance, provincial employment boards must be assigned with special tasks for fighting informal employment and clandestine foreign labour).
  - The enforcement capacity of the Turkish Labour Inspectorate must be increased.
  - A kind of 'good-example-policy' must be developed (for instance, to give employers who work according to the rules favourable publicity).

The social partners disagree in particular on the measures and courses of action proposed to improve flexibilisation and flexicurity. This disagreement exists not only between union confederations and employers: the union confederations themselves have different opinions about these proposed measures and course of action. The measures and courses of actions are as follows:

– The admittance of temporary work agencies which could be a useful instrument for labour market policies as they could create points of entry onto to the formal labour market.
– The improvement of the legal position of temporary work agencies. The government should consider changing the Labour Act, introducing a licensing system for temporary work agencies and agreeing on the development of vocational training programmes for employees working for temporary work agencies.
– The improvement of legislative provisions for flexible work. At this moment legislative provisions referring to flexible work contracts are relatively limited.

Tisk is in favour of all three measures and courses of action and finds them urgent. Hak-Iş is in favour of the first two measures and agrees with the urgency of the measures, though it doubts whether it is necessary to improve the legislation on flexible work. Türk-Iş agrees that there is a need for temporary work agencies to have a better legal position, but doubts whether the other two measures are useful. Disk strongly rejects the three measures. It rejects in principle all flexible forms of employment and also rejects another proposed course of action, i.e. the creation of more part-time jobs. Disk sticks to the principle of full-time job security.

The issue of flexicurity was another point of discussion. Strategies that seek to strike a balance between flexibility and security are labelled flexicurity strategies. The main message of the flexibility concept is that in modern labour markets flexibility should also be defined in terms of security and security should also be defined in terms of flexibility. Put differently, flexibility and security are not incompatible but should rather be seen as two sides of the same coin and as mutual preconditions. The implication is that flexible labour markets need *more,* rather than less security (be it different types of security), and that secure labour markets cannot exist without certain types of flexibility.[36]

Starting from the premise that you cannot have more flexibility without more security and knowing that other countries strike various and different balances between the use of full-time work (with more flexible rules in relation to hiring and firing) and part-time and temporary agency work (with increasingly better pay and labour conditions), we asked the Turkish social partners to choose between the following four options:

- Option 1: the strong position of full-time work and 'hiring and firing' regulations in Turkey can only be made more flexible if at the same time the weak position of part-time work is improved (for example, with increased rights and better labour conditions).
- Option 2: the strong position/situation of 'hiring and firing' in Turkey can only be made more flexible if at the same time the weak position of part-time and temporary agency work is improved (for example, with increased rights/better labour conditions).
- Option 3: improvements (in rights and labour conditions) for part-time and temporary agency work are acceptable as long as those improvements do not harm the position of formal full-time work.
- Option 4: even if flexibility contributes substantially to changing undeclared work into declared work one should never allow any form of flexibility and should always promote job security and full-time work.

On the assumption that flexibility will contribute to a substantial change of undeclared labour, the union confederations (Hak-Iş, Disk and Türk-Iş) chose option 3. Disk made this choice on the basis that 'full-time work is the basic type of work. The nature of part-time work and temporary work has to be identified in accordance with the workers and production needs and it should not adversely affect full-timers' positions and rights'. The choice made by Türk-Iş was motivated by its sense that

36 See Ch. 7.

there was a danger that flexibility as implemented in Turkey would deprive workers of social security and job security.

The position of Tisk can be placed within option 1 and option 2, although Tisk is against conferring new rights upon part timers. According to Tisk, flexible modalities of employment will become available in good time. More rights to part-timers may have adverse effects on employability. In other words: employers and establishments might be frightened by these new rights and make little or no use of part-time work. If it is not to the advantage of the employers (lower labour costs, easier hiring and firings) and if the rules on flexible employment are as strict as those on full-time workers employers will not be inclined to make use of the new forms of flexible work.

As a rule one can position the four social partners *and* 'flexicurity as a possible way-out' within a framework between more and less flexibility and more and less security.

Figure 4.1. Security and Flexibility and the Position of the Turkish Social Partners

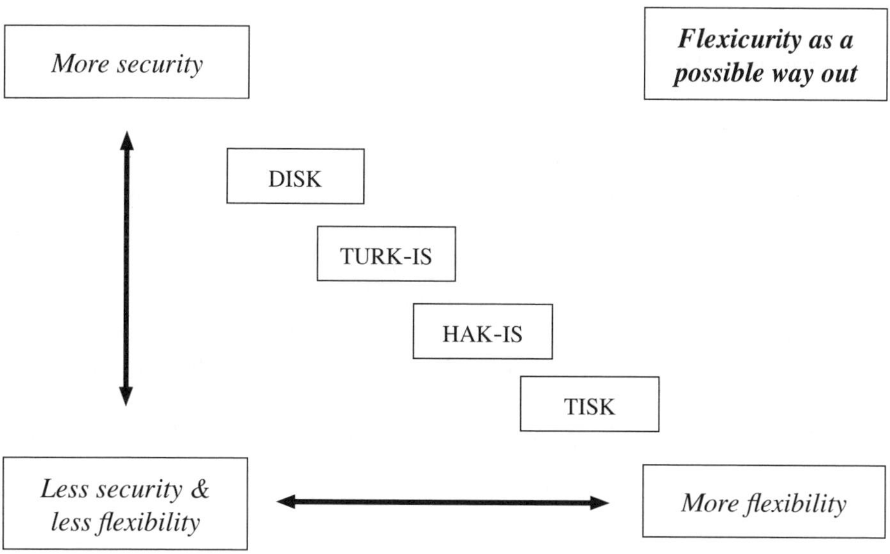

4.8 CONCLUSIONS AND RECOMMENDATIONS

The previous sections have discussed the structure of the Turkish social dialogue, how it functions and topics possibly relevant to the Turkish labour market. In this final section we will summarise the main conclusions. Naturally, the country's specific cultural and historical aspects have been taken into consideration in reaching these main conclusions. Section 4.8.2 will give some suggestions for improvements. These suggestions are fleshed out in the last section (Section 4.8.3).

4.8.1 Main Conclusions in Relation to the Structure, Practice and Contents of Turkish Social Dialogue

1. There are conflicting attitudes, confrontational approaches and much distrust between the social partners themselves and between the social partners and the government

One of the main conclusions that can be reached in respect of Turkish social dialogue is that at this moment there is hardly any real dialogue going on. The exchange of viewpoints can best be described as an exchange of slogans with a strong emotional appeal, a situation which blows the viewpoints out of all proportion. As outlined in Section 4.2, the conflicting and confrontational attitudes find their source in Turkish industrial relations and history (the automatic check-off system, the fierce struggle to become the authorised union, and so on). The situation can be described as a win-lose one: the other party must surrender, the winner takes all. There is an absence of integrative bargaining and instead distributive bargaining. This has been the traditional context for the unions themselves and is also evident in the behaviour of the social partners. It is quite illustrative that none of the union confederations make use of the term 'social partners', but refer to 'social *parties*'.

As a consequence – and enhanced by the absence of real progress – there is much distrust between the union confederations (issues as full representation and the authorised union), between unions and the employers' association (accusing each other of not taken care of the others/common interests) and between social partners and the government (accusing each other of not taking social dialogue seriously).

2. The fragmentation and rivalry on union side is having a paralysing influence on social dialogue

The fragmentation and rivalry on the union side has been discussed thoroughly in this chapter. To sum up: the confederations and many of the trade unions still see each other as a threat or at the best as a competitor for worker membership. As a result all of the confederations are preferring to stick to their own opinion than to make some progress by looking at common or shared interests. Changing your own position to get better results is not seen as a possibility but merely as a defeat, and thus open to criticism and negative publicity.

As a result the fragmentation and the confrontational attitudes on the union side is having a paralysing influence on social dialogue and especially on getting better results. The confederations are sticking to their positions. It is illustrative that the union confederations – being the organisations that are the closest to the interests of workers – have no organised structure, platform or whatever to overcome their conflicts and disagreements and to prepare common viewpoints to employ in consultations or negotiations with the employers' association and/or the government.

3. The social partners and the government have different opinions about the role the government should play within tripartite social dialogue

Section 4.4.2 discussed the role of the government within social dialogue as seen by the social partners. The discussion demonstrates that despite the claims of the Turkish government that it is prioritising social dialogue, the social partners do not share this opinion or at least would like the government to play another role. Simply put: the social partners are of the opinion that the role of the government is too dominant and that the government should take the role played by the others more seriously.

4. The bipartite structure is poorly developed

In theory, the tripartite consultation structure (with the Work Assembly, Tripartite Consultation Board, Economic Social Council) is quite impressive and seems to have been well devised. The social partners are quite optimistic that tripartite consultation will progress in the near future. In practice, there are flaws in its structure. While there is a platform for collective bargaining and some individual informal contributions there is no platform for national bipartite consultation. Considering the issues mentioned in 1–3 above, real social dialogue between social partners is, of course, still only a distant possibility and a good bipartite structure has not evolved. But now that there is some optimism this raises the question of whether the same is not true for a tripartite structure. Whatever the answer, it is hard to understand how national social dialogue can function without a platform or structure for the social partners to meet. For effective social dialogue, the bipartite structure must be strengthened.

5. Turkish social dialogue has achieved limited outcomes and had little success (especially at the bipartite national level)

Considering the other points it is not surprising that the social partners could hardly recall any really successful example of Turkish social dialogue. Of course, as has been noted, tripartite consultation in Turkey has been recently redeveloped and restructured. Regarding bipartite consultation there have been no successes identified at the national level. At the establishment and undertaking level some results in relation to collective bargaining and collective labour agreements can be identified.

6. There are few rules of conduct for and within Turkish social dialogue

With regard to the previous conclusion there appear to be few rules of conduct for and within social dialogue. In general one can say that in Turkey the 'rules, rights and competences' for making social dialogue more successful have been poorly devised.

7. The social partners disagree totally on the issue of flexibility and have adopted fixed positions with no alternatives to offer

Concerning the contents of social dialogue in relation to the Turkish labour market, the social partners in general agree on many measures for changing informal labour into formal labour, but they totally disagree on the issue of flexibility. This disagreement exists between the employers and the union confederations, but also between the union confederations themselves. In general employers want to have as much flexibility as possible while union confederations are strongly defending existing levels of protection and institutional arrangements and have been unable to offer alternatives for generating new formal employment (as an alternative for informal employment such as temporary or flexible work). Looking more closely at flexibility measures and courses of action (for example, admitting temporary work agencies or improving the legal provisions for flexible work) things are even more complicated. Tisk is in favour of these measures and courses of action and wishes to implement them as a matter of urgency. Hak-Iş is in favour of measures relating to temporary work agencies and underlines the urgency of these measures, but doubts the need for improving the legislative provisions in relation to flexible work. Türk-Iş agrees that there is a need for the legal position of temporary work agencies to be improved, but is in doubt about measures for flexible work. Disk strongly rejects all these measures or courses of action. As a matter of principle it does not accept any flexible form of employment. Disk sticks to the principle of full-time job security.

It seems that the unions and employers have reached a stalemate position. Consequently, the issue of flexibilisation has to be discussed within the arena of social expediency, where only with a lot of patience and through small incremental steps can some progress be made.

4.8.2 Improving the Framework for Turkish Social Dialogue

In this section we note some general factors that are required to create an appropriate framework for social dialogue. The next section then outlines specific recommendations.

1. Practice is now lingering behind theory

In general, the improvements within the legal framework are insufficiently utilised. For instance, the new Labour Code together with the Act on Organisation and Functioning of the Economic and Social Council provide good opportunities for social dialogue and, in particular, for tripartite consultation in platforms including the Economic and Social Council and the Tripartite Consultation Board. In practice, however, these opportunities are not sufficiently used. The social partners all agree that Turkish social dialogue has produced few results. Formal and informal meetings are conducted on the basis that one party must surrender. The concept of a 'win-win-situation' is not yet established, although all agree that it is important and expect social dialogue to improve in the near future.

2. The importance of personal input and individuals

The success of any social dialogue is based on personal input. However, in Turkey this is even more applicable, both in a positive and in a negative sense. To improve Turkish social dialogue more attention should be paid to the 'who question': individual and personal input may be more important than formal representation. Methods of rewarding personal input to social dialogue should be sought and applied more often.

3. The social dialogue paradox

Expanding consultation and social dialogue involves a paradox. Since social dialogue is based on finding common interest, there is a need for some trust and openness between social partners and the government. If, however, this is lacking, as is the case in Turkey, rules of agreement or even legal provisions and rights are required to protect social dialogue from coming to nothing. By using agreements, rights and provisions some trust can be created. Paradoxically, if there is more trust there is less need for these rules of agreement or legal provisions. Hence a balance has to be found.

4. The importance of research and statistic data

Where there is little trust, the use of independent data and research can serve social dialogue in two ways. Firstly, emotional viewpoints (often based on myth) can be dismantled using independent high quality data and research. Secondly, without these facts and figures it is much harder to develop a policy in relation to social dialogue and to make progress in this area.

5. Time and cultural change

Our interviews demonstrate that there is general consensus that time will improve social dialogue. Social dialogue (based on the search for common interest) is a new and foreign phenomenon in Turkey. The social partners and the government need time to make the necessary cultural changes. Our suggested improvements (see Section 4.8.3) could speed up this process.

4.8.3 Specific Suggestions for Improvement

Following on from the general factors outlined in Section 4.8.2 above we will suggest in this section some specific improvements for Turkish social dialogue, and for the flexibilisation of the Turkish labour market, drawing on our own analysis and the opinions of our interviewees.

Establish a formal bipartite structure

As already noted, the structure for national bipartite consultation is poorly developed in Turkey. The ideal would be a formal bipartite platform positioned within the existing formal consultation structure and with a formal status already in place or to be implemented in the future (and including, for instance, its own facilities and budget). Topics, decisions and timetables for the bipartite platform should correspond to those of the tripartite platforms in order to maximise the influence of the social partners. If the union confederations themselves also invested in a union confederation platform to precede the bipartite and tripartite platforms, the ideal structure would be as shown in figure 4.2:

Figure 4.2. The Ideal Structure for Bipartite and Tripartite Platforms

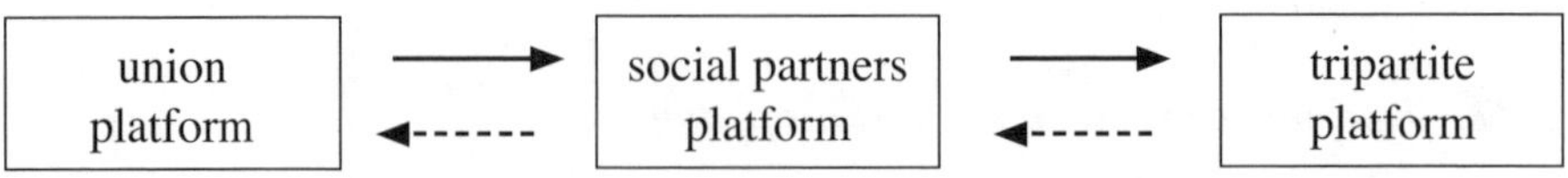

The creation of a formal bipartite platform for union confederations and employers' associations could help to build trust between the social partners as long as some basic rules (that still need to be formulated) are respected. One possible basic rule could be to find commonly shared objectives to work on together, such as the development of easy accessible training and schooling programmes or more programmes for child care.

Another rule for dialogue could include an agreement not to seek any publicity or media attention for bipartite consultation unless all parties are in agreement. As this structure would preclude direct interference by the government it would remove the ability of the social partners to blame failure on the government. In time the bipartite structure will serve as a pre-consultation forum for social partners to rehearse their contributions and viewpoints for the tripartite platforms. In every country there is evidence that the social partners approach tripartite consultation with less trepidation if they firstly reach some agreement amongst themselves.

Dealing with the problem of representation and fragmentation as a result of rivalry

We have seen that Turkish social dialogue is problematic because of the fragmentation caused by rivalry on the union side. This has caused several industrial relations problems. There could be less fragmentation and rivalry on the union side if the following three key recommendations were adopted:

- Decreasing the number of industries. Nowadays industrial unionism in Turkey is based upon twenty-eight industries. The number envisaged in a bill amending the Union Act 1983 is eighteen industries. A further decrease would diminish the potential for fragmentation.
- Changing or abolishing the check-off system. The check-off system is an important cause of rivalry among the union confederations. Changing this system (by limiting the scope of application) or abolishing it completely would diminish future rivalry.
- Changing the threshold requirement. The ten per cent rule was implemented in order to create bigger trade unions and less fragmentation. Raising the threshold for being the representative union higher could further assist in this aim, although, as said before, the ILO is critical of this ten per cent rule, making it not achievable.[37]

37 On the other hand, one can also say that this threshold requirement serves the aim of less fragmentation, though it could also increase the rivalry between unions since they are in competition with each other to meet the threshold. In that sense, abolishing the ten per cent rule would, in fact, contribute to less rivalry and conflict.

Although these recommendations may in the future decrease rivalry and fragmentation on the union side, there is no doubt that at this time and in the near future the latter two recommendations will certainly cause a great deal of unrest.

Consequently, a reduction in the number of industries from 28 to 18, as proposed by the draft laws, is the most feasible way forward, although this is also a sensitive issue.

Develop some rules of conduct for social dialogue

In Turkey there is a lot of misinterpretation and misunderstanding of what social dialogue can and cannot do and what the role of social partners and the government can or should be. Consequently the formation of a commission to develop rules of conduct for Turkish social dialogue, as desired by a number of the social partners interviewed, appears a sensible proposal. Such a commission should not be formed by the personal representatives directly involved, but could be formed – comparably to the commission on the enactment of the Labour Act – by academics, professors, independent experts and so on, who would be appointed as representatives by the social partners and the government. The central question should be how a more integrative social dialogue could be reached while taking account of the different interests and positions of the participants. These rules of conduct should at least bring forward matters concerning the following:

- Rights and competences in general. It must address issues such as the way the agenda is set, the contents of the agenda, the time schedules and the facilities for representatives participating in social dialogue (for example, the budget for hiring expertise and doing research).
- The role of the government. Issues to be addressed include the level of political will and commitment from the government, the value the government attaches to agreements between the social partners themselves, the role of the government and whether the government could adopt the role of mediator further.
- Decision making. For real dialogue all parties should be aware that there will be something gained by all parties and inevitably something lost by all parties. We need to consider how the government can deal with various situations in which the social partners either agree or disagree. It is necessary to create win-win situations instead of win-lose ones.
- Dealing with publicity and media attention. The issues are how to deal with publicity and media attention in relation to the issues discussed within consultation platforms and the possibility of a representative of one organisation taking turns in being the spokesperson for the other partners.

Look for improvements to create a positive change of mind and attitude.

Turkish social dialogue needs to adopt a different approach and to achieve successes. The relevant parties are concentrating too much on non-shared subjects and seem to be focussing less on concrete shared subjects and measures. The social partners need to demonstrate a positive approach towards each other. Such an approach requires the following:

- Discussing and researching commonly shared issues. All social partners underline the importance of effective social dialogue and all partners agree that the informal labour market in Turkey is a major problem and one that must be tackled. Table D in Appendix 1 shows that the Turkish social partners agree on many measures formulated for the three issues of the informal labour market, the position of women and sectoral policy. For commonly shared measures such as the development of easily accessible training and schooling programmes and more programmes for child care and educational programmes the social partners should arrange meetings and come up with a plan of action.
- Acquiring mutually applicable experience. Special attention should be paid to information exchange based on practical experience. For instance, the confederations of unions (either alone or in conjunction with the employer association) could work together on information-gathering in relation to the informal labour market. For example, using the media and an open telephone line they could jointly acquire information from society at large (including employers and workers) about the problems experienced by the informal labour market, flexibilisation, and so on.[38]

It may also be possible to work together on some implementation projects. The social partners generally agree that the enforcement capacity of the labour inspectorate should be increased. For certain sectors the social partners could strengthen this enforcement capacity by reporting unwanted situations concerning labour (both formal and informal). They should thus use their reporting and auditing capacity more often to meet common goals.

The development of a 'good example policy' is another way that the group could work jointly. Employers who, according to both social partners, are working according to the rules could be given extra attention or favourable publicity.

38 In many countries this kind of telephone report is often done by one or more of the social partners. A useful instrument could be the so-called 'week of reporting' during which interested parties and organisations interested report their experiences in relation to specific issues such as the informal labour market.

- Using a greater number of trusted experts or appreciated individuals. As a rule, this makes it easier for stalemate situations to be resolved. Personal input by people trusted and appreciated could help reach compromises in which each social partner feels that his/her position has not been too compromised.
- Professionalising social dialogue by training, education and support for social dialogue representatives. There is a need for more and better education of those who are involved in social dialogue in order to achieve a 'win-win situation'. Facilities and financing for training and education and for hiring experts must be developed, as the quality of representatives is an important condition for the success and impact of consultation. In practice this may impose a considerable financial burden.[39]
- Improving research, auditing and monitoring. Research is needed in the field of consultation. The need for research and statistics is not only a matter of knowing, improving and promoting. It is also a matter of political support and lobbying and of eliminating myths. Auditing and monitoring of progress is also necessary. As is shown in Table C of Appendix 1, the social partners do agree that there is insufficient *monitoring of progress* in the field of changing undeclared labour into formal labour.

Do not overload social dialogue

The Turkish social partners have rigid positions on the issue of flexibilisation. It seems that the unions and employers have reached a stalemate. The issue of flexibilisation can now really only be discussed as a matter of social expediency. Only with a lot of patience and by making small incremental steps in the area of flexicurity can some progress still be achieved.

Every country has issues that divide the social partners so much that it is impossible to imagine any progress being made to social dialogue. In Turkey it seems that this issue is that of flexibilisation in relation to part-time and temporary work. The positions of the social partners are too entrenched for major progress.

It goes far beyond the reach and responsibility of this chapter to claim that the Turkish situation has reached the stage of paralysis. But if such a stage is reached it would be unwise to retain flexibilisation as a cause to fight for, as it could hinder social dialogue in other areas. There are usually only three ways out of such a paralysis:

39 Because both employers and unions should benefit from education and training, there needs to be a more collective form of financing. For instance, federal organisations of employers and trade unions could establish a common service institution for participants from confederations of unions and employers. This service institution could finance or subsidise (to a certain amount and based on certain conditions) the training of individual social dialogue representatives.

a) *Freezing the controversial issue.* Doing nothing and consequently changing nothing except that the subject of flexibility is taken out of the social dialogue as a permanent source of conflict and left for another time or other partners, another government and so on.
b) *Government action.* One party, probably the Government, uses its power to make things happen. In this case it would have to be the government, no longer waiting for agreement from the social partners, that provides a better legal position for temporary work and agencies and improves the legislative provisions for flexible work.
c) *Win-win approach.* The issue of flexibilisation is broadened in such a way that all parties can win something and have a way out. For instance, not reducing the twenty-eight industries in which unions may be constituted to eighteen industries (a situation preferred by the union confederations) and in return the confederations agree upon some of the flexibilisation measures (for example, improvement in the legal positions of temporary work agencies).

APPENDIX 1: MAIN RESULTS QUESTIONNAIRE TURKISH SOCIAL DIALOGUE 2005

During the interviews with the representatives of the union confederations and the employers' associations a lot of topics were discussed. Due to lack of time some topics and questions were not thoroughly talked over with all of the partners. Consequently some topics had to be dealt with in a written form using a small questionnaire. The questionnaire made use of more or less standardised answers. The main results of this questionnaire are presented below in four tables. Answers to the more open questions on this questionnaire were used in the report that served as the basis of this chapter.

Table A: the Role of the Government in the Field of Social Dialogue according to the Social Partners

The role of the government. In the field of social dialogue (SD) government should …	*TISK*	*DISK*	*TURK-IS*	*HAK-IS*
… be less dominant	Yes	Yes	Yes	Yes
… listen more to social partners and not always impose its own will	Yes	Yes	Yes	Yes
… play the role of mediator/referee to reach agreement	Yes	Yes	Yes	Yes
… be more facilitating (for instance, organise more meetings, workshops, and so on)	Yes	Yes	Yes	Yes
… produce a 'code of conduct' for SD that all parties must respect	No	Yes	–	Yes
… take more initiative to make SD a success	No	Yes	Yes	Don't know
… go its own way because social partners can never agree	No	No	No	No
… only be obliged to take the viewpoints of social partners into consideration if the social partners themselves first reach agreement	No	Yes	Yes	Yes

Table B: the Style and Outcomes of Turkish Social Dialogue

	TISK	*DISK*	*TURK-IS*	*HAK-IS*
Good SD functioning is important	Yes	Yes	Yes	Yes
Good SD functioning is not important	No	No	No	No
SD should look for common interests	In between yes and no	No	Yes	Yes
SD should look for conflicting interests	In between yes and no	Yes	No	No
SD should be based on integrative bargaining	No	No	In between yes and no	No
SD should be based on distributive bargaining	Yes	Yes	In between yes and no	Yes
SD should produce results	Yes	Yes	Yes	No
SD does not have to produce any results	No	No	No	Yes
SD is successful at this moment	In between yes and no	No	No	Yes
SD is not successful at this moment	In between yes and no	Yes	Yes	No
SD can be expected to improve in the near future	Yes	Yes	–	Yes
SD cannot be expected to improve in the near future	No	No	–	No

Table C: Expectations of the Social Partners in relation to Three Tripartite Consultation Structures

Is the following platform functioning (or will function in the future)?	*TISK*	*DISK*	*Türk-Iş*	*Hak-Iş*
The Work Assembly	Yes	Yes	No	Yes
The Tripartite Consultation Board	Yes	Yes	Yes	Yes
The Economic and Social Council	Yes	Yes	Yes	Yes

Table D: Proposed Improvements or Courses of Action for Changing the Informal (Undeclared) Labour Market into a Formal (Declared) Labour Market

	Opinions and urgency			
	TISK	*DISK*	*Türk-Iş*	*Hak-Iş*
'Informal and Undeclared Market' Measures: Employment Guidelines 2/3/9				
a) Stimulate entrepreneurship especially among small and medium-sized enterprises	Yes ++	NO	Yes	Yes ++
b) Develop a more stable tax and social security policy (by, for example, simplification of legislation, more efficient tax and social security auditing and penal sanctions, and avoiding amnesty tax packages)	Yes ++	Yes ++	Yes	Yes ++
c) Develop easily accessible training and schooling programmes and extend the average length of education	Yes ++	Yes +	Maybe	Yes ++
d) Increase the enforcement capacity of the Turkish Labour Inspectorate.	Maybe –	Yes ++	Yes	Maybe +
e) Make greater regional effort and take more regional measures (by, for instance, giving provincial employment boards the task of fighting informal employment and clandestine foreign labour).	Maybe +	Yes ++	Yes	Yes +
f) Develop a 'good example policy' (by, for instance, giving favourable publicity to employers who work according to the rules).	Yes –	Yes +	maybe	Yes ++
'Position of Women' Measures: Employment Guideline 6				
g) Create more part-time jobs within the formal market.	Yes ++	NO	NO	Maybe +

	Opinions and urgency			
	TISK	*DISK*	*Türk-Iş*	*Hak-Iş*
h) Take measures to make part-time work and on-call work less expensive for employers	Yes + +	Yes -	NO	Maybe +
i) Take more measures against the social exclusion of women (for instance, by more programmes for child care and educational programmes for women).	Yes -	Yes +	Yes	Yes + +
j) In the light of the absence of an *integrated* approach for changing informal (undeclared) labour into formal labour, integrate the various measures within each field.	Yes + +	Yes +	Yes	Yes + +
k) In the light of the absence or poor *monitoring of progress* in the field of changing undeclared labour into formal labour, improve this.	Yes + +	Yes +	Yes	Yes +
'Sectoral Policy' Measures: Employment Guidelines 6/9				
l) In sectors such as the construction sector (where public expenditure is of great importance) give governments instruments (including the financial means) to prevent fraud, illegal work and the current extensive and uncontrolled subcontracting. Governments should use these instruments more often and more fully.	Maybe +	Yes +	NO	Maybe +
'Flexibility and Flexicurity' Measures: Employment Guidelines 1/3				
m) Create entrance opportunities to the formal labour market via temporary work agencies.	Yes + +	NO	Maybe	Yes +
n) Improve the legal position of temporary work agencies. The government could consider changing the Labour Act, introducing a licensing system for temporary work agencies and allowing vocational training programmes to be created for employees working for temporary work agencies.	Yes + +	NO	Yes	Yes + +
Improve legislative provisions for flexible work. At the moment legislative provisions relating to flexible work contracts are too minimalistic.	Yes + +	NO	Maybe	Maybe +

APPENDIX 2. FIGURES ON MEMBERS OF THE WORKER UNIONS

Table 1. Workers' Confederations and Affiliated and Unaffiliated Unions

Confederations	*No. of industries in which it is #1 union*	*Unions in total*	*Unions above the threshold*	*No. of members*
Türk-Iş	2	33	31	2,067,884
DISK		19	9	399,676
Hak-Iş	2	7	5	369,136
Unaffiliated unions	1	37	1	109,233
Total	5	96	46	2,945,929

Table 2. Public officials' confederations

Of 1,564,777 civil servants, 787,882 are unionised, giving an unionisation rate of 50.35 per cent.[40]

KESK (Kamu Emekçileri Sendikaları Konfederasyonu)	297,114
TÜRKİYE KAMU – SEN (Türkiye Kamu Çalışanları Sendikaları Konfederasyonu)	343,921
MEMUR – SEN (Memur Sendikaları Konfederasyonu)	137,937
BASK (Bağımsız Kamu Görevlileri Sendikaları Konfederasyonu)	5,228
HÜRRİYETÇİ KAMU-SEN (Hürriyetçi Kamu Çalışanları Sendikaları Konfederasyonu)	147
Unaffiliated	3,535
Total	787,882

40 http://www.calisma.gov.tr/CGM/4688_istatistik_2004.htm and *Official Gazette*, 28 August 2004.

5. THE IMPLEMENTATION OF FLEXIBLE WORK PROVISIONS IN THE LABOUR ACT

Frank Hendrickx and Karin Sengers[1]

5.1 INTRODUCTION

In this chapter we will investigate the flexible work provisions of the Turkish Labour Act. Work on the draft law began in June 2001, when the Ministry of Labour and Social Security formed a tripartite commission. The commission was composed of nine university professors: three appointed by the Government, three by the Turkish Confederation of Employers Association (Tisk) and one by each of the three labour confederations (Türk-Iş, Hak-Iş and Disk). This project was started in order to modernise labour law, in particular to take account of new developments, including part-time work and on-call contracts. An additional and explicit objective of the new Law was to take account of the Community *acquis* on flexible work.

In Chapter 1 we noted that the parliamentary proceedings relating to the bill did not run smoothly, as many compromises had to be made. Moreover, due to a lack of trade union support the Government withdrew the section on temporary agency work during the proceedings. Eventually this process produced the Labour Act of 2003.[2]

Since the Labour Act was to a large extent introduced in order to implement the *acquis communautaire*, we will first discuss the EU instruments relating to flexible work. Since these instruments allow alternative methods of implementation, it is useful to consider some examples of how Member States have regulated flexible work. For this reason we not only describe the *acquis* (Section 5.3.1), but will also discuss national examples (Section 5.3.2). After examining this aspect of the EU we will describe the relevant parts of the Turkish Labour Act (Section 5.4), followed by a critical discussion of the way the *acquis* has been implemented (Section 5.5).

1 The authors are very grateful to Toker Dereli and Nurhan Süral for their support in drafting this chapter.

2 Law No. 4857 of 22 May 2003, *Official Gazette* 10 June 2003.

Pennings, *Flexibilisation and Modernisation of the Turkish Labour Market*, 81–118

5.2 OVERVIEW OF THE EU INSTRUMENTS ON ATYPICAL WORK

On 29 June 1990, the European Commission submitted three proposals for directives on some specific types of employment relationship: part-time, fixed-term and temporary agency work. These proposals were subsequently discussed within the Council on various occasions between 1990 and 1994. Of the three proposals, only Council Directive 91/383/EEC, named *Supplementing the measures to encourage improvements in the safety and health at work of workers with a fixed duration employment relationship or a temporary employment relationship*, was adopted.

As no progress on other proposals for flexible work was made in the Council, the Commission decided to initiate the procedure by which the social partners are asked to develop agreements on flexible work relationships. The social partners broadly supported the idea that flexible workers have to be treated in the same way as full-time workers with contracts for an indefinite term. Although they differed considerably in their views as to the form and appropriate level of action to be taken in this area, most of the social partners were prepared to play an active part in defining the principles and putting them into effect, generally by way of collective bargaining at the appropriate level.

On 19 June 1996, the social partners at the EU level (UNICE,[3] CEEP[4] and the ETUC[5]) announced their intention to begin negotiations on an agreement relating to flexible work. On 6 June 1997, they concluded the European Framework Agreement on Part-Time Work, which was subsequently implemented in Council Directive 97/81/EC of 15 December 1997.[6]

On 23 March 1998 the same three parties announced their intention of starting negotiations on fixed-term work and concluded a Framework Agreement on 18 March 1999. They sent this agreement to the European Commission, asking for it to be implemented in a directive. They were, however, unable to conclude an agreement on temporary work. The most intractable problem was the definition of who is a 'comparable worker' of the temporary worker for the purpose of equal treatment. The European Commission then took the initiative to draft Community legislation on temporary agency work, but this has not been adopted yet.

A final instrument to be mentioned is Directive 93/104/EC of 23 November 1993,[7] which lays down minimum requirements with regard to the organisation of

3 Union of Industrial and Employers' Confederations of Europe.

4 European Centre of Enterprises with Public Participation and of Enterprises of General Economic Interest.

5 European Trade Union Confederation.

6 OJ L 14/9, 1998, and extended to the UK by Council Directive 98/23/ EC, OJ L 131/10, 1998. The drafting of the Agreement was much influenced by ILO Convention 175, Establishing Minimum Standards on Part-Time Work and the accompanying ILO Recommendation 182.

7 As amended by Directive 2000/34, repealed by Directive 2003/88 (codified version) (OJ L 299, 18 December 2003).

working time, with the aim of ensuring a better level of health and safety protection for workers. This directive is currently under review. In the view of the European Commission, the issue of working time has always been very closely linked with flexibility.

To summarise, the initiatives at European level have resulted in the following results, which now belong to the *acquis communautaire*:

- Council Directive 91/383/EEC of 25 June 1991 supplementing the measures to encourage improvements in the health and safety at work of workers with a fixed-duration employment relationship or a temporary employment relationship[8]
- Council Directive 97/81/EC of 15 December 1997 concerning the Framework Agreement on part-time work concluded by UNICE, CEEP and ETUC[9]
- Council Directive 1999/70/ EC of 28 June 1999 concerning the Framework Agreement on fixed-term work concluded by ETUC, UNICE and CEEP[10]
- Commission proposal for a Directive of the European Parliament and the Council on working conditions for temporary workers[11]
- Amended proposal for a Directive of the European Parliament and the Council on working conditions for temporary workers[12]
- Directive 93/104/ EC of 23 November 1993 concerning certain aspects of the organisation of working time.[13]

5.3 FIXED-TERM EMPLOYMENT CONTRACTS

5.3.1 Council Directive 1999/70/EC

Within the European Union, the issue of fixed-term work is primarily regulated at national level, but, as described in the previous section, the social partners at the level of the EU have concluded a Framework Agreement on Fixed-Term Work which was implemented in Directive 1999/70/EC. The European Framework Agreement sets out the general principles and minimum requirements for fixed-term employment contracts and employment relationships. The main purpose of the agreement was

8 OJ 29 July 1991, L 206/19.

9 OJ 20 January 1998, L 14/9.

10 OJ 10 July 1999, L 175/43.

11 Com (2002) 149 final.

12 Com (2002) 701.

13 OJ 13 December 1993, L307/18; amended by Directive 2000/34, repealed by Directive 2003/88 (codified version) (OJ L 299, 18 November 2003).

a desire to improve the quality of fixed-term work by ensuring the application of the principle of non-discrimination. Furthermore the objective was to establish an instrument to prevent the abuse of successive fixed-term employment contracts or relationships.

The Preamble of Council Directive 1999/70 points out that the main reasons for this instrument are the need to implement measures to increase the growth of employment, in particular by the more flexible organisation of work in a way which fulfils both the wishes of employees and the requirements of competition. The social partners are invited at all appropriate levels to negotiate agreements to modernise the organisation of work, including flexible working arrangements, with the aim of making undertakings productive and competitive and achieving the required balance between flexibility and security. The Preamble also indicates that in laying down the Framework Agreement, the Directive limits itself to the minimum required for the attainment of the objectives mentioned above and does not go beyond what is necessary for that purpose.

The Framework Agreement on fixed-term work obviously aims at facilitating the use of such contracts. However, in the preamble of the European Framework Agreement, the social partners 'recognise that contracts of an indefinite duration are, and will continue to be, the general form of employment relationship between employers and workers. They also recognise that fixed-term employment contracts respond, in certain circumstances, to the needs of both employers and workers'.

Hence, the social partners indicate that the Framework Agreement should provide a context for using fixed-term employment contracts on a basis acceptable to employers and workers, although it is not very clear what this means in practice. In the provisions of the Framework Agreement, no objective reasons for the first use of fixed-term employment contracts are required. This seems to have been a deliberate choice.[14] The 'prevention of abuse' is only regulated with regard to successive fixed-term contracts (see article 5 of the Framework Agreement).[15]

---

14 J. Murray, 'Normalising Temporary Work. The Proposed Directive on Fixed-Term Work', ILJ 1999, p. 273–274.

15 1. To prevent abuse arising from the use of successive fixed-term employment contracts or relationships, Member States, after consultation with social partners in accordance with national law, collective agreements or practice, and/or the social partners, shall, where there are no equivalent legal measures to prevent abuse, introduce in a manner which takes account of the needs of specific sectors and/or categories of workers, one or more of the following measures:

(a) objective reasons justifying the renewal of such contracts or relationships;

(b) the maximum total duration of successive fixed-term employment contracts or relationships;

(c) the number of renewals of such contracts or relationships.

2. Member States after consultation with the social partners and/or the social partners shall, where appropriate, determine under what conditions fixed-term employment contracts or relationships:

The most important provisions of the Framework Agreement relate, therefore, to employment conditions: fixed-term workers must not be treated in a less favourable manner than comparable permanent workers solely because they have a fixed-term contract or relation unless different treatment is justified on objective grounds. Where appropriate, the principle of *pro rata temporis* has to be applied. Qualifications relating to periods of service have to be the same for fixed-term workers as for permanent workers except where different length of service qualifications are justified on objective grounds.

5.3.2 Regulation of Fixed Term Employment in the Netherlands and Belgium

The European Directive on fixed term work does not provide definitive guidance on how the *acquis* has to be implemented in national law. A common characteristic of the national laws of EU countries is the basic division between contracts for an indefinite period and contracts for a fixed term. This can also be found in the Turkish Labour Act. The legal regulation of fixed-term contracts is strongly related to national dismissal law. While fixed-term contracts provide for contractual job security, the law normally favours the contract for an indefinite period, which is protected by statutory job security. Normally fixed-term contracts can be concluded for a specific period (a fixed term) or for the completion of a specific project or event. This corresponds to the definition of fixed-term employment in the directive. Most provisions addressing fixed-term employment relate to consecutive contracts and the flexible use thereof. These provisions are related to dismissal law, and in cases where the law deals with possible abuse of fixed-term contracts, allows the implementation of the normal system of statutory job security (for indefinite-period contracts).

We will now discuss the systems of some Member States in order to give examples of how the *acquis* is incorporated in national law.

In *the Netherlands* employers and employees are allowed to conclude a first fixed term contract for whatever purpose and whatever period. In principal, the use of these contracts is not legally restricted. However, until 1999 the Civil Code stipulated that a second consecutive fixed term contract could not be ended without giving notice and prior authorisation by the public authorities. These restrictions are the same as those relating to a contract for an indefinite period. Employers complained that this legislation was very restrictive. In order to allow for greater flexibility, the Flexibility and Security Agreement of 1996, made by the national organisations of employers and trade unions, enabled the Dutch government to introduce a new

---

(a) shall be regarded as 'successive'

(b) shall be deemed to be contracts or relationships of indefinite duration.

system of fixed-term contracts in the Act on Flexibility and Security 1999. The new Act allows three consecutive contracts for a definite period that may be ended without having to give notice, as long as they fall within a period of three years. The fourth contract, or the contract that causes the total working period to exceed 36 months, is converted automatically into a contract for an indefinite term. The latter contract provides the worker with enhanced protection against dismissal.

Three stipulations of the new law are meant to prevent the abuse of contracts for a definite period. The first is that contracts following each other within a period of three months are considered to be consecutive. The second is that for consecutive fixed-term contracts between the same employer and the same employee it is irrelevant whether the work done under the different contracts is identical or not. The third rule is that if the same employee works for two consecutive employers who can be considered to be each other's successor with regard to the work, the fixed-term contracts concerned are considered to be consecutive contracts. In addition, if the worker worked under some of the consecutive contracts for a temporary work agency, the protective rule is applicable. The fourth contract is decisive: the employer that employs the worker at that time is the employer that now has a contract for an indefinite term.

These rules are considered to be in line with the recent EC-directive on fixed-term contracts. However, the Directive also requires the introduction of the principle of equal treatment of permanent and fixed-term workers. This required new legislation in the Netherlands. In order to comply with Directive 1999/70/EC, the Dutch Parliament passed the Law regarding Fixed Term Contracts of 22 November 2002.[16] This new law inserted two new articles in the Civil Code. Article 7:649 of the Civil Code stipulates that the employer cannot make a distinction between employees as far as their working conditions are concerned on the basis of the fixed or permanent status of their employment, unless this distinction is objectively justified. The second new provision in the Civil Code is Article 7:657 that obliges the employer to inform the fixed-term worker clearly, and in time, of any vacant position which offers an employment contract for an indefinite period. This provision does not contain the right of the employee to be appointed to the vacant permanent position.

In *Belgium*, the 1978 Act on Employment Contracts limits the possibility of concluding consecutive contracts for a fixed duration. Consecutive (two at least) contracts for a fixed duration are considered to be concluded for an indefinite period, except when there is an interruption between contracts caused by the employee (e.g. military service or voluntary leave) or when the employer can prove that the consecutive contracts were justified by the nature of the work or for some other good reason (e.g. the unfavourable economic situation of the enterprise, or a dependence on uncertain subsidies).

16 *Stb*. 2002, 560.

In order to avoid the need for employers to justify the reasons for concluding consecutive fixed-term contracts and thus to increase flexibility, the legislator introduced a new provision in the 1978 Act on Employment Contracts: fixed term contracts that run consecutively may be concluded, with a maximum of four, with a term no less than three months for each contract, always providing that the total duration of the consecutive contracts not exceed two years. If this '4-3-2 rule' is respected, no objective justification has to be provided by the employer. Furthermore, subject to prior official authorisation, consecutive fixed-term contracts with a total duration of up to three years may be concluded, always providing that the fixed-term contract may not be less than six months in each case.

Whereas a contract for an indefinite period can be concluded verbally, a fixed-term contract always has to be in writing, to be produced at the latest when the employee starts to work. If not, the contract will be held *de iure* to be a contract for an indefinite period.

5.4 A COMPARISON OF THE TURKISH PROVISIONS ON FLEXIBLE CONTRACTS WITH THE *ACQUIS*[17]

5.4.1 The Rules Concerning Contracts for a Definite Period

5.4.1.1 Making a Contract for a Definite Period

Article 11/I of the Turkish Labour Act stipulates that an employment contract is deemed to have been made for an indefinite period where the employment relationship is not based on a fixed period. An employment contract for a definite period is one that is concluded between the employer and the employee in written form, for work of a specified term or which is based on the emergence of objective conditions such as the completion of a certain project or the occurrence of a certain event.

In the second consideration of the Preamble of the European Framework Agreement, the social partners recognise that contracts of an indefinite duration are, and will continue to be, the general form of employment relationship between employers and workers. This idea that the fixed-term employment relationship type is an *a-typical* form of employment, deviating from the typical permanent employment relationship, is also found in the presumption underlying Article 11/I of the Labour Act.

The Labour Act includes an additional condition concerning the required form of a fixed-term contract: namely that the contract must be in writing. In combination

17 This section is largely based on Toker Dereli, 'Turkey', in *International Encyclopaedia of Labour Law*, The Hague 2006.

with the presumption laid down in Article 11/I, this rule means that a fixed-term contract which is not in writing will be presumed to be a contract for an indefinite period. This rule can also be found in Belgian labour law (see Section 5.3.2). It is not clear from the text of the Labour Act whether this presumption can be refuted, or whether the parties can also conclude a fixed-term contract after the employee started to work. The requirement that all contracts for a definite period must be concluded in written form is contradictory to the provision of Article 8/I which stipulates that a written contract is required only for definite-term contracts whose duration is at least one year. Article 8/III suggests that a fixed-term contract could be delivered some time after the moment the employee is hired, but this contradicts the prior requirement of having a written contract in place before the employee starts work. The only solution to this contradiction would be to treat the written form requirement of Article 11 as a broad principle covering the requirement of a written contract as well as the duty to provide the employee with a written document in the case of no written contract having been drawn up. The original draft bill prepared by the committee of academics was not saddled with this contradiction and was more consistent with the EU Directive. Without referring to written form, it defined a fixed-term contract as one whose duration was determined in terms of a certain time and date or which could be inferred from objective factors such as the type, nature and purpose of the work undertaken by the employee, which was based on judgments of the Court of Cassation on fixed-term contracts. Also the notion in Article 11/II stating that a fixed-term contract once repeated should automatically turn into an open-ended contract had been emphasised by the Court of Cassation in various decisions.

That part of Article 11 which defines the contract for a definite period as a contract for a specified term or on the basis of objective conditions such as the completion of a certain job or the materialisation of a certain event suggests that an objective justification is required in order to be able to conclude a first fixed-term employment contract. The term 'objective conditions' suggests that the first use of a fixed-term contract also requires an essential reason, such as that the work in question must be of a certain duration. By restricting the freedom of the parties to fix an expiry date, this interpretation is likely to restrict the first conclusion of fixed-term contracts. While most EU laws do not require the presence of essential reasons for the first conclusion of fixed term contracts, the Labour Act has gone further than the Directive in protecting the fixed term employee and requiring an objective justification for the first conclusion of a fixed term contract. The original draft of the Labour Act simply mentioned for fixed term contracts the phrase 'whose duration is fixed by the parties in terms of time and date...rather than for work of a specified term' (Article 12, original draft). The government memorandum underlying the final text of Article 11 claims that there is no requirement for an objective justification for the first conclusion of a fixed-term contract. The prevention of abuse has been regulated only with regard to successive (chain) contracts, as indicated below. Some Turkish academics, however, argue on the basis of the text of Article 11 that an objective reason must be given in order to prevent abuse of the first time fixed-term contracts.[18] It is advisable to carefully reconsider the definition of fixed-term contracts to the extent that an objective reason need not be demonstrated for the first use of a fixed-term contract when the parties involved have determined its duration and/or expiration date.

5.4.1.2 Measures to Prevent Abuse

It is often feared that fixed-term contracts can be abused by giving an employee a series of contracts for a fixed term, a so-called chain of contracts. In this way the applicability of provisions concerning contracts for an indefinite term could be evaded. Prevention of such use (or rather, abuse) is regulated in Article 5 of the Framework Agreement. In the Turkish Labour Act such measures can be found in Article 11. Article 11/II stipulates that 'an employment contract for a definite period must not be concluded more than once, except when there is a substantial cause which may necessitate repeated (chain) contracts. Otherwise, the employment contract is deemed to have been made for an indefinite period from the very beginning'. Article 11/III confirms this: 'chain contracts based on substantial cause shall maintain their status as contracts made for a definite period'.

Some EU Member State labour laws[19] provide for a maximum duration of successive fixed-term contracts, or a number of allowed renewals of such contracts, without having to demonstrate a justification for contract renewal. In other words, a limited period of time (two to three years to be counted from the moment of hiring of the employee) is provided for, governed by conditional flexibility (no justification for renewal of fixed-term contracts). As a consequence, such a limited period of flexibility prevents a 'chain' of contracts from being modified into an open-ended employment relationship, even if there is no demonstrated justification for such chain. The Framework Agreement does not require such rules.

---

18 See N. Çelik, *İş Hukuku Dersleri,* revised 16th edn, Beta, 2004, p. 82; G. Alpagut, 'Belirli Süreli İş Sözleşmesi', *Mercek,* Ocak 2004, pp. 73–91. Ö. Eyrenci, S. Taşkent and D. Ulucan, who were members of the Committee that drafted the Labour Code state that the article requires the existence of an objective reason for the first conclusion of a fixed-term contract (Bireysel İş Hukuku, *Legal Yayıncılık,* March 2004, pp. 45–46).

19 See Section 5.3.2. for examples.

5.4.1.3 The Principle of Non-Discrimination

Parallel to article 5 of the Directive concerning the principle of equal treatment, article 12 of the Labour Act deals with limitations on the distinction between fixed-term and open-ended contracts. An employee working under an employment contract with a definite term must not be subjected to differential treatment compared to a comparable employee working under an employment contract with an indefinite period (article 12/I).

Divisible amounts for a given time period relating to wages and other monetary benefits to be given to an employee working under a fixed-term contract have to be paid in proportion to the length of time during which the employee has worked. In cases where seniority (length of service) in the same establishment or the same enterprise is treated as the criterion for an employment benefit, the seniority criterion foreseen for a comparable employee working under an open-ended contract shall apply to an employee with a fixed-term contract, unless there is a reason justifying the application of a different seniority criterion for an employee working under a fixed-term contract (Article 12/II).

A comparable employee is the one who is employed under an open-ended contract in the same or a similar job in the establishment. If there is not such an employee in the establishment, then an employee with an open-ended contract performing the same or a similar job in a comparable establishment falling into the same branch of activity shall be considered as a comparable employee (article 12/III).

These provisions are consistent with the provisions of the Framework Agreement and Directive 99/70. Since they were not contained in previous Turkish legislation, the interpretation of the comparable employee is likely to cause practical problems in the event of labour disputes. These will have to be solved by expert opinions and court decisions. In the past the same principles were applied in the computation of an employee's severance pay and entitlement to paid annual vacation. Under the new system, the same principles are also applicable to other employment conditions.

5.4.1.4 Information, Employment and Training Opportunities and Consultation

Article 6 of the Framework Agreement sets out the duty of the employer to inform employees of vacancies which become available in the undertaking or establishment and to facilitate the access of fixed-term workers to training opportunities. There is no provision in the Labour Act requiring employers to inform fixed-term employees of vacancies. Such a provision exists only with regard to part-timers: employers have to give consideration to requests by workers to transfer from full-time to part-time work and vice versa if there is such availability in the establishment (article 13/4). The Labour Act is silent on in-service training or on-the-job training. If such training is provided by management, however, on the basis of article 5 no discrimination is allowed. Regarding education on occupational health and safety issues, again no discrimination may be made, this time on the basis of article 77.

The Labour Act would be a suitable place to set out these duties, since it would then include all relevant provisions concerning contracts for a definite period.

Article 7 of the Framework Agreement contains provisions on how to take fixed-term workers into account when deciding whether the thresholds are reached for establishing workers' representative bodies and on giving information to such bodies. There is no provision in the Labour Act defining explicitly the scope of the terms 'workers' or 'fully employed'. But where the terms workers or fully employed are used for such cases, be it in the Labour Act, Unions Act or Collective Labour Agreements, Strikes and Lockouts Act, it is generally understood (and interpreted by the Court of Appeals) to include all part-timers, fixed-term workers, seasonal workers and temporary workers as well as indefinite workers.

5.4.1.5 Conclusions

In general, it can be concluded that the Turkish Labour Act has implemented the provisions of Council Directive 1999/70 well. The Labour Act not only contains the main minimum requirements of the directive, but has also adopted the general approach of most EU Member States for regulating fixed-term employment contracts.

However, a number of recommendations for improvements to the Labour Act to ensure that Turkish law conforms to EU labour law can be made. Firstly the definition of fixed-term work in article 11 of the Labour Act should be reconsidered in so far as it now requires an objective reason to be demonstrated for the first use of a fixed-term employment contract.

Secondly, we recommend the determination of a period of flexibility, conditional upon a maximum total duration of successive fixed-term employment contracts, and/or a maximum number of renewals of such types of contracts, in accordance with article 5(1)(b) and (c) of the Framework Agreement. Although this is not required, such provisions are part of most labour law systems in the EU Member States.

Thirdly, we recommend implementing the rules regarding the availability of vacancies and training opportunities, regulated in articles 6 and 7 of the Framework Agreement.

Finally the scope of the Turkish Labour Act has to be considered. Articles 4 and 10 seem to exclude workers who normally fall under the European directive on fixed-term work. All other Turkish laws and regulations covering these workers should also be brought in line with the European directive(s). The workers mentioned in articles 4 and 10 refer to workers in sectors or contexts of employment that are not excluded from the relevant European provisions. While those workers may be governed by specific Turkish laws and regulations, the application of rights and obligations of the European directive on fixed-term work cannot be excluded and should therefore be provided for, either in those specific laws, or as a better alternative, in the Turkish Labour Act.

5.4.2 Part-Time Work

5.4.2.1 General

Under the now repealed previous Labour Act No. 1475, there was no regulation of part-time employment, although part-time work has been a well known phenomenon in the previous decades. The void in legislation was filled by the rulings of the judiciary, but the new Labour Act introduced provisions on part-time work consistent with the EU standards.

The Act stipulates that an employment contract is considered a part-time contract if the normal weekly working time of the employee is considerably shorter than a comparable full-time employee (article 13/I). The basic criterion is thus a comparison with the normal weekly working time. Part-time work may be done in various ways: working part-time on all days of the week or working only a few days of the week full-time and in the remaining days shorter hours or not working at all. Domestic services, cleaning and preparatory work, work by company physicians, lawyers and engineers, work by women or students employed by supermarkets are typical examples of part-time work in Turkey.

The objectives of the directive are to prevent discrimination against part-time workers and to improve the quality of part-time work. It also seeks to facilitate the development of part-time work on a voluntary basis and to contribute to the flexible organisation of working time in a manner which takes into account the needs of employers and workers. Article 5 requires Member States to review any obstacles which may limit opportunities for part-time work and, where appropriate, to eliminate them. A similar requirement is placed on social partners within their sphere of competence.

These objectives are not expressly laid down in the Turkish Labour Act. Although most Member States have not explicitly laid down these objectives in their legal texts either, they in fact realise these objectives via their laws and practice.[20] Turkish labour law, however, has only a non-discrimination clause concerning part-time work. Consequently, the objectives of the directive are realised to a much lesser extent and there are no measures in place to stimulate part-time work.

20 Report by the Commission's services on the implementation of Council Directive 97/81 of 17 December 1997 concerning the Framework Agreement on part-time work concluded by UNICE, CEEP and the ETUC, 21 October 2003.

5.4.2.2 The Scope of the Rules and the Definition of Part-Time Work

The directive applies to part-time workers who have an employment contract or employment relationship as defined by the law, collective agreement or practice in force in each Member State. The directive gives the option to exclude, partly or fully, part-time workers who work on a casual basis if there are objective reasons. It does not define casual work and therefore this rule can be elaborated in national legislation and collective agreements. Some sectors and activities are excluded from the Labour Act and regulated by other laws (e.g. the Maritime Labour Act).[21] We recommend that these other laws and regulations also be brought in line with the European directives, since all employees have to be covered. Under the directive an exclusion is allowed only and where there are objective reasons for part-time workers who work on a casual basis. Turkish legislation makes use of this possibility in article 10 of the Turkish Labour Act, which excludes from its scope 'employment which, owing to its nature, lasts only up to 30 working days'.

The 'part-time worker' is defined in the directive as an employee whose normal number of working hours, calculated on a weekly basis or on average over a period of employment of up to one year, is less than the normal hours of work of a comparable full-time worker. The term 'comparable full-time worker' means a 'full-time worker in the same establishment having the same type of employment contract or relationship, who is engaged in the same or a similar work or occupation, due regard being given to other considerations which may include seniority and qualification or skills'. Where there is no comparable full-time worker in the same establishment, the comparison shall be made by reference to the applicable collective agreement or, where there is no applicable collective agreement, in accordance with national law, national collective agreements, or practice.

In article 13 of the Turkish Labour Act, part-time work is defined as follows: 'where the normal weekly working time of the employee is considerably shorter in relation to a comparable employee working full-time'. A remarkable difference between the definition in the directive and the definition in the Turkish Labour Act is the use of the term 'considerably shorter' in the Turkish Labour Act. Considerably shorter is interpreted as 'less than two-thirds of the contracted weekly number of hours of work' as it is stated in the explanatory memorandum to the article. Therefore, a part-time job above a certain weekly limit is considered a full-time job. For example, if the statutory number of weekly working hours (45) is the same as the contracted number of weekly working hours, work beyond 30 hours a week is deemed full-time work.

The rationale behind this rule is that insignificant reductions in normal working time should not qualify the work as part-time work. However, according to the definition of the directive all employees whose normal number of working hours is

21 Art. 4 of the Labour Act.

less than the normal number of working hours of a comparable full-time worker are considered to be part-time workers. This means that workers who only work a few hours less than the normal hours of work are part-time workers. It is recommended that the Turkish definition be brought in line with the definition of the directive.

The Labour Act describes what is meant by a 'comparable full-time worker'. It adds that where there is no comparable full-time worker in the establishment, reference should be made to individuals generally considered as being comparable full-time workers in the sector of activity concerned.[22]

With regard to the definitions of part-time workers and a comparable full-time worker, some Member States have definitions which are not exactly the same as those of the Framework Agreement, but which guarantee an equivalent level of protection.

Self-evidently part-time employment contracts may be concluded for an indefinite or definite term or for continual work or transitory work. In the computation of the employee's length of service (i.e. for severance pay, notice term or notice pay), the total period between the beginning and ending dates of the contract shall be considered, rather than the total actual time worked. Pursuant to article 13 of the Paid Anual Leave By-law, part-timers and on-call workers are entitled to annual vacation in full.

5.4.2.3 The Non-discrimination Clause

Discrimination against part-time workers is not always forbidden, as different treatment may be justified on objective grounds. The directive does not define objective reasons. In the *Bilka* case,[23] the Court of Justice EC formulated a test for objective justification. Treatment in a less favourable manner may be justified if, firstly, the measure answers a real need of the employer; secondly the measures are appropriate for achieving the objectives they pursue; and, finally, the measures are necessary to achieve those objectives. The Court of Justice left it to the national court to apply the proportionality test in this case.

The Court phrased the proportionality test slightly differently in the *Rinner-Kühn* case,[24] in which discrimination by the State rather than by the employer was the issue. The 'real need of the employer' mentioned in the *Bilka* case was replaced in the *Rinner-Kühn* case by a 'necessary aim' of social policy, and rather than requiring the means chosen to achieve that aim to be 'appropriate and necessary', the Court in the *Rinner-Kühn* judgment said it must be 'suitable and requisite'. In the *Danfoss* case, the Court considered what kinds of justification for indirect discrimination in

22 Art. 13 of the Labour Act.

23 Case 170/84 *Bilka-Kaufhaus v. Weber von Hartz*, [1986] ECR 1607.

24 Case 171/88, *Rinner-Kühn v. FWW Spezial-Gebaüdereinigung GmbH,* [1989] ECR 2743.

the criteria for supplementary pay might be acceptable.[25] The pay criteria included factors such as mobility, training and length of service of employees. 'Mobility' a term rather oddly used to describe characteristics such as enthusiasm and initiative, was in the view of the Court, a neutral criterion which should not disadvantage women unless the employer misapplied it. However, if mobility meant adaptability to hours and places of work, the Court considered that it could disadvantage women because of family and household duties for which they so often bear responsibility. The criteria of training and length of service, too, although apparently 'neutral', could disadvantage women. However, while ultimately leaving the issue for the national court to decide, the Court took the view that they could be objectively justified if the employer could show, for example, that it was of importance for the performance of specific tasks that the employee be adaptable and mobile, or had valuable experience due to length of service. In the case *Stadt Lengerich*[26] the Court ruled that there was no indirect discrimination where collective agreements restricted payment of overtime supplements to cases where the normal working hours fixed for full-time workers were exceeded. Under the more recently adopted Burden of Proof Directive,[27] all the employee must do is to establish 'facts from which it may be presumed that there has been direct or indirect discrimination, leaving it for the employer to prove that there has been no such discrimination, or that any differential impact is objectively justified'.

The principle of non-discrimination is at the core of the directive. This principle stipulates that in respect of employment conditions, part-time workers are not to be treated in a less favourable manner than comparable full-time workers solely because they work part-time unless different treatment is justified on objective grounds. Where appropriate, the principle of *pro rata temporis* shall apply.

Article 4(4) stipulates that when justified by objective reasons, Member States, after consulting of the Social Partners in accordance with national law or practice, may, where appropriate, make access to particular conditions of employment subject to a period of service, time worked or earnings qualification. Qualifications relating to access by part-time workers to particular conditions of employment should be reviewed periodically having regard to the principle of non-discrimination.

Discrimination is defined as individuals being treated differently where there is no relevant difference between them. A straightforward example of discrimination on grounds of sex would be a woman being paid a lower wage than a man for doing exactly the same job. Indirect discrimination occurs if an apparently neutral requirement, rule or practice does have a disproportionate negative impact on one of the groups that are protected against discrimination. An important implication of the concept of indirect discrimination is that the intention of the person who

25 Case 109/88, *Danfoss* [1989] ECR 3199.

26 Case 399/92, [1994] ECR 5727.

27 Council Directive 97/80, (1997) OJ L 14/62.

performs this specific act is not relevant: only the effects of the act count. This is important because indirect discrimination aims to reveal practices based on persistent habits which are often derived from dominant views, prejudices or stereotyped opinions.

Article 13/II of the Labour Act stipulates that an employee working under a part-time employment contract must not be subjected to differential treatment in comparison to a comparable full-time employee solely because his/her contract is part-time, unless there is a justifiable cause for differential treatment. The divisible benefits to be appropriated to a part-time employee in relation to wages and other monetary benefits must be paid in proportion to the length of his/her working time proportionate to a comparable employee working full-time (article 13/II). A comparable employee is one who is employed full-time in the same or a similar job in the establishment. If there is not such an employee in the establishment, an employee with a full-time contract performing the same or similar job in an appropriate establishment which falls into the same branch of activity is considered to be a comparable employee (article 13/III). These provisions of article 13 are in conformity with the framework agreement put into effect by Council Directive 97/81.

What this all means is that a part-time employee must have access to all the fringe benefits (e.g. bonuses, premiums, child allowances, heating allowances, holiday pay) granted to full-time employees but only in terms of divisible amounts in proportion to the length of his work unless there is an agreement to the contrary. As explained in the Act's statement of reasons on which the said article is based, a part-time employee who works fifteen hours a week will be entitled to only one-third of the benefits of a full-time employee working 45 hours a week. Similarly, an employee working only two days a week shall not have access to a paid weekly rest day; workers engaged in work only during afternoons will not take advantage of the transportation service assigned to employees who begin the workday in the morning. On the other hand, if employees are paid a transportation allowance, a part-time employee working every day shall receive that allowance in full while a part-time employee who is employed only on certain days will be paid the said allowance prorated in accordance with the length of his working time.

Remuneration for part-time employees may be freely determined by the parties, provided the wage to be paid for a given period of time is not less than the amount of the legal minimum wage corresponding to the same time period. Part-time employees have access to all the entitlements of collective labour law, and benefit from the provisions of the collective agreement in force, with the exception of those benefits granted exclusively to full-time employees.

5.4.2.4 Information Procedures

In line with Directive 97/81, the Labour Act stipulates that if there are vacant positions suited to the qualifications of employees working in the establishment, employees' requests to move into full-time from part-time jobs or vice versa must be taken into consideration. Such vacancies must be announced without delay (article 13/IV of the Labour Act).

The procedure for providing information on the availability of part-time and full-time posts has been transposed in Belgium, Denmark, Germany, Netherlands, Portugal, Spain and Sweden.[28] For example, in the Netherlands the employer has to fulfil the employee's request to adapt working hours unless the request conflicts with major business interests. The period within which the employer has to deal with the request has also been defined and the employer has the obligation to provide valid reasons for refusing the request.

Article 6 contains the provision that Member States or social partners may maintain or introduce more favourable provisions than set out in this agreement. Moreover, implementation of the provisions of this Agreement does not give valid grounds for reducing the general level of protection afforded to workers in the field of the agreement.

In general, implementing these provisions is not problematical as the principle of 'more favourable treatment' already exists in most Member States.

Article 13/IV of the Labour Act, as described above, is relatively neutral. It requires no action by the employer and is unlikely to stimulate part-time work.

In Belgium, France and Germany legal measures have been taken to identify and eliminate obstacles to part-time work and to facilitate transfers between full-time and part-time work. In Denmark collective agreements contain appropriate regulations. In the United Kingdom the implementation law was accompanied by a best practice guide. Ireland followed the same mechanism whereby the Labour Relations Commission prepared a Code of Practice to deal with the issue of full-time workers transferring to part-time and vice versa. Belgium created a special time-credit system offering a career break of one year, leave for specific purposes and the right to reduce the number of working hours.

5.4.2.5 Conclusions

The Part-Time Workers Directive codified the case law of the Court of Justice in relation to part-time work. On the basis of article 141 EC on equal pay and Directive

28 Report by the Commission's services on the implementation of Council Directive 97/81/EC of 17 December 1997 concerning the Framework Agreement on Part-Time work concluded by UNICE, CEEP and the ETUC.

76/207 the Court found that the less favourable treatment of part-time workers is indirectly discriminatory on the grounds of sex since the majority of part-timers are women. In practical terms, it seems that the Part-Time Workers Directive will help applicants to skip two stages in indirect discrimination cases. Firstly, the directive removes the obligation to show that less favourable treatment of part-time workers has an adverse impact on women. The employer now has the obligation to justify the measure: discrimination against a part-timer will always be unlawful unless it can be justified. Secondly, it appears that the inability to comply with a full-time work requirement will not have to be demonstrated in indirect discrimination cases: as described above, treating full-time and part-time staff differently must be justified. The Directive also gives rights to male part-timers who previously would have experienced difficulty in arguing that they were disproportionately affected.[29]

In the Labour Act provisions relating to part-time work have been implemented in a minimalist way. No measures have been taken to stimulate part-time work.

One of the targets set at the Lisbon European Council of March 2000 was to reach a 70 per cent overall employment rate in the EU by 2010, with the female rate set in general at sixty per cent. The Union counts paid jobs of more than one hour a week towards these targets. The stimulation of part-time jobs will help to reach the sixty per cent employment rate target for women. Consequently a more active policy to stimulate part-time work in Turkey is recommended.

5.4.3 On-Call Work

Work on call is a special form of part-time employment contract regulated by article 14 of the Labour Act. Work on call is defined as an employment relationship which foresees the performance of work by the employee upon the emergence of a need for his/her services, as agreed on by the parties in the written employment contract (article 14/I). Work on call, not unknown in past Turkish practices and referred to as a special form of part-time employment contract in various decisions of the Court of Cassation, is now regulated by the Labour Act which has bolstered it by certain protective measures.

Article 14/II stipulates that in the event that the parties have not defined working time in terms of time units such as a week, month or year, the weekly working time of the employee is considered to have been fixed at twenty hours. The employee is entitled to wages irrespective of whether or not he/she is engaged in work during the time announced for work on call. Implicit in this article is the notion of working time and wage flexibility, which should encourage the parties to agree on a contract longer or shorter than 20 hours. However, there is a strong likelihood that the twenty hours rule will be regarded as an absolutely binding minimum, taken

29 Catherine Barnard, *EU Employment Law*, Oxford 2000.

to mean that the parties may not agree on a lower number of hours in individual or collective agreements.

As well as this, unless the contrary has been decided, an employer in this situation must make the said call at least four days in advance. The employee is obliged to perform the contracted work within the said time limit (i.e. notice at least four days in advance). If the daily working time has not been decided in the contract, the employer must engage the employee in work for a minimum of four consecutive hours at each call (article 14/III, IV). As these provisions indicate, legislation has granted considerable freedom to the parties involved in the work on call contract while also introducing certain protective measures to apply in the absence of any agreement to the contrary. Notwithstanding such regulations, however, the trade unions were quite critical of work on call during the legislative debates on the grounds of its alleged infringement of secure and stable employment.

5.4.4 Temporary Employment Contracts

5.4.4.1 Characteristics of Agencies for Temporary Work in EU Member States

A 1999 study remarks that temporary work is on the increase in the entire EU. According to a study conducted for the International Confederation of Temporary Work Businesses, 6.5 million individuals gain work experience through temporary work agencies each year. This is a daily average of 1.7 thousand individuals a day. On a country-by-country basis, the UK leads the EU market followed by France, the Netherlands and Germany. These four countries together account, for 90 per cent of all temporary workers assigned through temporary work agencies in the EU, according to the report.[30]

In its proposal for a directive on working conditions for temporary workers[31] the European Commission pointed out that, while the basic common feature of all temporary agency work is a ‘three-way relationship' between a user undertaking, an employee and an agency, the legal situation varies considerably from Member State to Member State.[32] Despite such differences, the Commission was able to identify the following characteristics common to temporary agency work in the labour laws of the Member States:

> The temporary work agency is generally considered as the employer of the temporary worker. The worker can thus be considered an employee.

30 S. Clauwaert (ed.), *ETUI Legal Survey on Temporary Agency Work*, Brussels, 4 October 1999, p. 3.

31 Brussels, 20.3.2002, COM(2002) 149 final.

32 Ibid., p.5.

> The United Kingdom and Ireland are the exceptions to this: some UK and Irish temporary agencies explicitly give their recruits the status of employee; others consider temporary workers as self-employed. However, the final qualification will eventually depend on a court-based decision. In its capacity as employer, the temporary agency is bound to meet all the obligations this entails. However, the three-way relationship peculiar to temporary work frequently involves sharing of responsibilities with the user undertaking. The latter sometimes has to guarantee payment of wages and social contributions and has to apply health and safety rules. However, it is generally the temporary agency where temporary workers can enforce their collective rights; in some Member States (Austria, France and the Netherlands) they can enforce their collective rights in both the relation with the agency and the user company. Temporary workers are recruited on the basis of a fixed-term contract. In Germany and Sweden, by contrast, permanent contracts are the norm. In some States, particularly Italy and the Netherlands, fixed-term contracts are converted to permanent contracts under certain conditions. Temporary workers receive pay at least equal to that which a permanent worker in the undertaking carrying out identical or similar tasks would receive. A similar principle can also be found in the legislation, agreements or codes of conduct governing the temporary work sector in Austria, the Netherlands, Belgium, France, Italy, Portugal, Spain, Luxembourg and Greece. The principle that an employee who is on strike may not be replaced by a temporary worker is very often enshrined in the legislation, collective agreements or codes of conduct. The relevant legislation very often regulates access to the social services of the undertaking.[33]

The European Commission added that there were also areas in which there are still broad differences between the Member States, including the quality of temporary jobs, equal treatment with regard to pay and other conditions, such as training, and the willingness of workers to engage in temporary work.

The study shows that a division can be made between three approaches: prohibition, regulation and non-regulation of temporary work. In some countries the ban on temporary work has only recently been lifted. In other countries, temporary work is an accepted phenomenon and is integrated into the overall legal framework. In several countries, specific legislation has been introduced to regulate temporary work. Some countries have implemented very detailed rules in order to clearly determine the rights and obligations of the three parties involved (e.g. Belgium, France, Germany and the Netherlands). In other countries, including Denmark, Ireland and the UK,

33 Ibid., pp. 5–6.

the general principles of (labour) law apply without specific rules for temporary work. In a number of countries collective bargaining, in particular at the sectoral level, plays an important role in the regulation of temporary work (e.g. Belgium, France, Netherlands, Spain, Finland and Sweden). Codes of conduct produced by the temporary agency representative organisations are also significant.

5.4.4.2 The Turkish Rules

The only provision in the Labour Act on temporary agency work is article 90, which regulates private employment agencies. Article 7 of the Labour Act refers to the 'temporary employment relationship', but this is not temporary work normally understood as temporary 'agency' work. Article 7 of the Labour Act refers to what is, in Europe, usually called 'staff lending' or 'secondment' of personnel, whereby an employee is hired out to a third party without the involvement of a private employment agency.

Temporary employment relationships, based on a triangular employment relationship involving the temporary transfer of employees to other establishments within the structure of a holding company or the same group of companies, was a familiar practice in Turkey, generally with the purpose of meeting the needs of related companies for skilled labour or for undertaking joint projects. In some cases and with a view to avoiding layoffs, employers who faced financial difficulties assigned some of their staff to employers of related companies. The Labour Act has now brought some clarity to this complicated issue. From the wording of the article 7, it follows that temporary work agencies assigning their employees to third parties on a professional basis are illegal. The original bill contained detailed regulations on these agencies, but these were withdrawn.

A temporary employment relationship is established when, upon obtaining his written consent at the time of transfer, the employer transfers the employee to another establishment within the structure of the same holding company or the same group of companies or to another employer to undertake similar work. While after such transfer the employment contract between the employer and the employee continues to be in effect; the employee is obliged to perform work for the employer with whom the temporary employment relationship has been established (transferee). The employer who is the party to the temporary employment relationship has the right to issue directions to the employee but is also obliged to provide appropriate health and safety training. Temporary employment relationships, which must be concluded in written form, may be established for a period not exceeding six months, and may renewed twice if required (article 7/I, II).

In this triangular relationship, while the employment contract between the transferor and the employee exists, the employee is obliged to perform the work (i.e. the work which he/she had undertaken in the light of this contract) for the transferee employer, who has the right to issue directions to him/her. The transferee's right to issue directions to the employee is limited, however, to issues affecting the management of the establishment. In addition, the employer (transferor) who is the party to the employment contract may maintain his/her right to issue directions to the employee on such matters as access to paid annual vacation.

The transferor's obligation to pay the employee's wages continues to exist. The employer with whom the temporary employment relationship has been established (transferee) is jointly liable with the employer (transferor) for the employee's unpaid wages and social security contributions for the period during which the employee was engaged in the establishment, alongside the duty to protect the employee (article 7/III).

If the employee becomes liable for damages due to negligence, he/she is liable to the employer (transferee) with whom a temporary employment relationship has been established (article 7/IV).

Though the Labour Act is silent on this, it should be recalled that the employee has a duty of loyalty to both employers, implying for instance obligations such as refraining from keeping the trade secrets of the transferee as well as those of the transferor. Regarding the employer's obligation to treat the employee equally, both the transferor and the transferee are obliged to observe and respect the principle of equal treatment towards the employee. However, as the obligation to pay the employee's wages and wage-related supplements rests on the transferor, his/her duty of equal treatment is limited solely to such payments. The transferee, on the other hand, must uphold equal treatment in all areas relating to the right to direct and manage (i.e. the organisation of work), doing night work and the assignment of tasks between the transferee's employees and a temporary employee who has similar qualifications.

In establishments where collective dismissals have taken place, no temporary employment relationship may be established in jobs affected by the collective dismissal within the following six-month period after the collective dismissal (article 7/VII).

Unless the contrary is understood from the employee's temporary employment contract, the provisions of the Labour Act relating to other rights and obligations of the employee also apply to his relationship with the employer with whom temporary employment relationship was established (article 7/V).

In the event of the employer who has taken over the employee temporarily being a party to a collective labour dispute which has reached the strike and lock-out stage, the employee must not be engaged in work during the execution of the strike and lock-out. Provisions of article 39 of the Collective Agreements, Strikes and Lock-outs Law are, however, reserved. The transferor employer must engage such employees in work at his own establishment (article 7/VI). This means that the temporary employee must not work at the transferee's establishment affected by a strike or lock–out, without prejudice to a situation where the employee is designated among those who must not participate in a lawful strike or lock-out. In this case, he/she has to perform the obligation to work at the establishment of the transferor. The Act is silent, however, on the employee's participation in a strike or lock-out which has affected the transferor's establishment. As the employee is attached to the transferor with his employment contract, one could safely argue that he could be entitled to exercise his Constitutional and legal rights to participate in a lawful industrial action affecting his main workplace.

As for the temporary employee's union and collective bargaining rights, he/she may only become a founder of or join a union organised in the branch of activity which covers the establishment of the transferor employer, again by way of the nature of his/her employment contract. And for the same reasons, he/she may avail himself exclusively of the collective agreement covering the transferor's establishment if the conditions foreseen by the Collective Agreements, Strikes and Lock-outs Law are present. Nevertheless, provisions of the collective agreement covering the transferee's establishment relating to working time, rest breaks and employer's management rights apply to the temporary employee as well.

The original draft bill prepared by the tripartite academic committee had foreseen the operation of temporary work agencies, based on the same notion of a triangular relationship but on a professional basis. It envisaged certain protective rules, yet left further details to be covered in a regulation to be issued in conjunction with other provisions on labour market management. Due to intensive labour opposition, the said article was deleted from the bill during the parliamentary process. Article 90 now permits the operation of private employment agencies as an intermediary to provide employment services for job seekers and employers only. Private employment agencies must be licensed and supervised by the Employment Organisation of Turkey and they must not charge employees any fees, except for high-level managers and certain occupational categories as determined in the By-law of 19 February 2004 on Private Employment Agencies.

However, the triangular temporary work relationship is practised on a professional basis by certain agencies, albeit informally and with no legal basis. In so doing, these agencies rely for the most part on the principal employer-subcontractor relationship which, by way of its quite different nature, leads to controversy. Consequently there is an urgent need to legalise temporary work in Turkey with a view to supporting it via protective measures.

5.5 HEALTH AND SAFETY FOR TEMPORARY WORKERS

5.5.1 Introduction

Directive 91/383, adopted on 25 June 1991, provides for health and safety protection for workers with a fixed-term contract or a temporary employment relationship. This directive was produced in view of the special position of such workers given the nature of the risks they face in certain sectors. These risks justify special rules, particularly regarding the provision of information, training and medical care. The purpose of the directive is to ensure that in the area of health and safety at work, workers with a fixed-duration employment relationship or a temporary employment relationship are granted the same level of protection as other workers in the user undertaking and/or establishment, particularly regarding access to personal protective equipment.

According to the European Commission, research has shown that in certain sectors, workers with a fixed-term contract or who are working in a temporary employment relationship are generally more exposed to the risk of accidents at work and to occupational diseases than other workers. This higher risk which exists in some sectors is claimed to be partly linked to certain particular modes of integrating new workers into the undertaking. The Commission argued that the risks can be reduced by adequate provision of information and training as soon as the employee is engaged.

5.5.2 A Comparison of Turkish Law with the Health and Safety Directive

5.5.2.1 The Non-discrimination Provision of Article 2

We will now examine how the main provisions of the directive are implemented in Germany, Belgium, France and the Netherlands.[34]

The German Law on Health and Safety covers workers with a temporary employment relationship or a fixed-duration employment relationship under the same conditions as all other workers. The discrimination provision of article 2(2) of the Framework Agreement is not explicitly included in this law. Such provision is not necessary as any discrimination in the field of health and safety at work would fall foul of the general principle of equal opportunities enshrined in German labour law.

34 This overview is based on European Commission, *Report on the Implementation of Directive 91/383/EEC Supplementing the Measures to Encourage Improvements in the Safety and Health at Work of Workers with a Fixed-Duration Employment Relationship or a Temporary Employment Relationship*, Brussels, *s.d.*, 34 p.

Belgian law does not distinguish between workers with a fixed-duration or temporary employment relationship and other employees. Flexible workers are therefore entitled to equal treatment in respect of hygiene, health and medical surveillance. The conditions governing access to personal protective equipment are the same for all categories of workers.

The French law on fixed-duration and temporary employment relationships does not contradict the application of general protective measures applicable to all workers. In particular, the conditions governing access to personal protective equipment apply fully to these categories of workers.

Article 1(1)(a 2) of the Dutch Working Conditions Act states that, for the purposes of this Act, the employer of an assigned worker is not the temporary employment agency with which the employment contract has been concluded but the user firm. Consequently, the latter is subject to the same legal obligations towards temporary workers as those that apply to other employees. The Working Conditions Act does not contain any expressly non-discrimination rule corresponding to article 2(2) of the Directive. However, such a ban is not necessary: firstly, the employer or user has the same rights and is subject to the same obligations in respect of workers with a fixed-duration or temporary employment relationship that apply to other employees; secondly, to penalise these workers would fall foul of the general principle of equal treatment enshrined in the Netherlands Constitution (article 1). Workers with a fixed-duration employment relationship and workers assigned by a temporary employment business are entitled to equal treatment pursuant to the basic health and safety legislation.[35]

5.5.2.2 The Information Clause

In Germany the information provision of the directive is transposed by an amendment to article 11 of the *Arbeitnehmerüberlassungsgesetz*. Paragraph 6, sentence 2, of article 11 requires the user to inform the temporary worker before he/she starts work and whenever the work changes of the potential health and safety risks, as well as the measures and equipment required to eliminate these risks. Article 11(6), sentence 3 of the Law also requires the user undertaking to inform the temporary worker of the need for special occupational qualifications, skills or special medical surveillance, and of any increased specific risks that the job may entail.

In Belgium, the provision of information to workers is governed by Collective Labour Agreement No 38 of 6 December 1983 on the recruitment and selection of workers, which acquired force of law by the Royal Decree of 11 July 1984.[36] Pursuant to article 8 of this Agreement, the employer must provide the job applicants

35 Working Environment Act 1977:1160.

36 *Moniteur Belge* 28 July 1983.

with 'sufficient information on the job offered', notably 'the nature of the activity' and 'the requirements for performing the activity'. These rules cover particulars relating to qualifications and skills and the eventuality of special medical surveillance. Information on risks is prescribed by the Wellbeing at Work Code, which applies to all employees and hence to workers on a fixed-duration contract. Every employer is obliged to assess risks. Employees are informed of the risks which the job may entail, without prejudice to other information concerning safety in the undertaking.

Articles 2 and 3 of the Royal Decree of 19 February 1997 are the main rules governing the health and safety information to be provided to temporary workers. The procedure begins with the information provided by the user undertaking to the temporary employment business before a temporary worker is assigned. Hence the user undertaking must specify the occupational qualifications required and the specific features of the job in question, as well as the results of the assessment of the risks the job may entail. The temporary employment business must communicate to the temporary worker all the information provided to it by the user undertaking.

In France, pursuant to article L. 122-3-1 of the Labour Code, the fixed-duration employment contract must be in writing and must be given to the employee at the latest two days after recruitment. When the contract concerns the replacement of an employee on leave of absence, it must indicate the name and qualifications of the employee who has been replaced. The designation of the job must be indicated; this implies indirectly the qualifications required.

Moreover, collective branch agreements generally define the required qualifications. This means that employer has to indicate a precise qualification when recruiting an employee. As a result, the employee should be sufficiently informed.

Pursuant to article 8 of the Dutch Working Conditions Act, the employer must ensure that as soon as he/she takes up work every worker is precisely informed of the nature of the job and the associated risks, as well as the measures taken to address these risks. Pursuant to the Working Conditions Act, the user is considered to be the employer, and hence bears responsibility for informing the worker of the risks entailed. The obligation on the employer to inform the worker provided for in article 8 does, however, not expressly mention qualifications or particular occupational skills or special medical surveillance. The Dutch text merely prescribes in very general terms the provision of information on the risks and the measures taken to eliminate or reduce them. Article 6 of the Dutch Act mandates employers to inform the worker of all particular risks associated with the workplace.[37]

37 The text does not specifically require the employer to specify the additional specific risks linked to this workplace. However, since employers must provide details of all particular risks, one may consider that additional risks are also included.

5.5.2.3 The Provision on Training

In Germany, pursuant to article 12(1) of the Law on Health and Safety, the employer must provide workers with sufficient and appropriate training on occupational health and safety during their working hours. This training must include instructions and explanations related to the job or field of activity concerned. In the case of assigned workers, article 12(2) stipulates that this obligation is incumbent on the user. The latter must ensure that assigned workers receive training, taking account of their qualifications and experience.

In Belgium, just like other employees, safety training of employees with fixed-duration employment contracts is covered by the General Regulation on Protection at Work and other texts of a general scope. The provisions of Section III, Title I, Chapter III of the Wellbeing at Work Code require employers to provide sufficient and appropriate health and safety training to all workers, notably in the shape of specific information and instructions concerning the worker's job or function. The same provisions also require employers to ensure that workers receive all necessary information on health and safety risks, protective measures, and activities concerning the undertaking and the type of job or function in question.

The safety training of temporary workers is governed by the Royal Decree of 19 February 1997. Pursuant to article 5 thereof, the user is responsible for health and safety at work and must see to it that the temporary worker is afforded the same degree of protection as other workers in the undertaking.

In France, all employees on fixed-duration employment contracts must first receive safety training under the same conditions as permanent staff. This 'practical and appropriate safety training' (article L 231-3-1 of the Labour Code) must be designed in liaison with staff representatives. This article stipulates that having regard to the specific nature of their employment contract, employees on fixed duration employment contracts assigned to jobs that entail particular health and safety risks shall receive intensified safety training as well as appropriate guidance and information at the firm in which they are employed. All these rules also apply to temporary workers. The texts on basic training apply both to the undertaking's own staff and to workers assigned to it by temporary employment businesses.

The Directive's provisions on training have been transposed by article 8 of the Dutch Working Conditions Act. This article requires employers to notify the worker at the time of recruitment of the possible dangers and the measures to be taken to prevent them. Such information must also be provided during the course of employment if this is necessary for health or hygiene reasons, or to improve the worker's welfare.

5.5.2.4 The Use of Workers Services and Medical Surveillance

The German Health and Safety Law does not explicitly transpose the provision regarding the use of workers services and medical surveillance. However – just like its implementing decrees transposing the individual Directives relating to health and safety at work – German Law also applies to workers on a temporary or fixed-duration employment contract.

No provision in Belgian law prohibits employers from assigning workers with a fixed-duration employment relationship to dangerous work. However, the law requires special medical surveillance for certain categories of workers, including those performing dangerous work or workers exposed to certain job-related health risks. In the case of employees doing dangerous work or employees exposed to certain biological agents, surveillance begins on recruitment with a medical examination. The legal rules governing work subject to this special medical surveillance apply to all workers, irrespective of the nature of their employment contract.

No specific provision provides for an extension of medical surveillance beyond the end of the fixed-duration employment relationship. Only the nature of the risk to which the employee has been exposed may determine such an extension. The Royal Decree of 19 February 1997 specifies the types of work which may not be performed by temporary workers. The provisions on special medical surveillance apply to all workers, including temporary workers. This surveillance is incumbent on the temporary employment business and includes vaccinations, examination on assignment to hazardous jobs and regular check-ups.

French law prohibits the recruitment of workers with a fixed-duration employment relationship and the use of temporary workers for certain types of work.[38] There is no rule concerning special medical surveillance of employees recruited on a fixed-duration contract. They are subject to the same examinations and surveillance as any other employees in the undertaking. However, French law has adapted these general rules to the particular case of temporary workers.

The Netherlands has not availed itself of the option provided for in articles 1 and 3 of the Framework Agreement. Temporary workers are deemed to be employees of the user undertaking and are always entitled to the same medical surveillance as other employees of the undertaking.

5.5.2.5 The Provision on Protection and Prevention Services

In Germany, this provision was transposed by incorporation in the Safety at Work Act. These amendments require employers to inform the occupational physicians

38 The list of jobs in question was laid down in a Decree of 8 October 1990 for the non-agricultural sector and a Decree of 27 June 1991 (amended) for the agricultural sector.

and safety at work specialists whenever they recruit workers with a fixed-duration employment relationship or workers assigned to them to accomplish a specific task.

Belgian law does not require employers to inform persons and services responsible for health and safety to the effect that they are employing workers on a fixed-duration employment contract. The Law merely stipulates that a list of workers subject to special medical surveillance be made available to the workers' representatives on the safety, hygiene and improvement of workplaces committee, or if there is no such committee, to the trade union delegation and to various administrative bodies responsible for monitoring. However, temporary work is governed by specific provisions that satisfy the Directive's requirements. Pursuant to article 5(4) of the Royal Decree, the user must keep a list of all temporary workers, featuring in particular their names and the posts they occupy.

In French law no provision requires the undertaking to inform the bodies, services or persons responsible for prevention of risks and for safety of employees on a fixed-duration or temporary employment contract.

The Dutch Working Conditions Act does not contain any particular obligations regarding the position of information about the assignment of temporary workers. In principle these workers are on the same footing as other employees in the user undertaking: in theory, temporary workers are therefore under the responsibility of the services covered by article 8. However, the information requirement enshrined in this article must take account of the particular risks associated with the use of temporary workers.

5.5.2.6 The Responsibility for Temporary Employment Relationships

German Law stipulates that the activity performed by a temporary worker at the user undertaking is subject to the public law rules applicable to the latter in the field of health and safety at work (article 11[6], sentence 1). The obligations of the employer arising from public law are incumbent on the user undertaking, without prejudice to the supplier's obligations.

In Belgium, article 16 of Collective Labour Agreement No 36 concluded by the National Labour Council and given force of law by the Royal Decree of 9 December 1981 stipulates that the temporary employment agency may not assign a temporary worker to a user undertaking unless the latter undertakes to comply with the provisions of the legislation governing protection at work. These provisions concern the health and safety of workers and the quality of work and the workplaces. Article 19 of the Act of 24 July 1987 on temporary work stipulates that temporary work and the assignment of workers to user undertakings shall be subject to the same conditions as those set out in the aforementioned collective agreement. Article 5(1) of the Royal Decree of 19 February 1997 stipulates that the user undertaking be responsible for working conditions in respect of safety and hygiene at work such that the temporary worker is afforded the same level of protection as other workers in the undertaking.

In France, pursuant to article L. 124-4-6 of the Labour Code, the user undertaking is responsible during the term of the assignment for the conditions governing performance of the work as laid down by the laws, regulations and agreements which apply to the workplace.

In the Netherlands, pursuant to the Working Conditions Act (and in particular article 6[1][a 2] and articles 3, 4, 5 and 8), the user undertaking is deemed to be the employer and is therefore responsible for the conditions governing performance of the work during the term of the assignment.

5.5.2.7 Concluding Remarks

As a result of the report underlying this chapter, the Turkish Government was informed of the need to implement Directive 91/883. By means of a by-law of 15 May 2004, based on the general provisions of the Labour Act, Turkey intends to implement Directive 91/383. This was done, however, by a mere translation of the text of the directive into Turkish. Implementing EU law is, however, not simply a matter of translation. It generally requires an adjustment to national law. We recommend that the transposition of the directive be reconsidered.

5.6 THE RULES CONCERNING WORKING TIME

This section concerns Directive 93/104 of 23 November 1993.[39] The essential aims of the Directive are to ensure that workers are protected against adverse health and safety effects caused by working excessively long hours, having inadequate rest or having disruptive working patterns.

The Directive requires in particular:

- A minimum rest period of eleven consecutive hours for each twenty-four-hour period
- A rest break where the working day is longer than six hours
- A minimum rest period of one day per week

39 OJ L 307, 13.12.1993, p. 18. Directive as amended by Directive 2000/34/EC OJL 195, 1 August 2000, p. 41. Directive 2000/34 of the European Parliament and of the Council of 22 June 2000 was repealed by Directive 2003/88/EC (codified version), concerning certain aspects of the organisation of working time, OJ L 299, 18 November 2003, p. 92.

- Maximum weekly working hours of 48 hours on average, including overtime
- Four weeks of paid annual leave
- An average of no more than eight hours of work at night in any 24 hour period.

Member States may maintain or introduce more favourable provisions for the protection of the health and safety of workers than set out in this Directive.

5.6.1 The Scope of the Directive

The Directive applies to all sectors of activity, both public and private. Seafarers are, however excluded.[40] As regards the personal scope, the Working Time Directive uses the notion of 'worker', however this notion is not defined in Directive 93/104, but in article 3 of Directive 89/391: a worker is defined in this directive as any person employed by an employer, including trainees and apprentices but excluding domestic servants. An employer is defined as any natural or legal person who has an employment relationship with the worker and has responsibility for the undertaking and/or establishment.

The Turkish Labour Act applies to employees working under a contract of employment. The Labour Act excludes, however, sea and air transport activities, establishments and enterprises employing a minimum of fifty employees where agricultural and forestry work is carried out, any construction work related to agriculture which falls within the scope of family economy, works and handicrafts performed in the home without any outside help by members of the family or close relatives up to the 3rd degree, domestic services, apprentices (without prejudice to the provisions on occupational health and safety), sportsmen, persons undergoing rehabilitation, and establishments employing three or fewer employees and falling within the definition given in article 2 of the Tradesmen and Small Handicrafts Act.

Some of these categories fall under article 17 of the Directive, for instance family workers and activities in the agriculture sector. Article 17 allows derogations from some articles of the directive, but requires observation of the general principles of the protection of the health and safety of workers. It is recommended that all Turkish laws, including the Maritime Labour Act or regulations covering these workers, be brought in line with the Working Time Directive. Any person employed by an employer has to be covered.

---

40 As defined in Directive 1999/63/EC OJL 167, 2 July 1999, p. 332.

5.6.2 Definition of Working Time

Article 2 of the Directive defines working time as 'any period of time during which the worker is working, at the employer's disposal and carrying out his activities or duties, in accordance with national law and/or practice'. Article 2 defines rest period as 'any period which is not working time'. In accordance with the definitions expressed in the Directive, there is no interim category: any specific period can only be working time or a rest period, The two concepts are mutually exclusive.

The Labour Act does not contain express definitions on working time or rest periods. It only stipulates in article 68 that breaks are not reckoned as working time. Working time itself is not defined in the Turkish Labour Act. In general, it can be assumed that under Turkish law, working time is considered as being any period of time during which the worker is at the employer's disposal or carrying out his activities or duties.

However, some provisions of the Labour Act consider additional time periods as part of the statutory hours of work, i.e.:[41]

a. The time required for employees employed in mines, stone quarries or any other underground or underwater work to descend into the pit or workings or to the actual workplace and to return therefrom to the surface

b. Travelling time, if the employee is sent by the employer to a place outside the establishment

c. The time during which the employee has no work to perform pending the arrival of new work but remains at the employer's disposal

d. The time during which an employee who ought to be performing work within the scope of his duties in the establishment is sent on an errand for the employer or is employed in the employer's household or office

e. The time allowed to a female employee who is a nursing mother to feed her child

f. The time necessary for the normal and regular transportation of groups of employees engaged in the construction, maintenance, repair and alteration of railways, roads and bridges to and from a workplace at a distance from their place of residence.
Time for transportation to and from an establishment which is not a requirement of the activity but is provided by the employer solely as a form of amenity is not regarded as part of the statutory working time.

41 Art. 66 of the Labour Act.

It can therefore be concluded that, besides some specific statutory definitions, the notions of working time and rest periods will be defined by national practice and case law in Turkey.

5.6.3 The Rest Period Requirements

The definition of adequate rest is designed to establish the criteria which need to be taken into account if no numerical limits apply. According to the directive 'adequate rest' means that workers have regular rest periods, of sufficient continuous time units expressed in units of time to ensure that, as a result of fatigue or other irregular working patterns, they do not cause injury to themselves, to fellow workers or to others and that they do not damage their health, either in the short or in the longer term. The rest provisions which comply with articles 3, 4 and 5 of the Working Time Directive satisfy these criteria.

Article 3 of the Directive lays down a minimum daily rest period of eleven consecutive hours per 24 hour period. Derogations from article 3 are allowed in accordance with articles 17 and 18.

The Turkish Labour Act stipulates that daily working time must not exceed 11 hours. Moreover, article 69 stipulates that the employee whose shift will be changed must not be engaged on another shift unless allowed a minimum rest break of eleven hours.

To ensure the proper application of the directive, however, it is advisable to include a provision guaranteeing a daily rest period of eleven consecutive hours per twenty-four hour period in the Turkish Labour Act.

Article 4 requires a rest break for every worker if the working day is longer than six hours. The details of the rest break have to be laid down in collective agreements or other agreements between the two sides of industry or, failing that, by national legislation. This provision may be derogated from in accordance with articles 17 and 18.

Turkish law requires a rest break of fifteen minutes when the work lasts four hours or less, half an hour when the work lasts between four and seven and a half hours, and one hour when the work lasts more than seven and a half hours.

In most Member States, the implementation of article 4 of the Directive is carried out by a combination of legislative measures and collective agreements. The statutory rules tend to fix the maximum period a worker is allowed to work without a break and the duration of the break.[42]

---

42 Report by the European Commission, *State of Implementation of Council Directive 93/104/EC of 23 November 1993, Concerning Certain Aspects of the Organisation of WorkingTime*, Brussels, 1 December 2000, COM (2000) 787 final.

Article 5 of the directive requires an uninterrupted rest period of 24 hours for each seven-day period plus the eleven hours daily rest referred to in article 3. In other words, article 5 provides for a 35 hours rest period for every seven-day period. Article 16 provides for a reference period of 14 days.

Article 17 allows for derogations from these general rules under certain conditions and article 5(2) allows for a rest period of only 24 hours under special conditions.

Initially, Directive 93/104 contained a provision that the weekly rest period should in principle include Sunday. This provision was annulled by the Court in the case *United Kingdom of Great Britain and Northern Ireland* v *Council of the European Union.*[43] In this ruling the Court said that the 'Council has failed to explain why Sunday as a weekly rest day is more closely connected with health and safety of workers than any other day of the week'.

Under Turkish law, workers are entitled to a minimum weekly rest period of twenty-four hours.[44] In this law the provision concerning the eleven hours daily rest period is missing, although such a requirement could be deduced from the rule that there must be a maximum period of eleven working hours a day.[45] In order to avoid any misunderstanding and to be precise, it is recommended that the additional provision of eleven hours daily rest be included in the Act.

5.6.4 The Provision on the Maximum Weekly Working Time

Article 6 requires that the average working time for each seven-day period, including overtime not exceed forty-eight hours. For the calculation of the average, article 16 allows a reference period of four months, from which periods of annual leave and sick leave have to be excluded. It may be set at six months in cases where it is possible to derogate from article 16. By collective agreement it may be extended up to twelve months. Article 17 allows derogations under special conditions, for example where the duration of the working time is not measured and/or predetermined or can be determined by the workers themselves (e.g. by managing executives).

Article 17(5) contains a new derogation for a transitional period in respect of the maximum working week for doctors in training. Where there is an agreement between the employer and workers' representatives, the limit on the average number of weekly hours worked could be increased to fifty-four (i.e. one hour per day) over a four-month reference period. An immediate passage to a maximum working week of 48 hours on average would have serious consequences for the provision of health care. This is not only because of the increased costs involved, but also

43 Case C-84/94, [1996] ECR I-5755.

44 Art. 46 of the Turkish Labour Act.

45 Art. 63 of the Turkish Labour Act

because of the lack of trained doctors. The transitional period, should provide sufficient time for the hospital authorities to plan the necessary changes, including a modernisation of the organisation of work, in agreement with representatives of the doctors concerned.

Under Turkish law, according to article 63 of the Labour Act, the maximum weekly working time may not exceed forty-five hours a week. Overtime work is work that exceeds forty-five hours a week.[46] In cases where the principle of balancing is applied, work which exceeds a total of forty-five hours a week shall not be deemed overtime work, provided the average working time of the employee does not exceed the normal weekly working time. The Turkish provisions with regard to maximum weekly working time are in line with European legislation.

5.6.5 Annual Leave

Article 7 requires paid annual leave of at least four weeks and prohibits replacement of the leave by an allowance in lieu. The directive does not allow for any derogations from article 7. It is important to emphasise that article 7 requires accumulation of two elements: 'leave', which is a period off work during the regular work schedule as laid down by national law and/or practice; and 'payment', which is the right to normal wages or equivalent compensation during the leave period. The directive lays down an annual leave of at least four weeks. This means that if a worker normally works five days a week, he/she has the right to twenty working days off. If the worker works six days a week, he/she has the right to twenty-four working days off. In both cases annual leave implies a leave of four weeks. The average annual leave entitlement[47] across the old Member States stands at 26.5 days a year on the basis of a five-day working week. The total of agreed annual leave and public holidays in the EU varies from 44 days in Sweden to 29 days in Ireland.[48]

Article 56 of the Turkish Labour Act and article 6/V of the Regulation issued on 3 March 2004 both stipulate that national holidays, weekly rest days and public holidays which coincide with the duration of annual leave should not be included in the annual leave period.

Turkish Law has the following qualifying period for entitlement to annual leave:[49] 'employees who have completed a minimum of one year of service in the establishment since their recruitment, including the trial period, shall be allowed to take annual leave with pay. The provisions of annual leave are not applicable to employees engaged in seasonal or other occupations which owing to their nature,

46 Art. 41/1.

47 Without public holidays.

48 Source EIRO 2003.

49 Art. 53 of the Labour Act.

last less than one year'. Under these rules the length of the employee's annual leave with pay shall not be less than fourteen days if his length of service is between one and five years, twenty days if his length of service is more than five and less than fifteen years, and twenty-six days if it is fifteen years or more.

Article 53 of the Labour Act with regard to the qualifying period as well as the minimum leave period do not comply with the working time directive. Consequently, a revision of this article is necessary.

5.6.6 Night Work

According to article 8 of the directive, the normal number of working hours for night workers must not exceed an average of eight hours in any 24-hour period. The notion of 'normal hours of work' includes overtime as indicated in consideration 8 in the preamble to the Directive: 'Whereas there is a need to limit the duration of periods of night work, including overtime'. Article 16 of the directive provides for the option of laying down a reference period for night workers who fall under article 8. In such a case the weekly rest period as defined by article 5 is not counted in the calculation of the average. Night work according to Turkish law is limited to seven and a half hours.[50]

According to article 9, Member States have to take measures to ensure that night workers are entitled to a free health assessment before their assignment and thereafter at regular intervals. Night workers suffering from health problems which are recognised as being connected with the fact that they perform night work must be transferred, whenever possible, to day work to which they are suited. The free health assessment must comply with medical confidentiality and it may be conducted within the national health system.

Turkish legislation provides for a health examination of workers before they start night work and thereafter at least once every two years, paid for by the employer.[51]

EU Member States may make the work of certain categories of night workers subject to certain guarantees, under conditions laid down by national legislation and/or practice, in the case of workers who incur risks to their health and safety linked to night-time working.

The corresponding Turkish legislation prohibits children and young employees under the age of eighteen from undertaking industrial work.[52]

50 Art. 69 of the Labour Act.

51 Art. 69 of the Labour Act

52 Art. 73 of the Labour Act.

Article 11 of the directive requires Member States to take measures to ensure that an employer who regularly uses night workers brings this information to the attention of the competent authorities if they so request.

The Labour Act requires that the employer submit to the relevant regional directorate of labour a list of employees who will be employed on night shifts.[53]

Article 12 of the directive requires Member States to ensure that night workers and shift workers have health and safety protection appropriate to the nature of their work equivalent to those applicable to other workers, and that it be available at all times. Article 13 of the directive requires Member States to take those measures necessary to ensure that employers are alleviated from monotonous work and work at a predetermined work-rate, in particular by allowing breaks during working time.

In Turkey the general legislation on health and safety of workers is also applicable to night workers. Apart from this two special provisions are applicable. Article 69 of the Labour Act stipulates that shifts must be so alternated that employees are engaged on night work for no longer than one week and are then engaged on day work the following week. Alternation of work on night and day shifts may also be carried out on a two-week basis. An employee whose shift will be changed must not be engaged on the other shift unless a minimum rest break of eleven hours is allowed.

5.6.7 Preliminary Conclusions on the Implementation of the Directive

The Labour Act is predominantly in line with the requirements of the Working time Directive, apart from two important issues.

Firstly, Turkey has excluded those categories of workers who do not fall within the scope of the exclusions of the Working Time Directive or article 2 of Directive 89/391. The fact that some of these categories fall within the scope of article 17 of the Working Time Directive does not permit a total exclusion of these workers.

Secondly, under Turkish legislation there is a qualifying period for entitlement to annual leave. Article 7 of the Working Time Directive lays down a right to four weeks annual leave for all workers which, in appropriate cases, may be given on a pro rata basis. Furthermore, workers are not entitled to take any leave during the first year of their employment. This shortcoming is particularly relevant since it concerns workers under relatively short fixed-term contracts.

At least two provisions have to be added to or modified in the Turkish legislation to guarantee that the Working Time Directive has been incorporated into domestic law in a sufficiently clear and precise manner. As the Working Time Directive is intended to establish legal rights for individuals, the persons concerned must be

53 Art. 69 of the Labour Act.

able to ascertain the full extent of their rights and where appropriate, rely on them before national courts. The following provisions should be adopted:

- Adding a daily rest period of eleven consecutive hours per twenty-four-hour period into the Labour Act
- Changing the provision of the minimum weekly rest period of twenty-four hours into the provision of a minimum weekly rest period of twenty-four hours plus the eleven hours of daily rest.

5.7 CONCLUSIONS

The European directives on flexible work do not provide a complete picture or an overall model of regulation. For example, the Fixed-term Work Directive has had little impact on many Member States' national labour laws. The respect for significant national autonomy in this field can probably be better explained when the 'flexibility' issue is put in a broader context. The use of 'fixed term' and 'temporary' work is obviously very strongly linked to the law on dismissals. The regulation of flexible work cannot be separated from the regulation of employment termination of typical work (full-time workers hired for an indefinite period). Such dismissal law is, clearly, to be found at the national level. Not surprisingly, this limits the EU approach. It also implies that the Turkish view on flexibility will also be strongly linked to the Turkish law on dismissals.

This latter element lies at the centre of the above analysis. The Turkish legislator and actors in the field of social policy will need to reflect on certain options that are either left open or left unattended by the European *acquis*. Seen within a more technical perspective, the Turkish Labour Act generally appears to be in conformity with European legislation in the area of flexible work or a-typical employment (barring some details). If greater European guidance is required in this field, not only would the *acquis* become relevant but also comparative insights. Taking a broader view of Turkish labour law, however, some social and political options have been left open for discussion in the near future. The challenge here will be to combine the notions of flexibility and security, as used in EU language under the rubric of 'adaptability'. It was not the purpose of this contribution to depict national models showing how countries deal with this concept, although such an exercise remains useful, or even necessary. The limited experience with the Turkish Labour Act has strengthened the assumption that any synthesis between the *acquis* and national law is likely to be based on Turkey's own ways of dealing with the broader issue of flexicurity.

6. THE RELATIONSHIP BETWEEN SOCIAL SECURITY AND FLEXIBILITY

Frans Pennings, Nurhan Süral and Karin Sengers

6.1 INTRODUCTION

In this chapter we describe and analyse the relationship between Turkish social security law and its attitude towards flexibility. The relationship between labour market flexibility and the protection that social security provides has several implications. It may encourage and/or allow a worker to accept more insecurity in his or her working conditions. For example, a person who is working and who is offered a new job may be reluctant to accept the new job if he/she loses all social security rights as a result (e.g. pension rights connected with his or her previous work). The position of flexible workers is also implicated: traditionally, flexible workers belong to the informal labour market and tend to be excluded from social security protection. By extending social security protection to flexible workers, they can be drawn within the scope of the labour market.

In other words, flexibility and social security may be narrowly connected with each other. However, introducing greater social security for flexible workers is not an easy task as it requires enhanced implementation and supervision systems. Still, it is worthwhile to approach the social security system with this objective, in order to see whether changes are necessary and possible.

Following a description of the system, this chapter identifies several issues relevant to promoting flexibility and employment and giving adequate protection to marginal workers. It does not deal with all aspects of Turkish social security.

We describe the EU standards on flexibilisation and social security in Section 6.2. In Sections 6.3, 6.4 and 6.5 we describe the Turkish system and its relation to flexibilisation. In Sections 6.6 and 6.7 we analyse our findings and present our recommendations.

6.2 RELEVANT EU RULES AND POLICIES

In principle, EU Member States have the right to determine the contents of their social security systems. However, this freedom is restricted by legislation follow-

Pennings, *Flexibilisation and Modernisation of the Turkish Labour Market*, 119–152

ing from the *acquis*, including the rules on the protection of migrant workers and equal treatment (the 'hard' *acquis*). In addition there are recommendations and guidelines, which are not 'hard law', but which are important for the Member States (the 'soft' *acquis*). The Member States have to report on these aspects on a regular basis. Sometimes it is difficult to make a distinction between hard and soft *acquis*, since where both are closely linked, the binding effect of the soft *acquis* will be the same as that of the hard *acquis*. There is generally consensus within the EU on objectives such as those concerned with increasing competitiveness or increasing the number of jobs and encouraging older workers and women to participate in work, Member States do their best to reach these objectives.

In this section we discuss the relevant hard *acquis* and then the soft *acquis*, confining ourselves to the most essential elements.

6.2.1 Equal Treatment of Men and Women

The principle of equal treatment of men and women is a very important principle within EU law. Article 2 of the Treaty provides that the Community must aim to eliminate inequality and promote equality between men and women in all its activities. Directive 79/7 concerning statutory social security is particularly relevant to equal treatment. This directive covers those who have worked and left work because of illness, retirement, or unemployment; those who are in work and those who are seeking work. The directive covers statutory sickness, invalidity, old age, accidents at work and occupational diseases, and unemployment benefits. Family benefits are not included in these risks, except when they are due as a result of one of the five risks listed above.

The directive prohibits direct and indirect discrimination on the grounds of sex. A rule is considered as indirectly discriminating if it makes use of seemingly neutral criteria which in practice affect men more than women, or women more than men. However, such a rule is not indirectly discriminating if it can be justified objectively. Objective justification requires that the rule be suitable and necessary in order to comply with a legitimate objective of the Member State's social policy. Budgetary considerations alone do not constitute objective justification.

For example, statistical figures show that considerably more women than men work part-time. As a result, a rule which affects part-time workers negatively may be indirectly discriminating against women. The issue of objective justification here is somewhat complicated, as in the case of minimum income protection, the Court of Justice of the EC allows Member States a broad margin of discretion. In the *Nolte and Megner* judgements,[1] for instance, a scheme was justified whereby

1 Case C 317/93, *Nolte*, [1995] ECR I-4624 and Case C-444/93, *Ursula Megner*, [1995] ECR I-4741.

part-time workers were excluded from coverage as there was a demand for this type of minor employment and the supply of such employment could only be encouraged by excluding it from compulsory insurance. However, we should not assume that this case law allows discrimination against part-timers in general. The case law is restricted to minimum income situations and the policy measures concerned have to be justified

Article 7 of the directive allows Member States to exclude certain parts of their statutory social security systems from the scope of the directive. The most important aspect is the determination of pensionable age for the purposes of granting old-age and retirement pensions and the possible consequences therefore for other benefits. However, this is a temporary exception and Member States have to report on a regular basis on why the exception is still necessary. In most EU Member States that make a distinction between pension ages for men and women, legislation has been enacted which will gradually phase out these differences.

Article 141 EC concerning the principle of equal pay of men and women also has the effect of forbidding discrimination in non-statutory social security systems. This provision is more radical than the directive since it forbids, for instance, differential pensionable ages (with no temporary exceptions).[2]

Given the situation in Turkey, Directive 86/613 covering the principle of equal treatment between men and women engaged in activities such as agriculture or self-employment activity and the protection of self-employed women during pregnancy and motherhood is particularly relevant. This directive not only requires equal treatment on grounds of sex, but also requires Member States to examine whether, and under what conditions, female self-employed workers and the wives of self-employed workers may, during interruptions to their occupational activity owing to pregnancy or motherhood, have access to services supplying temporary replacements or existing national social services, or be entitled to cash benefits under a social security scheme or under any other public social protection system.

6.2.2 Employment Policy and Modernisation of Social Security Systems

One of the key aims of the EU is the enhancement of competition (Lisbon Agenda) requiring a co-ordinated approach to employment and social security policy. One of the main objectives of the Treaty of Amsterdam was the development of a 'coordinated strategy' for employment in order to reach a high level of employment and social protection. This implies the need for modernisation of the social protection system. Most European social security systems are based on a model of employment consisting of lifelong and permanent employment, with retirement from the labour

2 This is only a very short overview on the EU law on equal treatment; for more information, see Frans Pennings, *Introduction to European Social Security Law,* Antwerp, 2003.

market taking place at the end of a full working life. Eligibility for benefits depends on satisfying contribution conditions and sometimes on continuous service.

In the past decades, traditional work structures have changed with major implications for social protection policies in the long term. Such changes should not be perceived as a threat to social security: flexible working can be both beneficial to European economies and attractive to individual employees. The latter should not therefore be penalised for adopting alternative working patterns. The European Commission notes that mechanisms must be found for adapting European social protection systems to take account of these new patterns of work.[3]

The broad objectives for modernisation were defined in the Council conclusions of December 1999 on the basis of a communication by the Commission.[4] These objectives are making work pay and providing a secure income, making pensions safe and pension systems sustainable, promoting social inclusion, and ensuring the high quality and sustainability of health care. The key objective of making work pay and providing secure income is central to flexibility and security. In order to make work pay and to provide a secure income:

- Social protection systems must reflect and respond to the emergence of new working arrangements (temporary and part-time contracts, self-employment).
- Social protection systems must provide an adequate level of income and active assistance to prevent a temporary gap between jobs from becoming long-term unemployment.
- Social protection should contribute to reconciling work and family life.

Policy cooperation on social protection made a huge step forward when the Lisbon European Council (March 2000) outlined its vision of an integrated socio-economic strategy for Europe for the decade to 2010. To achieve the new strategic goals, the Lisbon conclusions attached considerable importance to the contribution required from social protection systems. According to the Council's conclusions, the social protection systems need to form part of an active welfare State in order to ensure that work pays, to promote social inclusion and gender equality, and to provide quality health services. The Council also recognised that as the population ages, the need to secure the long-term sustainability of such systems increases. The Lisbon conclusions also provided a clear mandate for joint work between the Member States and the Commission in the fields of social inclusion and pensions. The Open Method of Coordination was introduced as the mechanism for promoting this work and the annual Spring European Council was given a central role in the guidance

---

3 European Commission, *Green Paper – Partnership for a New Organisation of Work.*

4 European Commission, *A Concerted Strategy for Modernising Social Protection,* COM (1999) 347 final.

and coordination of work towards the production of a new strategy. This view of social protection as an important element in overall socio-economic policy was further strengthened in the Social Policy Agenda adopted by the European Council of Nice. The areas for policy development defined in Nice were:

- More and better jobs
- Anticipating and capitalising on change in the working environment by creating a new balance between flexibility and security
- Fighting poverty and all forms of exclusion
- Modernising social protection
- Promoting gender equality
- Strengthening the social policy aspects of enlargement and EU external relations.

The Council of Nice confirmed the goal of modernising and improving social protection in order to 'respond to the transformation to the knowledge economy and to the change in social and family structures and build on the role of social protection as a productive factor'. Starting in 2006, Member States will have to produce national reports setting out their strategies for reaching the common objectives defined in the Council.

The Employment Guidelines are also relevant. The European Employment Strategy is designed to be the main instrument for giving direction to and ensuring co-ordination of the employment policy priorities to which Member States are expected to subscribe. This co-ordination of national employment policies at EU level is built around several components:

- Employment Guidelines: following a proposal from the Commission, the European Council shall agree every year on a series of guidelines setting out common priorities for Member States employment policies.
- National Action Plans: every Member State shall draw up an annual National Action Plan describing how these Guidelines will be put into practise nationally.
- Joint Employment Report: the Commission and the Council shall jointly examine each National Action Plan and present a Joint Employment Report. This shall form the basis of subsequent provisions to the European Guidelines presented by the Commission.
- Recommendations: the Council may decide, by qualified majority, to issue country-specific Recommendations upon a proposal by the Commission.

The Employment Guidelines address flexibility and security. In the latest guidelines,[5] Guideline 3, *Address change and promote adaptability and mobility in the labour market*, is concerned with aspect of flexibility and security. The guideline requires Member States to facilitate the adaptability of workers and firms to change, taking account of the need for both flexibility and security and emphasising the key role of the social partners in this respect. Specific social security aspects are found in Guideline 8, *Make work pay through incentives to enhance work attractiveness.* Member States have to reform financial incentives with a view to making work attractive and encouraging men and women to seek, take up and remain in work. They have to review and, where appropriate, reform tax and benefit systems and how they interact with a view to eliminating unemployment, poverty and inactivity traps, and encouraging the participation of women, low-skilled workers, older workers, people with disabilities and those furthest from the labour market in employment. Finally, Member States have to review replacement rates and benefit duration, whilst preserving an adequate level of social protection.

6.3 GENERAL OVERVIEW OF THE TURKISH SOCIAL SECURITY SYSTEM

6.3.1 Basic Information

Turkey has state and occupational social security systems. There are two types of state social security systems: a contributory system providing social insurance benefits (contributory benefits, wage-related benefits) and a non-contributory system providing social assistance (means-tested benefits, safety-net benefits).

The contributory state social security schemes are regulated in separate laws as shown in Table 6.1.

5 Employment Guidelines 2005–2008 of 12 July 2005, Guideline 21.

Table 6.1 Overview of the Social Security System

Legislation	*Coverage*
Retirement Fund Act	civil servants
Social Insurances Act	workers
Tradesmen, Small Artisans and the Other Self-employed Social Insurances Act	self-employed
Social Insurances Act of the Self-employed in Agriculture	self-employed in agriculture
Agricultural Workers' Social Insurances Act	agricultural workers employed on a temporary basis in the private sector
Unemployment Insurance Act	workers upon loss of employment

The Turkish social security system is a complicated one and, as is the case in many other countries, subject to frequent changes. One of the reasons for the Turkish reforms is that the costs of the system are seen as being too high in relation to the State budget, thus destabilising the economy. With this in view the World Bank suggested some important changes.

The result was the recent introduction of draft laws establishing a new system. We are not in a position to consider the economic need and impact of these proposals and we will limit ourselves to commenting on their effect on the promotion of employment and flexibility. However, we suggest that it is important to introduce change at a measured pace in order to be able to monitor the effects and increase the chance of success of implementation.

Of all the OECD countries, Turkey has the highest rate of tax and contribution levels on wages. Due to the fact that tax and contribution rates are relatively high, many employers declare, in collaboration with their employees, the lowest possible monthly earnings and not the actual ones. Employers also register full-timers as part-timers with the SSK. Of course, this practice is illegal, but due to the inadequacies of the supervision system hard to prevent. As a result, differences often exist between actual and officially stated wages. This practice is beneficial for the insured, because traditionally there is a very low correlation between the level of retirement pensions and contributions. Therefore there is no incentive for workers to contest this practice. A combination of underdeclaration and the prevalence of informal sector employment has led to the SSK suffering financial deficits.

According to the 2004 Second Quarter Household Labour Survey Results, of the 22.2 million in employment, 5.7 million are registered with the SSK, 1.9 million with the Retirement Fund and 2.5 million with Bağ-Kur. In addition 11.9 million persons do undeclared work.

Definitions of undeclared work vary. The numbers we use are from the SIS (State Institute of Statistics). Undeclared work falls under the coverage of the Social Insurances Act and Acts covering the self-employed. However not all undeclared work is illegal work. According to SIS statistics, there were 10.7 million undeclared workers in 2003 (figures for fourth quarter unless stated otherwise). More than half of the undeclared workers were unpaid family workers, mainly in agriculture. 1.7 million undeclared persons were (paid) regular workers and 1,497,000 were (paid) casual (seasonal, temporary) workers involved in mainly illegal work. Undeclared work does not exist amongst those employees in the public sector covered by the Retirement Fund Act. Our figures also exclude those 179,000 persons who were employers.

In addition to seven million working people registered at the SSK in 2004, there are 26.8 million dependants and 4.1 million pensioners, meaning that a total of 37.8 million people are covered by the SSK. Of the total population, 12.1 million persons were outside social security coverage. It also appears that the proportion of actively to inactively insured persons is diminishing: in 2004, for each 1.69 actively insured, there was 1 inactively insured. This proportion was 24.30 in 1960 and has fallen steadily especially as a result of legislative amendments enacted in response to populist concerns. For more figures, see Tables 6.5 and 6.6.

During our interviews with the social partners and government bodies we were told that over time the Turkish social security system has been subjected to a great deal of political influence, resulting in more generous provisions for favoured groups.[6] The system is also criticised for being more generous than the country can afford,

6 For instance, in past general elections, the retirement age issue has been misused as a means of political propaganda and has therefore been subjected to frequent amendments causing great losses for the Social Insurances Institution. In 1950 the retirement age was 60 for both men and women. This was reduced to fifty-five for women in March 1965. The age limit was lifted in March 1969. Only the requirement of an insurance period of 25 years and 5,000 contribution-paid days remained. In May 1976, the insurance period was lowered to twenty years for women. In April 1985, 55 and 60 became the age limits for women and men respectively. Then in April 1992, the age requirements were lifted: women could retire following 20 and men 25 years of insurance with 5,000 contribution-paid days. It was possible for women to retire at the age of 33 and possible for men to retire at the age of 38 (13 being the minimum age for light work) until 1 April 1981 when the insurance period for disability, old-age and survivors benefits was said to become effective starting from 18 years of age. From 1 April 1981 onwards it was possible for women to retire at the age of 38, and men at the age of 43. This is regarded as one of the major causes of the financial collapse of the social insurance system in Turkey. For example, after 19.4 years of employment, a woman retiree is probably eligible to receive a pension for 35 years and a man for 28 years, some of the longest periods amongst OECD countries. Raising the age of eligibility for state pensions seemed to be the most sensible option. In 1999 there were great outcry within labour circles against the increase in retirement ages. 'Work till you drop' and 'retirement in the grave' were the most used slogans. Pensioner percentages are also quite high in Turkey. It is estimated that the percentage of 65+ers to that part of the population aged 0–64 will reach 7 per cent in 2012 and 14 per cent in 2039.

given the state of its economy. The large deficits of the social security systems have had a significant impact on the economy, causing inflation and instability.[7]

Another problem, closely related to the deficits, is the difficulties experienced by the competent body, the SSK, in collecting the contributions due from the insured and their employers. Employees have regularly been offered reduced interest or new payment plans to encourage the payment of contributions. This, plus the inflationary environment, has encouraged payments to be withheld until as late as possible.

During our discussions with the social partners and government officials it was freely admitted that the government has not always been very strict in enforcing the contribution and benefit rules. For this reason there are relatively few labour inspectors. This means that the problem of the informal market may be easier to tackle than sometimes thought. More supervision brings the danger, however, of higher unemployment levels and for this reason it is important to encourage work within the formal labour market.

6.3.2 The Draft Laws

In December 2004, draft laws on the Social Security Institution, Retirement Insurance, and General Health Insurance were finalised and sent to the social partners. This was followed by a fourth bill on Non-Contributory Benefits. Later, the draft laws on Retirement Insurance and General Health Insurance were combined under the title of Social Insurances and General Health Insurance.

- Under the Draft Act on the Social Security Institution, a new Social Security Institution is to be established as an umbrella institution replacing the current Social Security Institution. The General Directorates of Social Insurances, General Health Insurance and Non-contributory Benefits will be responsible for the supervision and implementation of the Social Insurances and General Health Insurance Act and Non-Contributory Benefits Act.
- The Draft Social Insurances and General Health Insurance Act provides protection against the risks of maternity, sickness, industrial accidents and occupational diseases, death, old age, and invalidity. Civil servants, workers, the self-employed, those self-employed in agriculture, and agricultural workers employed on a temporary basis in the private sector who have fallen within the scope of various pieces of legislation will all fall under the coverage of this Act once enacted. The provisions are more or less common across all categories of worker but with some exceptions. For example, Articles 12 and 13 of the draft Act envisaging joint liability for the hiring and user companies

7 See *Proposal for Reform in the Social Security System*, Ankara, 29 July 2004, p. 12.

as well as for main employers and subcontractors are to be applied only to employers employing workers.

– Non-contributory benefits that until now have been regulated in various laws will be covered by the new Non-contributory Benefits Act. The Act on Organisation and Powers of the Social Help and Solidarity General Directorate was the first step towards the systematic and integrated handling of non-contributory benefits.[8] The Draft Act on Non-contributory Benefits regulates family allowances, old-age benefits and disability benefits along with training and rehabilitation benefits for disabled children and general health insurance contribution payments for the needy by the State.[9]

One point of criticism we wish to raise is that under the new laws it is not clear how a particular law is funded and whether there are cross subsidies from contributory funds to non-contributory fund. It is recommended that such transparency be created.

At the time of writing this text – November 2005 – Parliamentary proceedings on these draft bills were suspended. The Parliament will start by discussing the Social Insurances and General Health Insurance Draft Act in February 2006. As these three bills are relevant to our discussion of flexible workers, their contents will be taken into account in what follows.

6.3.3 New Measures to Combat Undeclared Work

Unemployment, undeclared work, and social security benefit and contribution fraud feed on one another. Undeclared work has a significant impact on public finances, as demonstrated by the resulting tax and social contributions revenue losses. A vicious circle is the result: the government raises taxes and contribution rates on employment, thus creating greater incentive for undeclared work. There is a clear link between general policies aimed at combating unemployment and undeclared work, and removing disincentives in the tax and benefits system. To this end, the Social Security Institution published draft reform proposals for the social security system in July 2004. On 15 and 16 September 2004, the Work Assembly, a tripartite plus body, convened in Ankara and discussed the three items raised by these proposals: the creation of employment, courses of action and measures to eliminate undeclared work and establishment of a severance pay fund. In its Final Declaration, the importance of the long-term sustainability of social security systems and the creation of appropriate incentives in the tax and benefits system as part

8 Act 5263, *Official Gazette* 9 December 2004.

9 Art. 6.

of a comprehensive targeted strategy for reducing unemployment and combating undeclared work was emphasised.

A number of measures for combating undeclared work were identified. Employers have to notify the SSK of their place of work no later than the day they start employing an insured person. Where construction works are involved, the public body that has issued the construction permit has to inform the SSK of the contractor(s) and has to ask for a written clearance statement by the SSK before giving an occupancy permit. Where necessary, the SSK will also do surveys to determine the lowest number of workers to be employed on the construction site. In addition, the worker has to inform the SSK of his or her commencement of work for the purposes of cross-checking. Under the Draft Act on Social Insurances and General Health Insurance, the insured worker has to inform the SSK in writing and within thirty days of recruitment that he/she has started work.

6.4 COVERAGE BY THE SOCIAL INSURANCES ACT

In this section we will discuss the individuals and contingencies covered by the Social Insurances Act (hereinafter SIA)

6.4.1 Workers

All manual and non-manual workers (excluding agricultural workers employed on a temporary basis in the private sector) are covered by the SIA. This means that all industrial workers and agricultural workers employed in the public sector, be it on a permanent or temporary basis, and agricultural workers employed permanently in the private sector are covered by this compulsory social insurance scheme. A worker temporarily posted to a foreign country will continue to be covered by the national legislation.[10]

Workers are persons, nationals or non-nationals, employed under a contract of employment. Foreign insured persons and their dependants are protected under the same conditions as national workers.

Insurance is compulsory for workers employed in the public and private sectors. Workers employed by a single employer or a number of employers are considered insured.[11] Upon recruitment, the employee becomes insured automatically and a waiver or transfer of insurance rights is not permitted.[12] The Court of Cassation

10 SIA, art. 7.

11 SIA, art. 2.

12 SIA, art. 6.

interprets 'being recruited' as the day the worker actually starts working and not the day the labour contract is agreed. This is relevant if there is a difference between the two. If the worker is at the service of the employer but is given no work to do, the Court, in line with the Labour Act,[13] interprets being in service as commencement of work. Even if the SSK is not notified of the recruitment, the employed person becomes covered for insurance purposes in the interim period between recruitment and registration.[14] The SSK will pay any necessary benefits resulting from occupational accidents and industrial diseases, sickness or maternity in the interim period and claim the resulting expenses from the employer.

Homeworkers are also covered. Homeworkers are workers who undertake professional work alone or with help of their family members in their home or place of their choice in response to a request from a manufacturer or trader. Homeworkers may work for one or more employers (i.e. persons on whom they depend). This form of work is easy to hide and is (probably – there is a lack of data) to a great extent undeclared. Unlike German and Dutch law, a homeworker is not considered a 'quasi worker'. Turkish law[15] follows the Swiss system by considering a homeworker to be a worker. Homeworkers are therefore covered by the Labour Act. Homeworkers who are engaged in the production of handicrafts and are reliant solely on members of their own family up to kin of the third degree form an exception to this.[16]

Article 6 of the Draft Law on Social Insurances and General Health Insurance excludes a number of other groups.

– *Domestic workers*. Domestic workers employed on a temporary basis are not covered. Permanently employed domestic workers who make less than the monthly minimum wage (which can only be achieved by working less than 45 hours a week) are also not covered.[17] A domestic worker working for the weekly statutory hours has to be paid at least the statutory minimum wage to be compulsorily insured. The Draft Act on Social Insurances and General Health Insurance tries to clarify the categories of permanently employed domestic workers to be covered by the social security scheme. Permanently employed domestic workers not receiving the minimum wage from their employer due to working less than the normal weekly working time will fall outside the scope of the scheme. If they work for 45 hours per week for the same employer they have to be paid at least the minimum wage and hence will be compulsorily insured. There are many domestic workers

13 Labour Act, art. 66c.

14 SIA, art. 10.

15 Obligations Code, art. 322.

16 Labour Act, art. 4d

17 Art. 6c

in Turkey, mostly female. Some of them work on a daily basis, performing domestic work in different houses during the week. Some of them work on a monthly basis (i.e. in the same house or in different houses belonging to the same person/family). Some work two or three days a week for one person and on the remaining days for others. The draft Act would thus negatively affect part-time domestic workers: not only those working a few hours a week, but also those who only reach the minimum income by aggregation of jobs. Given the *Megner and Scheffel* judgment – see Section 6.2.1 – there may be objective grounds for justifying the exclusion of this group from coverage: for instance, the possible loss of jobs by these women. However, there must be sufficient reason to warrant their exclusion. Administrative burden is not sufficient reason and alternative systems – in particular for those concerning minimum income – have to be investigated, otherwise indirect discrimination is taking place.

- *Posted workers.* Workers posted to Turkey by a company abroad will be exempted if they officially declare that they will continue to be covered by a compulsory scheme in the country in which they normally work.[18] Apart from those falling under bilateral social security agreements providing for reciprocity, foreign teaching staff utilised by higher education institutions and foreign teachers utilised by public schools will benefit from short-term insurance during their stay in Turkey. Upon application, they may also benefit from the long-term insurance.[19]
- *Students of vocational training.* Students of vocational training are not covered if they perform work solely with the purpose of learning and practising.[20]
- *Rehabilitated persons.* Sick and disabled persons undergoing rehabilitation are not covered.[21]
- *Forestry and agricultural workers employed temporarily under a labour contract in the private sector* are not covered either.[22]
- *Workers employed on a one-day basis by different employers provided that the work can be accomplished in one day due to its nature* are not covered either.[23]
- *The spouse of the employer.* The if the spouse of an employer performs work without remuneration he/she is not covered.[24]

18 Art. 6/e corresponding to art. 3/I/G of the SIA.

19 Art. 5d.

20 Art. 6/f corresponding to SIA art. 3/I/H.

21 Art. 6/g corresponding to SIA art. 3/I/J.

22 Art. 6/I corresponding to SIA art. 3/I/A/b.

23 Art. 6/I – new.

24 Art. 6/a corresponding to SIA article 3/I/B.

6.4.2 Extension of Coverage to Persons with Work Relationships other than Labour Contracts

The coverage of the SIA has been extended over time. As a result there are groups of persons not employed under a labour contract, but still covered by the SIA. They include the following:

- *Apprentices*. The Vocational Training Act regulates apprenticeship, craftsmanship and master workmanship.
- *Part-time university students*. University students employed as part-timers are covered only for industrial accidents and occupational diseases under the SIA. Students of public universities are provided with health care by their universities.[25]
- *Artists, performers, authors employed by one or more employers,*[26] *and licensed prostitutes*.[27]
- *Persons performing domestic work on a permanent basis*.[28] Persons such as maids, servants, or cooks who do domestic work such as cleaning, cooking and ironing are not covered by the Labour Act,[29] but they are covered by the SIA if they are permanently employed.
- *Prisoners*. Where work is done by prison inmates, on a voluntary basis, under the general supervision of the public authority, and with protective guarantees, prisoners are covered.

6.4.3 Dependants

All insured contributors (breadwinners) and their dependants are covered by social security schemes.[30]

Dependants are:

- *Spouses*: a spouse who is not working or receiving benefits and therefore not covered by any social security scheme in Turkey or abroad is considered a dependant.

25 Paragraph added to Art. 46 of Act no. 2547 on Higher Education by Act no. 5234.

26 Additional art. 10.

27 Additional art. 13.

28 Art. 3/1d.

29 Art. 4e.

30 The spouse and children are standard beneficiaries whereas parents are beneficiaries under certain circumstances.

- *Children*: age limits apply for male children. A male child is considered a dependant until he reaches eighteen years of age. This age limit is increased to twenty if he is undertaking secondary education and to twenty-five if he is a student in tertiary education. If the male child is disabled to an extent which makes it impossible for him to work, there is no age limit. There is preferential treatment for female children: there is no age limit as long as the female child is unmarried, divorced[31] or widowed and not covered by any social security scheme. In October 1996 the Constitutional Court ruled that such preferential treatment for female children did not violate Article 10 of the Constitution on equality before the law. It is beyond the scope of this chapter to discuss this ruling in more detail, but it is clearly incompatible with EU law (in respect of the schemes covered by Directive 79/7, mentioned in Section 6.1.2). This rule may also discourage women from taking up paid employment. It is also an example of poor use of insurance.
- *Parents*. Parents who depend on the insured for their subsistence are dependants.

6.4.4 Voluntary Insurance

Under the SIA a formerly compulsorily insured person can apply for voluntary insurance for certain long-term insurance. A person who has paid contributions towards disability, old age and survivors' benefits for at least 1080 days but who is no longer an insured person may continue to be insured for these benefits by continuing to pay contributions.[32] In order to be eligible for voluntary insurance it is necessary to be a previously insured person. This requirement applies to both typical and atypical workers.

Under the SIA Long-term insurance is calculated and paid on the basis of a ranking related to the minimum and maximum amount of earnings subject to contributions (between the minimum wage and 6.5 times the minimum wage). Voluntarily insured workers can choose their ranking depending on the level of contributions they must pay and the benefits they wish to receive. As such, a voluntarily insured person is privileged compared to a compulsorily insured person, who can only ascend up the rankings after certain time periods. This is a point of criticism of the voluntary insurance scheme. The voluntarily insured person pays contributions each month, on a thirty-day basis. From 6 July 2004 the contribution rate is 25 per cent.

Under the Draft Law on Social Insurances and General Health Insurance, any person who has reached eighteen years of age may apply to the SIA for voluntary

31 In the event of divorce or if they become widowed they can return to their parents and can be co-insured again.

32 Art. 85.

insurance provided that he/she is not compulsorily insured or entitled to benefits.[33] The requirement for contribution-paid days as condition for benefit entitlement will be removed; hence the applicant need not be a formerly insured person. The applicant must apply to the Institution, choose one of the ranks between the minimum and maximum amount of earnings subjected to contributions and pay old-age, disability and survivors' contributions. The voluntarily insured has to determine the number of days to be covered per month, but this number can at most be thirty days, the number representing the calendar month. The applicant has to make payments on a monthly basis; contributions for a particular month have to be paid until the end of that month. If contributions are not paid then the days for which there has been no payment will not be considered.[34] Voluntary insurance will terminate upon commencing work and becoming compulsorily insured.

Part-timers form an exception to this rule[35] as they may be compulsorily insured, and for the remaining number of non-working days, voluntarily insured. Consequently, the bill assists atypical workers who have difficulty in fulfilling the contribution-paid days requirement under the present system.

The Government promotes the use of voluntary insurance as a way of improving the position of flexible workers. The social partners are divided on this: trade unions consider the voluntary insurance rates to be too high and so only encourage working within the informal market.

6.4.5 Contingencies Covered

The following risks are covered under the present law: maternity, sickness, industrial accidents and occupational diseases, death, old age, invalidity, and loss of employment as shown in Table 6.2. Under the present law there are no family allowances. The Draft Act on Non-contributory Benefits will change this. This act introduces family allowances for the following groups: needy families living on the streets with children exposed to beggary, prostitution, physical or sexual harassment and drug-addiction, and families permitted to foster such children.[36] The level of family allowances cannot exceed half the net minimum wage. If there are two children, half of the benefit paid for the first child will be paid for the second; there will be no additional payments to families with more than two children.[37]

---

33 Arts 69–74.

34 Art. 72.

35 Art. 73a.

36 Art. 6, 8a.

37 Art. 3d, 10.

Table 6.2 Contingencies covered and qualifying periods within the present law

Benefits	*Qualifying periods*
Sickness	Medical care: 90 premium-paid days (Art. 32/last par.) 120 premium-paid days (for dependants) (Art. 35/2) 300 premium-paid days (for treatment abroad) (Art. 32/E)
	Short-term incapacity benefits: 120 premium-paid days (Art. 37)
Maternity	Medical care: Insured woman: 90 premium-paid days (Art. 48/A) Wife of an insured man: 120 premium-paid days (Art. 48/B)
	Short-term incapacity benefits for an insured woman: 120 premium-paid days (Art. 49/1)
Disability / survivors	1800 premium-paid days (5 yrs) (Art. 54/b; 66/c), or 5-year insurance period, an average of 180 premium-paid days/yr (Art. 54/b; 66/c[38])
Old-age	Women: 58 / Men: 60[39] 7000 premium-paid days (19 yrs, 5 m, 10 days) (Art. 60/A/a) Or Women: 58 / Men: 60 25 years of insurance with 4500 premium-paid days (12 yrs, 6 m) (Art. 60/A/b)

38 Art. 66/c on qualifying periods for survivors benefits has been deleted by the Constitutional Court (*Official Gazette*, 18 October 2005). This annulment decision is to become effective a year after its publication in the *Official Gazette*. The decision will also have an effect on article 54/b envisaging the same qualifying periods for disability benefits.

39 An important area temporarily exempted from the scope of the equality principle in the relevant Community directives is the determination of pensionable ages. Member States are temporarily allowed to make a difference in pension age for men and women in statutory schemes. In non-statutory social security no difference in pension age is allowed, after the case law of the Court on article 141 EC. In order to abide by the requirement to remove the difference in pension age the Turkish Draft Social Insurances and General Health Insurance Act envisages equalisation of pensionable ages for men and women by 2075 (art. 38).

The Draft Social Insurances and General Health Insurance Act envisages new retirement ages to become effective starting from 2036 (art. 38):

Benefits	*Qualifying periods*
Unemployment	600 days during the 3-year period preceding contract termination and to have worked continuously during the last 120 days preceding termination by paying premiums[40] (Unemployment Insurance Act, Art. 51) Premiums for 600 days – benefits for 180 days (Art. 50) Premiums for 900 days – benefits for 240 days Premiums for 1080 days – benefits for 300 days
Voluntary insurance	1080 days (as from 24.4.2003) (1080/360=3yrs) (Art. 85) Contribution rate: 25% 122.175 YTL minimum contribution (16.29 YTL *30*25%)[41] 794.175 YTL maximum contribution (105.89*30*25%)

6.4.6 Insurance Period and Contributory Days

To understand the Turkish system it is important to understand the concepts of insurance period and contributory days. These are important concepts in the implementation of the SIA, since for several benefits, claimants have to satisfy a certain number of contributory days for entitlement to benefit. If they do not reach these thresholds, they are not entitled to any benefit.

Years	*Men*	*Women*
2036	61	59
2037–2039	62	60
2040–2041	63	61
2042–2043	64	62
2044–2045	65	63
2046–2047	65	64
2048–2054	65	65
2055–2064	66	66
2065–2074	67	67
2075	68	68

The Proposal for Reform in the Social Security System aims at an average of 19 and 16 years of retirement period for women and men consecutively.

40 There is a draft law simplifying conditions for entitlement and increasing the length and amount of unemployment benefits.

41 YTL = new Turkish Lira, which is about EUR 0.6 euro. YTL 122 is thus about EUR 73.

The insurance period starts at the time of recruitment. At the earliest, recruitment is possible upon reaching the minimum age at which a person can be employed. Until 1 April 1981, the insurance period for all insurance started at the age of thirteen, then the minimum age for light work. From 1 April 1981 the insurance period for disability, old age and survivors insurance starts upon reaching eighteen. Any period of employment preceding eighteen is not regarded as part of the insurance period for disability, old age and survivors insurance, but contributory days before this age are considered in calculating the number of contribution-paid days.[42] Individuals who become disabled or die before their nineteenth birthday have no right to benefit. If these risks materialise later, the resulting benefits are higher as a result of taking these periods pre eighteen into account. The insurance period ends on written application by the insured to be paid benefits or at the time of death. The insurance period therefore consists of an accumulation of employed and unemployed periods in between[43] and is not the same as an employment period.[44]

Table 6.2 shows a clear link between contribution days and benefit entitlement. To be eligible for old age insurance, for instance, a person must have worked 7000 days. As we will see below, this may cause problems for flexible workers. Under the draft laws it may be even more difficult for a flexible worker to be entitled to long-term benefits unless supported through other means such as voluntary insurance.

As indicated in Table 6.2, under the present system, there are two options available in order to be entitled to old-age benefits. In both options, the contingency covered is survival beyond the legally prescribed ages of 58 for women and 60 for men. A certain number of contributory periods are also required. Under the first option, at least 7000 contribution-paid days are required. The second option requires a 25-years insurance period and at least 4500 contribution-paid days. Both options are valid at the same time but there will be differences in the amount of old-age benefits due to the differences in the number of premium-paid days. The Draft Social Insurances and General Health Insurance Act prescribes the same age limits until 2036 but increases the minimum amount of contributory days to 9000 to discourage early retirement.

---

42 Art. 60/G.

43 Art. 108.

44 For example, A becomes insured on 1 February 1980 and works for three years under a contract of employment and his employment terminates on 1 March 1983. A does not work for about ten years and works again between 1 May 1993 and 1 May 2000. The insurance period is the total period between 1 February 1980 and 1 May 2000. Contribution-paid days are the number of days for which contributions have been paid while insured. The SIA requires certain periods of insurance and contributory days for entitlement to insurance benefits (Table 6.2).

6.4.7 Contributions

The employer calculates the contributions and deducts the worker's share from his/her wages. Wages consist of two parts: basic wages and wage supplements. Basic wages have to be paid in cash and cannot be less than the minimum wage. Wage supplements (fringe benefits) may be paid in cash or in kind. In the calculation of contributions some payments are disregarded.

The minimum and maximum amounts of earnings which are subject to contributions have been a topic of discussion and frequent amendments. Article 78 of the SIA as amended by Article 9 of Act no. 5198 envisages a new formula: as from 1 July 2004, the minimum daily earnings subject to contributions is the daily minimum wage determined for those above sixteen years of age (16.29 YTL).

The ceiling is 6.5 times the daily minimum wage (105.89 YTL per day). The draft bill maintains the same formula.[45]

Effective from 1 January 2005, the monthly gross minimum wage for workers above sixteen is 488.70 YTL (around 293 euro) with a net amount of 350.15 YTL (210 euros). The cost of the minimum wage to employers is 593.77 YTL (355 euros) per month.[46]

Social insurance schemes are to be funded through contributions by the insurer and the insured. Only unemployment insurance is funded by the State (Table 6.4 in the appendix). Where an employer employs flexible workers there will be no reductions in contributions and taxes. In this context, the labour costs will be more or less the same for all employers. Details of how flexible work affects labour costs will be discussed in the next section.

6.5 SOCIAL SECURITY RULES RELEVANT TO FLEXIBLE WORKERS

Until recently, labour law and social security law were designed with the full-time worker in mind, resulting in the exclusion of part-timers and temporary workers. The regulation of flexible work has lagged behind changing employment patterns. The growth of atypical types of employment, the increase in female labour and the potential impact of changing work types on employment policies necessitated legal regulations. To the extent that they take account of flexibility, the draft laws do prevent fraud and abuse, but they do little to improve the position of flexible workers.

The 2003 Labour Act regulates atypical types of work that were previously governed on the basis of the principle of *pro rata temporis* as a result of court

45 Art. 112.

46 The daily minimum wage is calculated by taking calendar days into account instead of working days (21 per month). The threshold is therefore lower than the actual minimum wage.

decisions. Some corresponding amendments have been made in the SIA to integrate atypical types of employment into the insurance scheme in order to facilitate alignment with the Labour Act.

The First Medium-term Program (2006–2008)[47] prepared under Act no. 5018 on Public Financial Administration and Control[48] envisaged the creation of 1.6 million jobs during the three-year period. If atypical work is targeted as one of the means of reducing unemployment in the country then it has to be promoted under the SIA. Otherwise atypical workers will prefer to remain undeclared.

6.5.1 Reference Periods

The previous Labour Act was inflexible in relation to working time, making it difficult for employers to adapt their establishments to changing demands. The 2003 Labour Act introduced flexitime.

The maximum number of weekly working hours is forty-five. This total is to be distributed over the workdays in such a way as not to exceed eleven hours a day. An equal distribution of 45 hours into six working days makes 7.5 hours of daily work. This is recognised as normal daily working time but employers and employees may agree on a different distribution of weekly working time: for example, nine hours of daily work on the basis of five working days. There is a reference period of two months that through collective labour agreements can be extended to at most four months. During a period of high demand, workers may work beyond forty-five hours a week provided that the maximum number of daily working hours (eleven hours) is not exceeded. If the average weekly working time throughout the reference period of two or four months is 45, then there is no question of overtime work and thus no overtime wages. Consequently, employers have flexibility in their deployment of staff and lower labour costs can be achieved by abolishing overtime. Reference periods are thus conducive to flexibility.

The SIA stipulates that each calendar month has thirty days, with a year equalling 360 days[49] and uses this assumption for the completion of contribution forms. Filling out the contribution forms for thirty days each month (it cannot be more than this) may cause problems for the newly introduced reference periods since if the total monthly hours of work are divided into days of 7.5 hours each the resulting number of worked days may be above thirty. So far, there have not been corresponding provisions in the SIA. If the working time is going to be averaged out over a longer

47 *Official Gazette* 31 May 2005, 2nd bis.

48 *Official Gazette* 24 December 2003.

49 The Draft Social Insurances and General Health Insurance Act maintains the same rules (article 3p, r).

term (whether it be over two or four months) at 45 hours per week this may not be so important and employers may proceed on a thirty-day basis.

6.5.2 On-Call Work

On-call work is based on the worker being asked to work when required. A potential job is promised to the worker. An analysis of the provisions on on-call work shows that on-call work is expensive for employers for two reasons:

1. If the duration of work is not specified in the contract, it is deemed to be twenty hours a week. Whether the 'twenty hours' constitutes at the same time the minimum number of weekly hours to be decided by the parties is currently subject to legal dispute. The Court of Cassation has not yet decided on this issue. It is generally expected that the court will interpret this provision as an absolutely binding one. If such a decision is made then even if the on-call worker is employed for a shorter period, he/she will be paid for 20 hours per week.
2. As reported by SSK officials, twenty hours will then serve as the minimum weekly hours worked by the call worker when calculating the contributions of the on-call worker. The gross daily minimum wage (16.25 YTL) is also the minimum daily amount of earnings subject to contributions. The hours worked monthly will be aggregated and divided into 7.5 hours (normal daily hours of work). For example, an on-call worker who works for 150 hours on a monthly basis will be considered to have worked for 20 days. If paid the minimum wage, that will equal the daily minimum wage multiplied by twenty which will also be the amount of earnings subject to contributions. The employer will be solely responsible for paying the due contributions in respect of any remaining period less than 7.5 hours. If that period is, say, four hours, that difference will have to be made up. If the worker has received less than the daily minimum wage the contributions have to be paid as if he were receiving the daily minimum wage. This is also true for a part-timer.

On the other hand, it will be very difficult for an on-call worker and a part-timer to qualify for pensions if he/she is not employed in various jobs. If we make a rough calculation for an on-call worker on the basis of twenty hours per week we can see that the conditions for qualification are not appropriate and discriminate against on-call workers (see Box 6.1).

This means that both the employer and the call worker may prefer to remain undeclared. The Draft Social Insurances and General Health Insurance Act maintains the same principles[50] but it also introduces voluntary insurance and indebtedness to overcome the threshold problem.

Box 6.1. Example of the effects of the thresholds on benefit entitlements

52 weeks x 20= 1040 hours per year
1040/7.5 = 138.7 days per year
To fulfil 4500 contribution-paid days: 4500/138.7 = 32.44 years
To fulfil 7000 contribution-paid days: 7000/138.7 = 50.47 years

6.5.3 Lump-Sum Payments

Lump-sum payments may be an insufficient remedy for an on-call worker or a part-timer who is not entitled to long-term benefits. An insured person who ceases to be liable for being insured without being entitled to a benefit arising from the contributions credited to his/her account is entitled to a lump-sum payment equal to the total amount of paid disability, old-age and survivors insurance contributions.[51] If the insured person is re-employed, the lump-sum payment does not have to be returned but if the insured wants to aggregate periods of employment, the lump sum must be paid back with accumulated interest. There are two types of lump-sum payments which may be made to the insured person from old-age insurance: old-age and marriage lump-sum payments.

An old-age lump-sum payment is made to an insured person who has left work without qualifying for disability or old-age benefits but who has:

1. Reached fifty-eight or sixty years of age for women and men respectively (fifty and fifty-five prior to 8 September 1999), or
2. Reached fifty years of age, meaning that he/she has not yet reached the retirement age but for medical reasons (as certified by a medical report) is treated as having reached retirement age.[52]

Only insured women can benefit from marriage lump-sum payments. To be entitled to a marriage lump-sum payment, an insured woman has to meet the following requirements:

50 Arts 56/b, 73/a, 110/7, 112.

51 Art. 64, additional art. 1

52 Social Insurances Health Issues Regulation art. 32.

1. Resignation from employment following marriage or marriage following resignation from employment
2. Resignation and marriage taking place within a period of one year

There are also survivors' lump-sum payments. Where the survivors have not been entitled to pensions upon the death of the insured, they shall be paid the total amount of disability, old age and survivors' contributions paid so far by the insured and the insurer.[53] The surviving spouse and any children are the main beneficiaries of this lump-sum payment. Where the amount to be paid to the surviving spouse and the children is less than the total amount of paid premiums, the remaining amount shall be paid in proportion to the surviving parents.

Lump-sum payments are paid without any increase to the original contributions. As such, they are not a sufficient alternative to insurance benefits. The Draft Social Insurances and General Health Insurance Act envisages an increase corresponding to the changes in the consumer price index, which will help maintain their value.[54]

6.5.4 Part-Time Work

A part-timer is a worker whose normal number of working hours, calculated on a weekly basis, is substantially lower than the normal number of working hours of a comparable full-timer.[55] In the explanatory memorandum to the article and the Working Time By-Law,[56] 'substantially less' is interpreted as 'less than two-thirds of the contracted weekly hours of work'. Therefore, a part-time job above a certain weekly limit is considered a full-time job. For example, if the statutory number of weekly working hours (forty-five) is at the same time the contracted weekly hours of work, work beyond thirty hours a week will be deemed full-time work and the contribution forms will be filled out accordingly.

Previously, where part-time work was performed, the SSK considered each worked day as a fully worked day for satisfying the conditions of long-term insurance schemes. The amount of time worked during a day was not relevant. The Court of Cassation found this unjust and ruled that the hours worked had to be aggregated and divided by 7.5 to find the number of worked days during a month.[57] The system was not only considered unfair to a comparable full-timer but also conducive to unequal treatment between part-timers. Part-timers working lesser periods of work

53 Art. 71.

54 Art. 42.

55 Labour Act, art. 13.

56 Art. 6.

57 Memduh Yelekci, *Sosyal Sigortalar Kanunu Serhi*, Ankara 1999, p.722.

than, for example, those working one full day a week and those working an hour six days a week are deemed to have worked a greater number of days.

In May 2004 a circular was issued by the Insurance Contributions Directorate of the SSK specifying the implementation of substantive and procedural issues in line with the amendments made in the SIA and the new Social Insurance Transactions By-law.[58] This circular uses the formula of the Court with regard to completing contribution forms, calculating the number of contributory days and calculating contributions. This makes it difficult for an atypical worker to qualify for benefits unless he/she works for more than one employer or opts to pay voluntary insurance on the basis of Article 85. Where the number of days specified is less than 30 per month, it is up to the employer to substantiate it with documents.[59] If a written contract is not submitted to the SSK or if submitted documents are not considered valid by the SSK, the contributions will be calculated *ipso facto* on the basis of thirty days. Verification is entirely up to the discretion of the SSK. Consequently, employers have to submit a written labour contract for part-time work. Under Article 20 of the Social Insurances Transactions By-Law, where employers of public enterprises and employers of enterprises with collective labour agreements inform the SSK in writing for the reasons for working periods of less than 30 days, substantiation for each individual worker is not required. The main concern of the SSK is preventing fraud: a full-timer must not be declared as a part-timer, leading to partially undeclared work.

Box 6.2. shows a example of how contributory days are calculated, based on the circular.

Box 6.2. Example of how contributory days are calculated

A teacher is employed in a private education institute to teach during two hours a day and is paid 10 YTL (about 6 euros) per hour. To determine contributory days the working hours have to be recalculated as monthly contributory days.

30 (days)[60] x 2 (hours) = 60 (hours)

60 (hours) / 7.5 (hours) = 8 days per month

To figure out the teacher's earnings to serve as a basis for the payment of contributions,

10 YTL x 60 (hours) = 600 YTL per month

58 *Official Gazette* 16 January 2004. The by-law became effective on 1 May 2004.

59 Art. 79.

60 Thus each calendar month is regarded as comprised of thirty days (which is to the advantage of workers, as this example demonstrates).

We also have to consider the minimum and maximum amounts of earnings which are subject to contributions. As stated above, starting from 1 July 2004, the minimum statutory amount of daily earnings subject to contributions is the basic daily wage determined for those over 16 years and the ceiling is 6.5 times the minimum daily wage. Consequently, the minimum monthly amount of earnings subjected to contributions is 488.70 YTL and the monthly maximum 2,886 YTL (2005).

A part-timer may be employed by various employers. In such a case, each employer will fill out separate contribution forms. The SSK will aggregate the contributory periods. Where the total amount of paid contributions exceeds the amount of contributions corresponding to the maximum amount, the worker's share from the exceeding part will be returned upon application to the SSK.[61] None of the employers will receive any refunds.

It can be concluded that the SIA rules are not aimed at encouraging part-time work. They are mainly aimed at part-timers working for more than one employer. As explained in Section 6.5.2, it is difficult for an on-call worker or a part-timer to gain entitlement to long-term benefits unless they work for various employers and benefit from voluntary insurance for the periods they are not compulsorily insured. The Draft Social Insurances and General Health Insurance Act has come up with two different options for such workers: voluntary insurance[62] and indebtedness.[63]

Under the current system, a person cannot be compulsorily and voluntarily insured at the same time (Section 6.4.4). The Draft Social Insurances and General Health Insurance Act makes it possible for a flexible worker to be voluntarily insured for the remaining periods (periods between worked days found by aggregating worked hours and dividing by 7.5 and 30 days) during the time that he is also compulsorily insured.

Indebtedness is possible for periods specified by the law and individuals can have these periods added to their actual services by paying contributions. A person may, for example, become indebted for periods spent as a law apprentice or a PhD student or as a graduate student abroad, time spent in a strike and lockout, or for military service. Likewise, a flexible worker may become indebted for unworked periods. To become indebted, a written application has to be made. The applicant will specify the rank between the minimum and maximum amount of earnings subjected to contributions and must pay the long-term contributions within six months following notification of the amount of the total debt. If the debt is not paid within the six-month period, no aggregation of periods will take place.

61 Art. 78/4.

62 Arts 69 and 73a.

63 Art. 56/1b.

6.5.5 Temporary Work

Under the revised Article 79, both the hiring and user companies are jointly liable for contributions due in respect of the temporary worker for the period that he/she is employed by the user company. The hiring company has to complete paperwork specifying the temporary work relationship. The user company also has to specify the temporary work relationship, but uses the establishment registration number assigned to the hiring company to complete the paperwork. The commercial books and documents of the hiring company and the user company that has undertaken payment of contributions for the temporary worker have to be consistent with each other. The Draft Social Insurances and General Health Insurance Act maintains the same rules.[64]

6.6 ANALYSIS

The rules described in the previous sections make part-time and on-call work expensive for the employer, and do not favour compliance with the *acquis*, which requires equal treatment of part-timers and full-timers. The present rules do not encourage the taking on of flexible work and are at odds with EU objectives which aim to encourage part-time work (done by women) and to reform social security in order to promote growth of employment. The discussions we had with the SSK made it clear that this organisation is mainly concerned about part-timers having more than one job and effectively working (almost) full-time and thus acquiring a disproportionate number of contribution days. However, the discussion on social security and part-time work should also be about those taking on small jobs, as this type of employment (which encourages women in particular to take up work) must encouraged.

Another problematic aspect of the system is that workers have to satisfy a certain number of contribution days before they are entitled to benefit. If they fail to reach the threshold, they are outside the protection of the law in question. The distinction between those in possession of a written contract (where the monthly number of working hours is divided by 7.5) and those without a contract (who acquire one contributory day for each day of work) is also problematical. Although *pro rata* rules apply for part-timers, if they work a relatively low number of hours limited to one or two days a week, they may still be unable to reach the threshold. Seasonal workers may experience similar problems.

A benefit system based on contributory days will always cause problems for marginal workers and may also have a discouraging effect on the taking on of work: it may not be rewarding to work more hours if the thresholds are still not within

64 Arts 12, 117/3 and 117/6.

reach. The threshold for old-age benefits is higher in the Draft Social Insurances and General Health Insurance Act but it also introduces voluntary insurance and indebtedness to overcome the threshold problem.

The present system is characterised by very low pension ages. While some variation in pension age is desirable (in particular, lower pension ages for dangerous jobs), there would seem no reason not to fix the pension age. This should not constitute a suggestion to do so: pension age is always dependant on factors such as political circumstances and life expectancy. However, the extremely long transition period before men and women may retire at the same age and the low pension ages during coming decades should be investigated to see whether they are consistent with equal treatment and employment policy rules (Section 6.2). For the time being 40 per cent of insured workers will pay contributions on the basis of the minimum wage (488.70 YTL gross, 350.15 YTL net). The minimum amount of old-age pension is 449.76 YTL (28.4 per cent more than the minimum wage) thus encouraging those on minimum wages to retire once the contributory days conditions are fulfilled. They may see no other reason for remaining in the system. The relationship between the number of contributory days and the pension level needs to be examined.

The German system, which does not work with contributory days, may be a suitable alternative. A value point is awarded for each year in which contributions are paid and the value of the point reflects the level of contribution. If a person pays, for instance, 2000 YTL, he/she receives 1 point. If he/she pays 1000 YTL he/she receives half a point. Credits are given in cases of pregnancy or raising young children. At the pension age a person may have, say, forty points. This would represent a full pension (forty times a particular fixed amount). If he/she has thirty points, it will be thirty times this amount. In this system there are no problems with inflation, as the basic amount is fixed every year.

There are several ways of reforming the Turkish system and the example of the German system is merely given to show an alternative. Whatever the system, a fixed pensionable age is to be recommended as a way of encouraging employment. It might be 65 for most jobs and a lower age for hazardous jobs. By relating the level of the pension with the number of contributory days, working beyond this age will lead to a higher pension. This would not disqualify flexible workers for not reaching a threshold.

During our discussions alternative proposals were made, including a lower threshold for part-timers than applies now. This would not, however, solve the main problems, as there will always be persons under that threshold. Moreover, this system would not encourage part-timers to work longer hours. We do not support this alternative.

In order to make the system work, it is very important to make it simple and to give it publicity, thereby encouraging workers to insist on the payment of contributions, as these will lead to a higher pension. This will lead to a smaller informal market and to less undeclared work.

Moreover, both the threshold and the reimbursement rules are not in line with the *acquis*, which requires sustainable and good pension systems (Section 6.2.1).

6.7 CONCLUSIONS AND RECOMMENDATIONS

The Turkish social security schemes covering workers are suffering from a financial deficit to such an extent as to threaten the national economy. Among the major causes are:

- Misappropriation of accumulated funds
- Increasing 'generosity' of the system for political gain
- Benefit and contribution fraud
- Undeclared work.

Starting in 1999, and especially in response to with the Urgent Action Plan of the 58th Government, significant amendments have been made to the SIA, as well as the enactment of new legislation with the objectives aimed at:

- Strengthening the institutional framework
- Contributing to transforming undeclared work into regular employment
- Including newly emerging work relationships
- Alignment with the relevant EC directives.

Focusing on the relationship between social security and flexible work, the following conclusions can be drawn:

1. The Turkish system has a broad concept of the term 'worker', one which covers both permanent and temporary workers. With the exception of workers such temporary domestic workers, any person employed under a labour contract, whether a typical worker or not, is covered by the SIA..
2. In so far as flexible workers are concerned, the recent plans for reforming the system are mainly focused on strengthening the maintenance of the rules and transforming undeclared work into regular employment. For this purpose legal gaps have been closed, making social security benefit and contribution fraud more difficult.
3. There is a regulatory gap in social security coverage, with exclusionary consequences due to underinsurance. The social security system must reflect and respond to the emergence of new work forms. The general practice of undeclared and under-declared work has implications for social security

and tax revenue, as well as for the social rights and working conditions of workers.

4. The new draft laws now also regulate those forms of work relationships which were newly regulated in the Labour Act of 2003. In particular, this means that these forms are now explicitly covered by the laws, but there is a need for special rules which take account of the particular position of these workers.
5. Part-timers and on-call workers are expensive for employers. The new Labour Act rules do not really encourage the taking on of flexible work and hence may not be fully implemented. This does not conform to EU objectives which aim to encourage part-time work (of women) and to reform social security in order to promote employment growth.
6. Another element of the system is that workers have to satisfy a certain number of contribution days before they are entitled to benefit. If they fail to reach the threshold, they are without the protection of the law in question. This encourages undeclared work. We also have to be aware of the risk of indirect discrimination arising from these rules as they mainly affect women. While such discrimination may justifiable, it should not justified in terms of system difficulties or for budgetary reasons. Valid justifications are likely to be few and far between. A fixed pension age and relating the level of the pension with the number of contributory days represents a useful alternative.
7. Another issue is that more than half of the undeclared workers are unpaid family workers (mainly in agriculture). These are most likely to be women. This issue needs special attention, as it may be an indication of indirect discrimination. In any case, the employment policy guidelines require special attention to be paid to the position of women on the labour market. Adjustment of the rules to make sure that family members are registered and good supervision systems to oversee such registration are therefore important. Another relevant point is that Directive 86/613 requires investigation into whether support can be given to young mothers (see Section 6.2.1).
8. In order to make the system work, it is very important to keep it simple and give it plenty of publicity so that workers will demand payment of their contributions, as these will lead to higher pensions. This should lead to a smaller informal market and to less undeclared work.
9. There is no 'one size fits all' solution. There is a need to adapt solutions to meet particular national circumstances. In the Turkish context, it is unrealistic to make any attempt to introduce flexibility without the cooperation of the unions. Meeting economic targets such as employment creation and efficient enterprise operation apply not just to the Government but to all stakeholders, implying that there is the need for consensus rather than conflict. Working relations based on participation and confidence rather than on opposition and conflict is the gaol.

APPENDIX

Table 6.3 Contributory State Social Security Schemes

Contributory state social security schemes	*Act no.*	*Adoption date*	*Coverage*
Retirement Fund Act	5434	8.6.1949	civil servants
Social Insurances Act	506	17.7.1964	workers
Tradesmen, Small Artisans and the Other Self-employed Social Insurances Act	1479	2.9.1971	self-employed
Social Insurances Act of the Self-employed in Agriculture	2926	17.10.1983	self-employed in agricul-ture
Agricultural Workers' Social Insurances Act	2925	17.10.1983	agricultural workers employed on a temporary basis in the private sector
Unemployment Insurance Act	4447	25.8.1999	workers on loss of employment

Table 6.4. Contribution rates

Contingency	*Contribution rate*	*Insured persons share*	*Insurers share*
Sickness	11%	5%	6%
Industrial accidents and occupational diseases	1.5% – 7%	–	1.5% – 7%
Maternity	1%	–	1%
Disability, old-age and death	20% (22% for miners [Art. 70] and those perform-ing heavy, arduous and toxic work [add. Art. 7])	9% (9%)	11% (13%)
Unemployment	4%	1%	2% | State: 1%
Total	36.5 – 42%	15%	21.5 – 27%

Table 6.5. The labour force of Turkey in July 2005[65]

	Total	*Urban*	*Rural*
Non-institutional Civilian Population (000)	71,645	44,350	27,295
Population 15 years old and over (000)	50,833	31,658	19,174
Labour force (000)	25,544	14,610	10,934
Employed (000)	23,227	12,812	10,415
Unemployed (000)	2,317	1,798	518
Labour force participation rate (%)	50.3	46.1	57.0
Employment rate (%)	45.7	40.5	54.3
Unemployment Rate (%)	9.1	12.3	4.7

Table 6.6. The distribution of persons covered by the SSK[66]

	2000	*2001*	*2002*	*2003*	*2004*	*2005 (Jul.)*
Total Insured	6,565,167	6,136,107	6,563,187	6,750,460	6,952,848	7,254,225
Compulsorily Insured	5,254,125	4,886,881	5,223,283	5,615,238	6,181,251	6,671,350
Apprentices	253,301	191,187	215,259	231,915	219,000	118,623
Voluntarily Insured	843,957	888,675	942,024	697,630	327,962	253,582
Collectively Insured	29,109	27,058	33,458	40,409	47,918	27,670
Insured in Agric. Sect.	184,675	142,306	149,163	165,268	176,717	183,000
Number of Pensioners	3,339,327	3,560,638	3,747,573	3,935,523	4,120,866	4,221,967
Dependants	22,541,181	1,592,466	2,993,730	4,610,697	6,771,763	8,536,105
Total Pop. covered by SSK	32,445,675	31,289,211	33,304,490	35,296,680	37,845,477	40,012,297

65 die.gov.tr. Starting with January 2005, Household Labour Force Survey results are published on a monthly basis and usually relate to three-month periods. The results are referred to by the name of the month which is the second of the three-month period for simplicity reasons. As such, the results of July 2005 indicate the results of the three months covering June, July and August 2005. A total of 31,105 sample households and 85,939 household members 15 years old and over, were interviewed during this term.

66 die.org.tr.

Table 6.7. Distribution of compulsory insured persons by gender and sector

Year	*Public*		*Private*		*Total*				
	Number of work places	*Number of compulsory insured persons*	*Number of work places*	*Number of compulsory insured persons*	*Number of work places*	*Number of compulsory insured persons*	*Female*	*Male*	*Total*
1998	25,024	660,791	756,887	4,169,265	781,911	4,830,056	475,965	4,354,091	4,830,056
1999	28,202	783,567	784,808	4,515,966	813,010	5,299,533	518,148	4,781,385	5,299,533
2000	20,263	756,929	749,411	4,248,474	769,674	5,005,403	965,231	4,040,172	5,005,403
2001	20,493	762,684	732,782	4,491,441	753,275	5,254,125	1,027,332	4,226,793	5,254,125
2002	20,928	751,958	702,575	4,134,923	723,503	4,886,881	972,744	3,914,137	4,886,881
2003	21,767	702,402	705,642	4,520,881	727,409	5,223,283	1,046,732	4,176,551	5,223,283
2004	23,848	686,157	753,329	4,929,081	777,177	5,615,238	1,166,739	4,448,499	5,615,238
2005	25,585	661,380	825,343	5,519,871	850,928	6,181,251	1,254,166	4,927,085	6,181,251

Table 6.8. Employment by status for social security registration

2004	*Quarter II*		*Quarter III*		*Quarter IV*	
	Total employm't	*Unregistered (%)*	*Total employm't*	*Unregistered (%)*	*Total employm't*	*Unregistered (%)*
Total	22 188	53.8	22 874	55.4	21,870	52.3
Regular employee	9 114	20.9	9 376	22.2	9 600	21.6
Casual employee	1 949	91.8	1 968	91.5	1 815	92.6
Employer	1 000	25.5	1 080	25.0	1 081	24.1
Self employed	5 476	64.0	5 425	67.6	5 275	65.7
Unpaid family worker	4 648	96.5	5 026	96.7	4 098	96.5
Agriculture	7 820	89.4	8 222	91.3	7 200	89.8
Regular employee	97	45.2	115	57.6	104	51.3
Casual employee	415	98.9	456	98.5	461	98.1
Employer	120	80.6	120	86.1	94	70.4
Self employed	3 102	78.1	3 080	81.9	2 967	80.2
Unpaid family worker	4 084	98.4	4 450	98.1	3 574	98.4
Non-agricultural activities	14 367	34.4	14 652	35.3	14 669	33.9
Regular employee	9 016	20.7	9 260	21.7	9 497	21.3
Casual employee	1 534	89.9	1 512	89.3	1 354	90.7
Employer	880	17.9	960	17.4	986	19.7
Self employed	2 374	45.5	2 345	48.8	2 308	47.0
Unpaid family worker	563	83.2	576	85.3	524	83.3

7. IN SEARCH OF A BALANCE: FLEXIBILITY AND SECURITY STRATEGIES IN EMPLOYMENT PROTECTION LEGISLATION, TEMPORARY WORK AND PART-TIME WORK

Martijn van Velzen and Ton Wilthagen[1]

7.1 INTRODUCTION

7.1.1 The Concept of Flexicurity

Two main issues dominate the current European debate on labour market and employment policies: increasing labour market flexibility and adaptability and providing security for workers affected by flexibility.[2] This demand for further flexibilisation of labour markets, employment and the work organisation, set against an equally strong demand for providing security to employees, especially to vulnerable groups of employees and outsiders in the labour market, may seem like a 'double bind', imposing conflicting requirements on labour market actors. This 'double bind' can be referred to as the 'flexibility-security nexus'.[3] Policy strategies that deliberately seek to strike a balance between flexibility and security are labelled 'flexicurity' strategies.[4] In other words: flexicurity strategies are trade-offs between degrees and modes of flexibility and security. The main message of the flexicurity concept is that in modern labour markets flexibility should also be defined in terms of security while security should also be defined in terms of flexibility. Put differently, flexibility and security are not incompatible but should rather be seen

1 The authors are grateful to Nurhan Süral for comments on an earlier version of this chapter.

2 High Level Group, *Facing the Challenge: the Lisbon Strategy for Growth and Employment*. Office for Official Publications of the European Communities, Luxembourg, 2004.

3 T. Wilthagen, 'The Flexibility-Security Nexus: New Approaches to Regulating Employment and Labour Markets', *British Journal of Industrial Relations Conference, the Politics of Employment Relations*, Windsor, 2002.

4 T. Wilthagen and F. Tros, 'The Concept of 'Flexicurity: a New Approach to Regulating Employment and Labour Markets', *Transfer* 10(2) (2004), pp. 166–186.

Pennings, *Flexibilisation and Modernisation of the Turkish Labour Market*, 153–182

as two sides of the same coin and as mutual preconditions. The implication that follows from this point of view is that flexible labour markets need *more* rather than less security, albeit different types of security, and that secure labour markets cannot be achieved without a degree of flexibility.

The aim of this chapter is to show how different modes, combinations and equilibriums of flexibility and security exist in different national employment systems. By analysing these modes we hope to find some indications of what factors contribute to good practices in enhancing both flexibility and security. We analyse three modalities of employment flexibility and security: dismissal policy, part-time work and temporary agency work. For each modality we compare two contrasting national examples: the United States and Denmark, Spain and the Netherlands, and the United States and the Netherlands respectively.

The reasons for choosing these three distinct areas of policy making/legislation relate to the fact that they represent important forms of numerical flexibilisation, that is, forms that provide for a timely adjustment of either the number of workers (dismissal policy, temporary agency work) or the labour hours of thse workers already employed (part-time work). Many European organisations (European Commission, OECD, European Central Bank) advocate numerical flexibilisation as a key strategy in reforming the labour market.

7.1.2 The Introduction of Flexibility in Turkey

In Turkey, recent legislative measures to enhance labour market flexibility have focused on the three domains of employment protection, temporary work and part-time work. The 2003 Labour Act provides for forms of flexible employment including temporary work, part-time work and on-call work. Traditionally, flexibility is a characteristic of the informal segments of the labour market. However, informal employment, with its flexible nature, has not been limited to grey and black economy firms. State-owned enterprises, much of the formal sector and foreign firms have benefited from flexibility through the use of subcontractors.

Under the Labour Act, the employment protection provisions ('regular' job security) of the previous Code have been maintained for firms employing fewer than thirty workers. There is increased employment protection for workers of establishments employing thirty or more workers.[5] Consequently, there are two sets of rules when a contract is terminated after a term of notice: one for workers with regular job security and one for those with enhanced job security.[6] The Labour

5 The number of firms employing fewer than thirty employees is 747,975. Over 2.6 million workers have regular employment protection. Almost three million workers in 29,202 firms employing thirty workers or more have increased employment protection (data from www.ssk.gov.tr).

6 Labour Act, arts 17 to 21.

Act provides enhanced job security for workers employed under open-ended labour contracts who have been working for a period of at least six months in an establishment where at least thirty workers are employed.[7] Employers' representatives responsible for administration and with the authority to recruit and dismiss workers cannot benefit from increased job security provisions.

The 2003 Labour Act restricts the use of fixed-term contracts. An objective reason for making such a contract is required at the time of its first conclusion and a substantial cause is required for its renewal (for the exact rules, see Chapter 5). This Act tries to prevent abuse arising from the use of successive fixed-term employment contracts, the so-called 'chain contracts', by stating that unless there is a substantial cause justifying the renewal, fixed-term employment contracts cannot be renewed. If renewed, the fixed-term employment contract must be reclassified as an indefinite contract.[8] Prior to the introduction of the new Act, flexible modes of employment including part-time work were governed by individual or collective labour contracts and judicial precedents. The governance of such flexible arrangements is now part of the 2003 Labour Act.

Moreover, private employment agencies have been introduced. These for-profit agencies, previously banned, are tasked with improving the allocation of labour by matching vacancies and jobseekers. The fact that these bureaus are profit-driven has raised expectations that they will be more efficient than the public employment service, İş-Kur, in job matching. However, the bureaus are not allowed to establish pools of flexible workers who can be sent to different employers. Current legislation does not allow for the existence of a triangular relationship between private employment bureau, employee and company.

The private employment bureaus (seventy-five in September 2005) thus have a much more limited function than agencies such as Adecco and Manpower in North America and many Western European countries. Enabling private agencies in the Turkish labour market to function as brokers between employers and employees may be a first step in the development of flexible staffing arrangements, as witnessed often in Western countries. Agencies specialising in job-vacancy matching have, over time, become external human resources departments of user-firms, providing recruiting, screening, selection, training and pay-rolling services to these firms. Initially, Articles 8 and 93 of the draft Labour Act had provided for 'agency work', on the basis of contracts between firms and temporary work agencies. Under Article 7 of the 2003 Labour Act, an employer may hire out a worker to another establishment within the group or conglomeration of identical companies, for, at most, six months. Where such hiring out occurs, the worker has to be utilised in a similar job and the arrangement can only be renewed twice, to a maximum of eighteen months.

7 Labour Act, arts 18.

8 Labour Act, art. 11, Sections 2 and 3.

The 2003 Labour Act was described by employers' and employees' organisations as a 'fair' balancing of flexibility and protection objectives, and it was welcomed by formal sector employers as an improvement.[9] However, Türk-Iş and DISK were opposed to the flexibility sections of the Labour Act. In the view of the unions, the informal sector, estimated at roughly forty percent of total employment in Turkey and fifty percent of its GDP, already provides flexibility without any restrictions.

Prior to the introduction of the new Labour Act, Turkey was ranked the second most rigid labour regulatory regime in the OECD index on employment protection legislation. A recalculation of the OECD index showed that the new law would lower the employment protection legislation index for Turkey, ranking the country as the tenth most flexible labour market among the thirty OECD Member States.

7.1.3 A Study of Flexicurity in Selected Countries

The reason for choosing and comparing our particular sets of countries is, as indicated, to present contrasting cases as summarised in Table 7.1 below. We intend to show that high levels of numerical flexibilisation can co-exist with either (relatively) high or low levels of security. The lesson to be learnt is that – as the saying goes – all roads lead to Rome and a combination of flexibility and security is not necessarily impossible. Consequently, it is important that Turkey, along with other countries, reflect on the flexibility-security nexus. The following matrix displays the structure of our comparative exercise.

Table 7.1 Contrasting Accounts of Flexibility and Security

Modalities creating high flexibility levels	*High security level*	*Low security level*
Loose employment protection legislation	Denmark	United States
Growing use of temporary agency workers	Netherlands	United States
Part-Time work	Netherlands	Spain

9 OECD, *Economic Surveys: Turkey*, Paris, 2004.

7.2 FLEXIBILITY, SECURITY AND THE EUROPEAN EMPLOYMENT DEBATE

The pursuit of a new balance between 'flexibility' and 'security' is especially manifest within the European Employment Strategy. The 2001 European Employment Guideline 13, under the Adaptability pillar, explicitly addressed both flexibilisation and security goals, as it invited the social partners: 'to negotiate and implement at all appropriate levels agreements to modernise the organisation of work, including flexible working arrangements, with the aim of making undertakings productive and competitive, achieving the required balance between flexibility and security, and increasing the quality of jobs'.

In the Council Decision on the revision of the Employment Guidelines[10] it is stated that 'providing the right balance between flexibility and security will help support the competitiveness of firms, increase quality and productivity at work and facilitate the adaptation of firms and workers to economic change'.

The 2003 European Employment Guidelines contain three overarching objectives, including 'improving quality and productivity of work', which encompasses 'flexibility and security'.[11] Moreover, Guideline 3 (Address change and promote adaptability and mobility in the labour market) stresses that 'Member States will facilitate the adaptability of workers and firms to change, taking account of the need for both flexibility and security and emphasising the key role of the social partners in this respect'.

The views of the European Commission on actually striking a good balance between flexibility and security are fairly optimistic. In the European Commission's overview of industrial relations in Europe for the year 2000, it is contended that 'all Member States have tried to improve flexibility in the labour market by launching active employment and vocational training policies. Modernising the way in which the labour market operates means finding a new balance between flexibility and security. This is reflected at Community level in the framework agreement on part-time work, concluded by the social partners'.[12] However, some studies are fairly pessimistic regarding the new trade-offs adopted. As Ozaki claims on the basis of a comprehensive comparative study: 'the flexibilisation of the labour market has led to a significant erosion of workers' rights in fundamentally important areas which concern their employment and income security and the (relative) stability

10 Council Decision of 22 July 2003 (2003/578/EC).

11 In March 2005, the Heads of State and Government of the EU endorsed the revision of the Lisbon Strategy as proposed by the Commission. The Spring European Council approved the simplified governance arrangement with one set of 'Integrated Guidelines for Growth and Jobs (2005–2008)' dealing with macro-economic, micro-economic and employment issues (COM [2005] 141 final).

12 European Commission, 2000, p. 83.

of their working and living conditions.[13] Regarding the trade-offs arising from flexibility bargaining, there has not been an attempt to drastically change the present paradigms of economic and social policy'. While Streeck posits that where flexibility is gained, rigidities need to be created,[14] Blank and Freeman conclude that 'there is little empirical evidence for large trade-offs between labour market flexibility and social protection programs in general'.[15]

In order to create support for flexibility, workers need security, as also stated in the 2003 report of the European Employment Taskforce. In the view of the Taskforce, security is about building and preserving people's ability to remain and move up in the labour market. It is thus not limited to job security. It is also related to decent pay, access to lifelong learning, working conditions, protection against discrimination or unfair dismissal, support in the case of job loss and the right to transfer acquired social rights when moving jobs. A similar set of suggestions can be found in the OECD's *Employment Outlook 2004*, urging governments to combine job strategies with other social objectives, including an individual's need for job security and work-life balance.

7.3 MODALITIES FOR EMPLOYMENT FLEXIBILITY AND SECURITY

7.3.1 Levels of Employment Protection

7.3.1.1 The United States

The US labour market is characterised by a high degree of flexibility, predominantly in terms of loose dismissal protection. This is best exemplified by the employment-at-will doctrine. This rule essentially gives an employer a right to hire and fire employees at his discretion, and a worker a right to resign at any given moment, in the absence of any expressed contractual provision to the contrary.[16] As long as

13 M. Ozaki (ed.), *Negotiating Flexibility: the Role of Social Partners and the State*, ILB, Geneva, 1999, p. 116.

14 W. Streeck, 'Comment on "Rigidities in the Labour Market"', *Government and Opposition*, 23(4) (1988), pp. 413–423.

15 R.M. Blank and R.B. Freeman, 'Evaluating the Connection between Social Protection and Economic Flexibility', in R.M. Blank (ed.), *Social Protection versus Economic Flexibility: Is There a Trade-off?*, University of Chicago Press, Chicago and London, 1994, p. 36.

16 As expressed by the Tennessee Supreme Court in *Payne* v. *Western & Atlantic Railroad* (1884): 'Men must be left without interference to buy and sell where they please and to discharge or retain employees at will for good cause or for no cause, or even for bad cause, without thereby being guilty of an unlawful act per se. It is a right which an employee may exercise in the same way, to the same extent, for the same cause or want of cause, as the employer'.

employment duration has not been specified in the employment contract, a contract is considered to be at-will. Employees in the public sector and unionised workers are to a lesser extent affected by the at-will doctrine. The Civil Service Reform Act of 1978 protects federal civil service employees from wrongful dismissal, and many State employees are covered by similar civil service and constitutional protection.[17] Workers represented by a union negotiate job security in their collective agreement along with avenues for grievance procedures in the event of dismissal.[18] Typically, legislation regarding at-will employment is drafted at the state level.[19] Given the fact that most employment relationships in the United States are at will there is reason to expect workers to be relatively insecure about their employment relationship. In 1995, almost one in every two US workers reported frequently worrying about lay-offs, compared to twenty-two percent in 1988. Over the same period, the percentage of workers that was confident that they could keep their job if they performed well dropped from seventy-three percent to fifty percent.[20] In addition to declining workers' perception of job security, the idea has taken root among certain US scholars and policy advisors that employment relations have become increasingly flexible, with job insecurity on the rise.[21] Farber shows that the incidence of long-term jobs (ones that last ten years or more) has declined among male workers, especially those with less than twelve years of education.[22] This is part of a more general development of worsening labour market opportunities for the low skilled. Overall job security, however, has remained the same, showing

---

17 S. Jacoby, 'The Duration of Indefinite Employment Contracts in the United States and England: a Historical Analysis', *Comparative Labor Law* 5(1) (1982), pp. 85–128.

18 R.N. Block, 'The Legal and Institutional Framework for Employment Security in the United States: an Overview', in K. Koshiro (ed.), *Employment Security and Labor Market Flexibility: An International Perspective*, Wayne State University Press, Detroit, 1992, pp. 127–149.

19 See, for instance, California Labour Code, Section 2922: 'An employment, having no specified term, may be terminated at the will of either party on notice to the other. Employment for a specified term means an employment for a period greater than one month'.

20 D. I. Levine, *Working in the Twenty-First Century: Policies for Economic Growth through Training, Opportunity, and Education*, M.E. Sharpe, Armonk, NY, 1998.

21 See, for instance, K. Barker, and K. Christensen (eds), *Contingent work: American Employment Relations in Transition*, Ithaca, Cornell University Press, New York, 1998; C. Benner, *Work in the New Economy: Flexible Labor Markets in Silicon Valley*, Blackwell Publishers Ltd, Oxford, 2002; W. Bridges, *Job Shift: How to Prosper in a Workplace without Jobs*, Addison-Wesley Publishing Company, Reading, Mass. etc, 1994; Commission on the Future of Worker-Management Relations (Dunlop Commission), *Fact Finding Report*, Department of Labor and Department of Commerce, Washington, D.C., 1994; J. Rifkin, *The End of Work: The Decline of the Global Labor Force and the Dawn of the Post-Market Era*, G.P. Putnam's Sons, New York, 1996.

22 H.S. Farber, 'Are Lifetime Jobs Disappearing? Job Duration in the United States: 1973–1993'. Working paper no. 5014, National Bureau of Economic Research, Cambridge, Mass., 1995; H.S. Farber, 'Trends in Long Term Employment in the United States', 1979-96, Working paper no. 384, Princeton University, Princeton, N.J., 1997.

no evidence that long-term employment relationships are disappearing.[23] Freeman and Rogers find that job tenure averages fifteen years, adding that US workers are more mobile than workers in most advanced countries.[24] This is not a feature of the overall labour force, but is primarily caused by frequent job shifting by new entrants in the labour market, as they search for the right match.

In the past two decades, state courts have carved away at the at-will doctrine, weakening the employer's right to dismiss at-will employees. Three categories of exceptions to the doctrine can be identified. Action for wrongful discharge can be granted to a worker if 1) the discharge violated public policy, or 2) breached an implied contract of employment arising from a handbook, a policy or some other representation, or 3) breached an implied covenant of good faith and fair dealing[25] As of October 2001, 43 states had recognised the public-policy exception, 38 states the implied-contract exception and 11 states the covenant of good faith and fair dealing.[26]

7.3.1.2 Denmark

The Danish labour market is characterised by, among other things, high worker mobility, providing employers with the potential for external numerical flexibility. This mobility is probably best reflected in low average job tenure, in which Denmark strongly resembles the United States (and the United Kingdom, for that matter). The high level of worker mobility may be explained by the 'liberal' regime of employment protection. The overall strictness of Danish employment protection legislation was ranked the fifth lowest in a 1999 OECD study. In this ranking, only the Anglo-Saxon nation states of Canada, Ireland, the UK and the US trailed behind the country. Contrary to the situation described above in the United States, high worker mobility combined with low levels of employment protection do not cause high levels of insecurity among Danish workers. Madsen gives three explanations

23 D. Neumark, 'Changes in Job Stability and Job Security: a Collective Effort to Untangle, Reconcile and Interpret the Evidence', Working paper 7472, National Bureau of Economic Research, Cambridge, Mass. 2000.

24 R.B. Freeman, and J. Rogers, *What Workers Want*, Cornell University Press, Ithaca, NY, 1999; L. Golden and E. Appelbaum., 'What Was Driving the 1982–88 Boom in Temporary Employment?', *American Journal of Economics and Sociology* 51(4) (1992), pp. 473–493.

25 Within the states that have adopted these exceptions California has been the most active in applying them. See W.B. Gould, *A Primer on American Labor Law*, MIT Press, Cambridge, Mass./London, 1993; A.B. Krueger, 'The Evolution of Unjust-Dismissal Legislation in the United States', *Industrial and Labor Relations Review* 44(4) (1991), pp. 644–666.

26 Alaska, California, Idaho, Nevada, Utah, and Wyoming recognised all three exceptions. See C.J. Muhl, 'The Employment-at-Will Doctrine: Three Major Exceptions', *Monthly Labor Review* 124(1), (2001), pp. 3–11.

for the relative security that Danish workers experience.[27] Firstly, the predominance of small and medium-sized firms in Denmark implies that strong internal labour markets are less important than in other countries, where large firms – with extensive internal labour markets – may be more prominent. Given the limited employment protection in place, hiring and entry barriers are relatively modest, which makes it easier for workers to move from one firm to another. A second factor that may play a role is the overall improvement in the Danish labour market since the mid-1990s, causing workers to feel more comfortable with the possibility or need for a job change. The third, and according to Madsen the most credible, explanation lies in the social security system: the generous income replacement schemes for unemployed workers may be the prime cause for the low levels of insecurity experienced among Danish workers. The employment protection regime, facilitating easy hiring and firing of Danish workers by employers, and the generous state-financed unemployment benefit system are both supported by trade unions and employers' associations alike. While the substantial replacement rates may initially cause the social security system to function as a hammock instead of a safety net, the broad array of active labour market measures makes the system look more like a springboard. Job training and other measures are targeted at the unemployed in order to prepare them for a transition back into the labour market, making them, with newly acquired skills, attractive to hire for employers. This activation system has been reformed into an effective tool that has helped reintegrate unemployed jobseekers in the 1990s. This reform has been the outcome of a negotiated compromise between the government and social partners. Clearly, corporatism has played a key role in striking a balance between flexibility and security in Denmark. Recent proof of this comes from the united response of employers' associations and unions to the government attempt to cut expenditure on unemployment benefits.[28]

While the Danish case is not an entirely positive story (a substantial number of people, e.g. ethnic minorities, are excluded from the labour market) the performance of the Danish labour market during the second half of the 1990s has been impressive. Rather than seeing 'flexicurity' as the main driver for these performances – other, macro-economic, factors are also at play – it is important to note that 'flexicurity' is an important result of the joint efforts of social partners over the course of many decades.

27 P.K. Madsen, 'The Danish Model of "Flexicurity": Experiences and Lessons', *Transfer* 10(2), 2004, pp. 187–207.

28 Ibid.

7.4 TEMPORARY AGENCY WORK

7.4.1 The United States

The use of temporary agency workers in the US has boomed, particularly during the 1980s, as firms undertook large-scale downsizing. Firms continued their flexible staffing strategies throughout the 1990s, even when the labour market became tighter and most flexible workers preferred a permanent job instead of a temporary one. Katz and Krueger conclude that the growth of the temporary staffing industry has possibly led to improved efficiency of job matching and may therefore at least partially account for the decline in unemployment and wage pressure in the 1990s.[29] The growing interest of firms in temporary agency workers even under tight labour market conditions has been traced back to an erosion of the at-will doctrine.[30]

The erosion of the employment at-will doctrine in the past two decades is exemplified by two court cases in the 1980s which held that 1) an employer's indirect statements about the manner in which termination decisions are made can imply legally binding employment contracts and 2) workers are entitled to ongoing employment even in the absence of written statements if contractual rights are implied via the context of the employment relationship (e.g. through longevity of service, a history of promotion or salary increases). This 'implied contract exception' has led employers to circumvent the suggestion of an employment contract, most importantly by using temporary agency workers. [31]

In addition to intensified regulation of the labour market, firms use temporary agency workers to avoid the costs of permanent workers, particularly the costs associated with benefits such as health care, family leave and retirement benefits. Other employer costs evolve from litigation (when a lay-off case is brought to court), retraining workers who would otherwise be laid off, and extra screening and

---

29 L.F. Katz, and A.B. Krueger, 'The High-Pressure US Labor Market of the 1990s'. Working paper no. 416, Princeton University, Industrial Relations Section, Princeton, N.J., 1999.

30 K.G. Abraham, 'Introduction', in K.G. Abraham and R.B. McKersie (eds), *New Developments in the Labor Market: Toward a New Institutional Paradigm*, MIT Press, Cambridge, Mass./London, p. 1–17, 1999; L. Golden and E. Appelbaum, 'What Was Driving the 1982–88 Boom in Temporary Employment?', *American Journal of Economics and Sociology*, 51(4) (1992), pp. 473–493; A. Kalleberg, *Non-standard Work, Substandard Jobs: Flexible Arrangements in the U.S.* Economic Policy Institute, Washington D.C., 1997; B. Lips, 'Temps and the Labor Market: Why Unions Fear Staffing Companies', *Regulation Spring* (1998), pp. 31–39; D.H. Autor, 'Outsourcing at Will: Unjust Dismissal Doctrine and the Growth of Temporary Help Employment', Working paper no. 7557, National Bureau of Economic Research, Cambridge, Mass., 2000.

31 D.H. Autor, 'Outsourcing at Will: Unjust Dismissal Doctrine and the Growth of Temporary Help Employment', Working paper no. 7557, National Bureau of Economic Research, Cambridge, Mass., 2000

background checks.[32] Another factor explaining the growth in temporary agency work may come from the substitution of temporary hires by agency workers for cost reasons including the selecting, screening, testing and training that temporary work agencies may undertake.[33] Search costs may be particularly high when the labour market tightens and firms therefore look towards temporary work agencies.[34] Some empirical support for this possible change in the hiring behaviour of firms is provided by Estevão and Lach.[35] According to the American Staffing Association, an important reason for firms to rely on temporary agency workers is the lost confidence of employers in the ability of the American education system to prepare young people for the workplace. Many firms rely on the recruiting and screening function of temporary work agencies in order to attract new personnel. Furthermore, temporary work agencies enable firms to observe a worker for a trial period before deciding to permanently hire the worker.[36]

7.4.2 The Netherlands

In the early 1990s a recession hit the economy of the Netherlands, albeit to a lesser extent than in the 1970s and 1980s. Downsizing operations in 1992 and 1993 spurred a need among firms for a more flexible organisation of work. In a Labour Foundation recommendation, *A New Course* (1993) concerning the collective bargaining agenda, the social partners jointly signalled a need for flexible employment patterns. With this recommendation social partners paved the way for future trade-offs between worker flexibility and reduced working hours. While central unions were convinced of the need for employment flexibility, individual union members were divided. The majority of union members regarded the eventual growth in the use of temporary agency workers with suspicion. In particular, union organisers and older male workers were concerned about the increase of temporary (agency) contracts, as they saw this development as threatening permanent jobs. Interestingly, while thirty-eight percent of union members thought that unions should actively oppose the growth of temporary work, forty percent wanted unions to negotiate

32 D.R. Lee, 'Why Is Flexible Employment Increasing?', *Journal of Labor Research*, 17(4), (1996), pp. 543–553.

33 A.E. Polivka, 'Are Temporary Help Agency Workers Substitutes for Direct Hire Temps? Searching for an Alternative Explanation of Growth in the Temporary Help Industry', Paper presented at the Society of Labor Economists Conference, Chicago, 3–4 May, 1996.

34 S.N. Houseman, A.L. Kalleberg, and G.A. Erickcek, 'The Role of Temporary Help Employment in Tight Labor Markets', Working paper no. 01-73, Kalamazoo, Mich., 2001.

35 M.M. Estevão and S. Lach, *The Evolution of the Demand for Temporary Help Supply Employment in the United States*, NBER, New York, 1999.

36 E.A. Lenz, *The Staffing Services Industry: Myth and Reality*, American Staffing Association, Alexandria, Virg., 2002.

this phenomenon at the bargaining table.[37] The latter reflects the general inclination of Dutch workers, and employers alike to reach consensus over delicate issues, in line with the *Polder model* tradition.

By the mid-1990s the unions were ready to settle for liberalisation of the market for temporary work agencies, provided that the legal position of agency workers was secured. In 1995 the Dutch government responded to the growing use of flexible staffing arrangements by issuing a memorandum on flexibility and security, setting out the need and desirability of expanding employment flexibility while at the same time safeguarding an appropriate level of worker security.[38] This memorandum was followed by the Labour Foundation's 1996 recommendation *Flexibility and Security*. This recommendation was accompanied by a covenant between the social partners in the temporary work industry. This 'temporary agency covenant' included an agreement to identity several phases in the career of an agency worker, each stage providing the agency worker with more entitlements. In the most recent collective agreement there are three phases, describing the transformation of a temporary agency worker's status through increased tenure.

The process leading up to the introduction of the flexibility and security legislation is at the very core of Dutch corporatism. Or as FNV President Johan Stekelenburg stated after the Labour Foundation agreed on the Flexibility and Security recommendation: 'This agreement is in line with the Wassenaar Agreement…and with [the Foundation's 1993 agreement] *A New Course*'.[39] In retrospect, the relatively short time it took to reach consensus in the Labour Foundation epitomised to some the heyday of the *Polder model*.[40] The Labour Foundation's recommendation essentially blueprinted the legislative package enacted in 1998–1999.

The revision of employment law for permanent workers and temporary workers has been influenced by two phenomena: the growing number of workers in flexible employment and a more deeply rooted desire to simplify the dual dismissal system. The 1999 *Wet flexibiliteit en zekerheid* (Flexibility and Security Act) mirrors the attempt of the Dutch government to redistribute employment flexibility and security: workers in flexible staffing arrangements (such as temporary work

37 J. Visser and C. van Rij, *Vakbeweging en Flexibiliteit*, Welboom, Amsterdam, 1999.

38 Ministerie van Sociale Zaken en Werkgelegenheid, *Flexibiliteit en Zekerheid*, Sdu, The Hague, 1995. See also P.F. van der Heijden, 'The Flexibilisation of Working Life in the Netherlands', Contribution to the 15th International Congress of Comparative Law, Bristol, United Kingdom, 1998; T. Wilthagen, 'Flexicurity: A New Paradigm for Labour Market Policy Reform?', Discussion paper FS I 98-202. Social Science Research Center Berlin, Berlin, 1998, for a discussion of the process leading to the legislation.

39 Press statement, 3 April 1996.

40 W.G.M. Plessen, 'Drie jaar Flex en zeker, goede regulering of goede economie?' *Sociaal Maandblad Arbeid* (5) (2002) pp. 287–291; D. Storrie, *Temporary Agency Work in the European Union*, European Foundation for the Improvement of Living and Working Conditions, Dublin, 2002.

agency employees, on-call workers and direct temporary hires) are provided with more employment security, while employers face fewer obstacles in the dismissal of permanently employed workers.[41] This legislation was preceded in 1998 by the introduction of the *Waadi* Act,[42] which reformed manpower allocation by private intermediaries and liberalised the temporary work industry. The legislative package providing flexibility for employers and security for flexible workers has been dubbed 'flexicurity'.[43] Much of the revised employment law evolved from a government search to remove legal barriers that obstruct an efficient operation of the labour markets, a search that started in the early 1980s.[44]

The 1998 Waadi Act liberalised the temporary agency industry: agencies were no longer required to have a licence for the temporary placement of workers at a client firm.[45] However, currently legislation is being prepared to reintroduce the licence requirement following reports of deployment of illegal workers, fraud and other misdemeanours. Furthermore, there was no longer a limit on the duration of a temporary assignment: temporary agency workers could be placed indefinitely at a client firm's job site. The freeing up of the temporary agency market through the Waadi Act was paired with the securing of the legal position of agency workers through the Flexibility and Security Act: the relationship between an agency and its temporary workers is an employment relationship. With the acknowledgment of the agency as the employer and the worker as its employee the relationship was brought under the governance of Civil Code Title 7.10, notably sections 7:690 and 7:691.

Another important change brought about by the Flexibility and Security Act is that workers on a temporary contract become permanent if they have been employed temporarily for 36 months or if three consecutive temporary employment contracts have expired.[46] A similar transformation from temporary to permanent employment has evolved from the 'phases model' as included in the temporary agency covenant discussed above.

---

41 See the November 2000 recommendation by the Commission on the Dual Dismissal System ('Commissie ADO').

42 Waadi is the acronym for *Wet allocatie arbeidskrachten door intermediairs* (Act on Manpower Allocation by Intermediaries).

43 T. Wilthagen, 'Flexicurity: A New Paradigm for Labour Market Policy Reform?', Discussion paper FS I 98-202, Social Science Research Center Berlin, Berlin, 1998.

44 A.T.J.M. Jacobs and W. Plessen, 'Deregulering in het arbeidsrecht'. SEW 40(2) (1992), pp. 83–111.

45 Temporary agency legislation only applies when the supply of temporary personnel is the very nature of the supplying firm's line of business. If a firm temporarily provides workers to carry out an assignment under supervision and direction of this firm at the job site of another firm, then temporary agency legislation is not applicable.

46 Civil Code section 7:668a.

The phases model was incorporated for the first time in the two temporary agency work collective agreements, covering the 1999–2003 period.[47] The two collective agreements for the temporary work industry are named after the acronym of the respective employers' associations with which unions concluded the agreements. The collective agreement of the *Algemene Bond Uitzendondernemingen* (ABU) covers 280,000 temporary agency workers at 280 large temporary work agencies whose revenues totalled 4.4 billion euros in 2002. The collective agreement of the *Nederlandse Bond van Bemiddelings- en Uitzendondernemingen* (NBBU) includes 15,000 temporary workers employed at 320 small and medium-sized agencies.[48] The two collective agreements cover all temporary agency workers employed through members of the ABU and NBBU respectively. The collective agreements for temporary agency workers are an elaboration of Civil Code section 7:691, which governs expiration and continuation of the employment relationship between the temporary work agency and its worker.

The social partners in the temporary employment sector had decided on a collective agreement that covered the 1999–2003 period. The main provision of this agreement was a so-called four-phase system that gradually grants more rights to workers depending on their tenure at the agency. For instance, once workers have completed twenty-six weeks with the agency they have a right to participate in a pension scheme at the agency and, moreover, the agency has to discuss the training needs of the worker. After another six months, the worker will be offered a fixed-term employment contract. After a total of eighteen months at the same client firm or after 36 months of working at different client firms this contract will be converted into a permanent contract. Thus, temporary agency work is increasingly considered a 'normal' type of work with the equivalent accompanying rights and obligations. Previously Dutch legislation and collective bargaining had successfully removed the legal disadvantages of part-time work, which is nowadays more or less seen as the standard labour contract, notably for women.[49]

In September 2003 the ABU employers' association and the trade unions concluded a draft agreement relating to a new collective labour agreement. On the basis of research,[50] recommendations had been issued with respect to the new collective

47 The relative complexity of the four phases has led some scholars to wonder whether the legal position of temporary agency workers would not have been sufficiently secured with only the legislative framework, thus without the collective agreement and its four phases (E. Verhulp, 'De uitzendkracht in het flex(s)t(r)ijdperk', *Sociaal recht* 13(11) (1998), pp. 321–333).

48 Data are from the Netherlands Trade Union Confederation collective agreement database.

49 J. Visser, T. Wilthagen, R. Beltzer and E. Koot-van der Putte. 'The Netherlands: from Atypicality to Typicality. Employment Policy and the Regulation of Part-Time Work in the European Union: a Comparative Analysis', in S. Sciarra, P. Davies and M. Freedland, *Employment Policy and the Regulation of Part-time Work in the European Union : a Comparative Analysis*, Cambridge and New York, 2004, pp. 190–223.

50 NEI, Instroom uitzendkrachten 2000, Rotterdam, 2001.

agreement, the main recommendation being a further differentiation of working conditions as the temporary employed workforce is relatively heterogeneous (e.g. students earning some extra income versus 'stayers' that do not use temporary agency work as a stepping stone). Both the phase system and the wage provisions were considered too complex and not transparent enough. Moreover, at that time the economic situation had changed significantly. From 1995 till 2001 the Netherlands experienced a prosperous period with very low official unemployment rates, a tight labour market and steady economic growth. However, in 2003 unemployment figures were rising, economic growth approaching zero and productivity growth declining.

This led to a different trade-off with respect to the new agreement: external numerical flexibility was enhanced a) by prolonging the period during which temporary agency workers can be dismissed without notice in the event of the client firm ceasing to deploy them (the so-called 'agency clause') and b) by extending the period during which fixed-term contracts can be used. The other part of the deal consisted of a) improved income security for temporary workers by applying (after half a year) the working (pay) conditions of the client firm to the worker (instead of the provisions of the collective agreement of the temporary agency sector) and b) granting temporary agency workers more concrete and individualised entitlements to training. In fact, one could argue that temporary agency work has been further normalised as the working conditions of these workers have become quite similar to those of 'standard' workers. Client firms simply pay extra money (to the agency) for the extra (external) flexibility gained through using temporary agency workers. The second collective labour agreement came into force on 29 March 2004. Another change worth mentioning is the recent announcement by the Ministry of Social Affairs and Employment that in the future a compulsory deposit of 75,000 euros will be required for new temporary agencies in order to curb fraud and the use of illegal workers. Figure 7.1 lists the main features of the two subsequent collective labour agreements in the Dutch temporary agency work sector.

In comparison with the first evaluation, positive experiences among both employers (including temporary work agencies) and flexible workers now generally outweigh negative experiences. Half of the employers involved in the second evaluation had a favourable opinion of the Act (compared to a third in 1999). However, the views of those running temporary work agencies are less favourable, with only a third expressing positive opinions (in 1999, a quarter of these employers had been positive about the Act). Flexible workers are less likely to attribute negative developments in their employment relationship to the Act. The researchers conclude that firms and workers are getting used to the new rules. Knowledge of the law is fairly widespread, though it is still important to provide information for those engaged

Figure 7.1 Main Features of the Collective Labour Agreements in the Dutch Temporary Work Agency Sector

	1999-2003 agreement	*2004-2009 agreement*
'Phase system'	*Phase 1:* First 26 weeks of agency work. *Phase 2:* Second half year of agency work. *Phase 3:* Begins after Phase 2 has ended and lasts 6 months if employed by the same agency or 24 months when working via different agencies. In this phase, agency has to offer fixed-term contract lasting a minimum of 3 months. *Phase 4:* At the end of Phase 3 (after 18 or 36 months of total agency employment) the worker is offered a permanent contract with the temporary work agency.	*Phase A (previously Phases 1 and 2):* Either contract for the duration of the assignment during which agency clause (see below) applies or fixed-term contracts are offered which can be unlimited in number but in total should not exceed 78 weeks of employment. Fixed-term contracts cannot be terminated prior to the end date mentioned in the contract. After 78 weeks of work with the same agency a worker reaches Phase B. *Phase B (previously Phase 3):* Temporary contract with the agency, maximum of 8 temporary contracts in a 2-year period. At the end of Phase B, worker reaches Phase C. *Phase C (previously Phase 4):* Permanent contract with the agency, after a maximum 3.5 years of temporary agency work.
Coverage by other collective agreements	The so-called 'SMU arrangement'[1]: collective agreements for other industries may explicitly include agency workers, who are then covered by these more generous provisions instead of the ABU agreement.	SMU arrangement has been abandoned. Worker salaries now compliant with industry in which they work after 26 weeks of employment (see 'Wage').
Training	Worker in Phase 2 is entitled to 'training-need assessment'. 'Assessment' is not clearly defined. 1.02 per cent of total wages to be spent on training.	1.02 per cent of total wages to be spent on training. 1 per cent of wage is used for individual training account after 26 weeks of work. Once in Phase B, worker is entitled to use money from this account for training purposes. If money is not used during tenure with agency, cash payment is made to the worker upon him/her leaving the agency.

	1999-2003 agreement	*2004-2009 agreement*
Vacation	Vacation rights are accrued for each day worked. Pay is continued during holidays for Phase 3 and 4 workers.	Vacation rights are accrued for each day worked. Pay is continued during holidays for Phase B and C workers (unchanged).
Agency clause[2]	During first year of agency employment (Phases 1 and 2 combined).	During first 78 weeks (Phase A): Contract ends when user firm no longer needs agency worker. Worker can terminate contract without reason.
Temporary contract	Worker cannot be offered temporary contract after having worked on temporary contracts for more than 18 months at one and the same user firm.	Worker cannot be offered temporary contract after having worked on temporary contracts for more than 3.5 years at one and the same user firm.
Pension	Worker in Phase 2 is entitled to pension if he/she is 21 years or old.	After 26 weeks of agency work and if agency worker is aged 21 and over (unchanged).
Wage	User firms that are covered by industry agreements applying an 'SMU arrangement' may deviate from ABU wage	Pay according to ABU agreement during first 26 weeks. After 26 weeks salary corresponding to permanent workers in similar positions with user firm. Continuation of pay during underemployment when worker is on fixed-term or permanent contract (90 per cent of last earned income).

Notes

1 In 1991 employers and employees in the temporary work industry established a body (*Stichting Meldingsbureau Uitzendbranche* or SMU Foundation) through which user-firm collective agreements could be registered. Once registered at the SMU Foundation the collective agreement of a client firm applies to all temporary agency workers employed at the client firm's job site. In practice this means that temporary agency workers may be entitled to the same provisions (for instance, pension rights, vacation pay and training) as regular workers of a client firm. Because of the new wage system in the second ABU collective agreement, the arrangement has been abandoned and the Foundation has been dissolved.

2 Or 'temporary employment clause'. This clause now applies during Phase A under the second collective labour agreement, unless otherwise agreed. If a firm no longer wishes to use a worker from a temporary work agency then this also means the end of the employment contract between the agency worker and the agency. During the first twelve weeks of the employment relationship, no notice of termination is required. As long as the clause applies, an agency worker may terminate the contract at will, with a day's notice.

in collective bargaining as well as to individuals.[51] The Minister of Social Affairs and Employment has stated that he agreed with the researchers that the results of the study were influenced by the current favourable economic conditions, but he also concluded that the legislation on flexibility and security did not represent a barrier to favourable developments in the labour market.

The results of a third evaluation[52] were generally in line with the previous evaluations. An initial observation was that the percentage of flexible workers had decreased between 1998 and 2000 (from 9.8 per cent of the working population to 7.7 per cent), notably due to a decline of on-call workers. The tight labour market situation has, in practice, limited the scope for using the new opportunities to increase the flexible deployment of labour. Employers preferred to use overtime and variable working hours to enhance flexibility in their company. A successive use of fixed-terms contracts was the most frequently applied element of the new legislation.

A quarter of the temporary agency workers interviewed report that their legal position has been improved by the flexibility and security legislation. The presumptions of law which were introduced by the new legislation appear to have had a preventive effect in the form of differently and more adequately formulated contracts. Only in a minority of cases (about ten percent) where workers work more hours than agreed by contract, is an appeal made on the basis of presumptions of law. Many flexible workers do not rely on the presumptions because they wish to maintain *their* flexibility towards the employer. The legislator's expectations regarding the guaranteed wage for on-call workers have not been met yet. One-sixth of the employers state that they do not pay the guaranteed minimum of three hours, whereas one-third of the on-call workers claim that they are not paid according to the legal requirements.

The four-phase system is well-known among temporary agency workers: half of the workers report being informed by their agency of the phase that applies to them. Ninety percent of temporary work agencies have introduced a pension scheme for the temporary workers; more than half of the workers report that they are building up pension rights. Temporary agency workers in phases 1 and 2 are entitled to sickness benefits and workers in phases 3 and 4 are entitled to continued pay. One-third of the latter category of workers is not aware of this entitlement and a quarter of the workers do not receive a benefit when they fall ill. Workers in phases 3 and 4 seem to have more problems than their counterparts in phases 1 and 2.

---

51 P.M. de Klaver, D.J. Klein Hesselink, E.P. Miedema, and C. Schlangen, *Ervaringen met en effecten van de Wet flexibiliteit en zekerheid: tweede meting 2000*, Ministry of Social Affairs and Employment, The Hague, 2000.

52 J.P. van den Toren, G.H.M. Evers and E.J. Commissaris, *Flexibiliteit en zekerheid: effecten en doeltreffendheid van de Wet flexibiliteit en zekerheid – eindrapport*, Ministry of Social Affairs and Employment, The Hague, 2002.

Most flex workers who involuntary quit their job and become unemployed do not receive unemployment benefits. The most prominent reason for this is that the workers do not apply for such a benefit (the largest category of these workers, some twenty-five percent, refrain from applying for a benefit because they already have a new job, or expect to have one soon; seventeen percent report 'no need' for a benefit, fifteen percent think they are not entitled to a benefit and seven percent feels applying for a benefit is too much bother). Eighty percent of applications for benefit are granted by the benefit administration. Cases in which the application is turned down are often related to the existence of a continued pay obligation on the part of the employer. The social insurance agencies have become stricter in view of this continued pay obligation: workers are being referred back to their employer, but then stop pursuing their rights (notably in the building and agricultural sectors) or must make more effort to carry through their claim. In the latter case a higher income is obtained, in the former case this has a negative effect on flexible workers' income protection.

7.5 PART-TIME WORK

7.5.1 The Netherlands

Part-time work is often seen as a form of flexible or non-standard employment. In the Netherlands, part-time work has become such a common type of employment that it can hardly be seen as non-standard. In 2003, 46 percent of all employees worked part-time, a fact that has significantly contributed to the increase in employment. Part-time work can enable workers to combine work with duties outside the labour market, such as caring for dependents. Thus it facilitates the flexibility of workers.

Given the widespread use of part-time work arrangements, this type of employment is highly regulated. Article 7:648 of the Civil Code, which makes it illegal to discriminate against workers in relation to the terms of agreement, renewal or termination of an employment contract on the grounds of working hours alone, unless such discrimination can be objectively justified. The Working Hours Adjustment Act 2000 confers on workers (in companies and services that employ ten or more workers) the right to adjust their contractual working-time by working either more or fewer hours.[53] Employers can deny workers an adjustment

---

53 It was drafted by the Deputy Minister of Social Affairs and Employment and is part of the larger Framework Act on Work and Care. The new legislation is also in line with a recommendation issued to the parties to collective bargaining by the Dutch Foundation of Labour in 1993 under the title 'Promotion of Part-Time Work and Differentiation of Working-Time Patterns. A study by the Dutch Labour Inspectorate' (Arbeidsinspectie, *Voorjaarsrapportage CAO-afspraken 1999.*

of working time only if 'major corporate or organisational interests' are likely to be adversely affected. The Working Hours Adjustment Act is expected to promote further part-time work, especially among men, and to facilitate the balancing of work and care commitments. Even before the new law came into force, part-time rates in the Netherlands were unparalleled in Europe. Some scholars have called the Netherlands the first part-time economy in the world.[54] Equal opportunities and labour market policies in the Netherlands are increasingly based on the assumption that each household has 1.5 jobs in total. This 'one-and-a-half earners' model[55] is called the 'combination scenario', in which men and women both have a (substantial) part-time job and share work and care responsibilities.[56] Eighty per cent of Dutch men working part-time and ninety-three per cent of women state as their reason that they 'do not want a full-time job'.[57] Figure 7.2 below gives a short overview of the legal terms of employment and social security for part-time workers in the Netherlands.

7.5.2 Spain

While Spain is not among the highest ranking European countries in terms of the level of part-time work (eight percent in 2002), it makes for an interesting case in this paper because of the legislative changes governing part-time work during the 1990s. Part-time workers in Spain have traditionally been subject to less favourable conditions than workers in full-time positions. Part-time jobs have been

---

The Hague, 1999) reveals that 19 per cent of the 118 collective agreements studied (covering 3.8 million workers) contain substantial provisions on part-time work. Sixty-four per cent of the collective agreements stipulate that an employee may request his or her employer to adjust his or her working-hours. None of the collective agreements contains all of the core elements of the 1993 recommendation issued by the Foundation of Labour. Nineteen agreements make a distinction between long and short-hours part-time jobs (the latter usually involving 12 or 13 hours a week). The question is whether this is against the law. The Secretary of State has asked the Foundation of Labour for its opinion on this matter. It is important that part-time workers be granted positive rights to vocational training, promotion and career structures, especially when part-time work is considered an employment strategy. Neither the Proposal for a Council Directive on Voluntary Part-Time Work (OJ C 62/7, 12 March 1982) nor the 1994 ILO Convention Concerning Part-Time Work (Convention No 175) and the Council Directive 97/81/EC on Part-Time Work have gone so far. See J. Murray, 'Social Justice for Women? The ILO's Convention on Part-time Work', CELRL Working Paper no. 15, 1999.

54 R.B. Freeman, 'War of the Models: Which Labour Market Institutions for the 21st Century?' *Labour Economics* 5(1) (1998), pp. 1–24.

55 J. Visser, 'The First Part-time Economy in the World: a Model to be Followed?', *Journal of European Social Policy* 12(1) (2002), pp. 23–42.

56 SCP, *De kunst van het combineren*, The Hague, 2000.

57 Ministerie van Sociale Zaken en Werkgelegenheid, *Part-Time Work in the Netherlands*, Ministerie van Sociale Zaken en Werkgelegenheid, Directorate of Industrial Relations, The Hague, 1997.

Figure 7.2 Legal Terms of Employment and Social Security for Part-time Work in the Netherlands

Salary

Persons who do the same kind of work should receive the same (gross) hourly wage regardless of working time. As from January 1, 1993 all employees are entitled to a salary based (proportionally) on the legal minimum wage regardless of working time.

Holidays

A part-time worker is entitled to the same number of days off as full-time workers, in proportion to the hours he or she works. For example, if somebody working full-time gets 20 full free days a year, somebody working half time gets 20 half free days a year. (According to the law 20 days is the minimum; collective agreements generally grant approximately 25 days a year.)

Probationary period

The maximum is 2 months for permanent contracts and possibly shorter for fixed-term contracts, but this is regardless of working time.

Dismissal law

Is exactly the same for all workers regardless of working time.

Special leave

In principle a part-time worker is entitled to special leave in the same cases as full-time workers. Divergence from this principle could be justified if the activities could also be fitted in during the part-timer's free time. If a bank holiday falls in the time that a part-time worker is not working, he/she cannot claim a free day at some other time.

Parental leave

Under the terms of the Parental Leave Act, persons employed by the same employer for a year or more are entitled to unpaid part-time leave. A new bill is currently being debated in Parliament. This stipulates, among other things, that employees working 20 hours or fewer will also be entitled to this kind of leave; up to now this category of employees has been excluded from this possibility.

cont. >

Figure 7.2 (cont.)

Overtime

Most collective agreements contain clauses on overtime and overtime pay. Under these clauses, granting overtime pay if full-time working hours are exceeded is not considered unequal treatment. The social partners may well have good reasons for granting overtime pay as soon as working time exceeds the contractually agreed level (whether full-time or part-time).

Pensions

Under the National Old Age Pension Act, every person is provided with a monthly pension. On top of that, employees can, as a rule, build up additional pension rights through company pension schemes. There are some 1000 private pension schemes. As from 1994 an employee can no longer be excluded from participation in a pension fund because of working time. If a wage limit is applied in pension schemes, then part-timers' wages have to be converted to full-time level. A part-time employee acquires pension rights in proportion to the volume of his/her working hours.

Social security

Every employee who has an employment contract with a private employer is insured against unemployment and disablement, regardless of the length of working time. Neither the number of working hours nor the amount of pay exerts any influence on this. In the event of sickness an employer is legally obliged to pay 70 per cent of the employee's salary for a maximum of 52 weeks.

Social security contributions are usually calculated on the basis of a fixed percentage of pay or income. Working time does not enter into the calculation.

Unemployment

Part-time employees receive unemployment benefits for the same period of time and under the same conditions as a full-time employee. The benefits are based on 70 per cent of the previous gross pay.

Sickness

Both part-time and full-time employees (whether on permanent or fixed-term contracts) receive at least 70 per cent of their gross salary in the event of illness (but not less than the minimum wage, calculated proportionally for part-timers) paid by the employer for a period of one year.

Figure 7.2 (cont.)

Disablement

Part-time employees receive disablement benefits for the same duration of time and under the same conditions as a full-time employee. The benefits are based on 70 per cent of previous income (in the event of complete incapacity) and varies in accordance with the age at which it is first paid.

Health insurance

Up to a certain salary limit (in 2004: €32,600 a year) all employees are insured under the terms of a Compulsory Health Insurance Scheme, which provides medical and dental care, hospital, nursing and other services. Above this limit employees have to insure themselves privately. There is no difference in the conditions that apply to part-time and full-time employees. Both pay the same percentage of their income plus the same nominal contribution.

Working conditions

Employers are legally obliged to apply the same safety regulations and measures at work for both part-time and full-time workers.

Working hours

The Working Hours Act, which came into effect on 1 January 1996, includes a clause obliging employers to take account of employees' care responsibilities. This means that employers have to give reasonable consideration to individual preferences when planning and allocating working times and schedules.

Taxes

There are no specific or special measures in the tax system to encourage part-time work. As the tax system is based on progressive taxation for higher incomes, the net income losses in the case of part-time jobs are smaller than the gross reduction of income.

Source: Ministry of Social Affairs and Employment (1997, 17–20).

mostly filled by young people with low skills. Part-time workers predominantly work on temporary contracts, many of very short duration. In 1998, nearly half of all temporary contracts for part-time workers were for less than one month.[58] Furthermore, part-time workers lack equitable social protection, making it hard to qualify for social security benefits. Not surprisingly, only 4.5 percent of part-time workers were happy with their type of employment.[59] Nearly 20 percent of part-time workers preferred to work full time.[60]

Until the early 1980s, part-time work in Spain was highly unregulated. The government's *laissez-faire* attitude was based on the hope that in the free market part-time work would stimulate employment growth or would enable a more flexible organisation of work. Restrictions were imposed with respect to who was eligible for part-time work: the unemployed and youth under the age of twenty-five. As a result part-time work was essentially left to the margins of the labour market.

In 1984, part-time work was 'normalised' by law in the sense that it was opened up for all workers: restrictions no longer applied as a means of creating employment. However, the subsequent tripling of part-time work in the ten years following the new legislation is seen by some as the result of a government policy that sought to maximise flexibility in the use of fixed-term contracts, be they full-time or part-time. In this view, the 1984 legislation is seen as a 'mere by-product of the use of temporary or fixed-term contracts' and explicitly considered as a tool created by the legislator to enable the flexibilisation of a firm's workforce.[61]

The idea that part-time work could contribute to employment growth was entirely dropped with the introduction of a new law in 1993 which converted part-time work exclusively into an instrument for the adjustment of work in order to meet production requirements.[62] The 1994 revision of the law contained a further erosion of worker security, by redefining 'part-time work' as all work where the number of hours was less than a full-time job. Further revisions concerning part-time work legislation and policies took place against the backdrop of a divided social partner front. In the late 1990s and early in the twenty-first century, successive changes initially steered away from flexibility (favouring the views of the principal worker organisations) but then returned to the flexibility-championing employers. Finally, in December 2001 Spain's most representative employee and employer organisations made the important decision to focus on finding a balance between flexibility and

58 F. Valdés Dal-Ré, 'The Difficulty of Reconciling Flexibility and Security in Spain: the Paradigmatic Case of Part-time Work', *Transfer* 10(2) (2004), pp. 248–262.

59 Ibid.

60 Eurofound, *Part-Time Work in Europe*, European Foundation for the Improvement of Living and Working Conditions, Dublin, 2004.

61 F. Valdés Dal-Ré, 'The Difficulty of Reconciling Flexibility and Security in Spain: the Paradigmatic Case of Part-Time Work', *Transfer* 10(2) (2004), pp. 248–262.

62 Ibid.

security, a first in the history of the Spanish industrial relations.[63] The potential of this consensus for regulatory reform that actually reconciles flexibility and security should be realised in the near future, as Spanish legislation needs to be aligned with EU policy on part-time work.

7.6 INTERLUDE: EUROPEAN INDICATORS ON FLEXIBILITY AND SECURITY

7.6.1 A Flexicurity Index

Tangian[64] has made a first attempt to establish a 'flexicurity index' of European countries, thus trying to measure the 'state' of flexicurity in these countries. In Tangian's paper the definition of flexicurity is limited to flexible employment: 'Flexicurity is the employment and social security of atypically employed, that is, other than permanent full-time'.[65]

Our own estimations and OECD data are used to assess different aspects and levels of security. In the econometric analysis the Netherlands shows the highest rate of flexicurity and Sweden displays the highest 'all security' (i.e. security for all workers). Denmark, often referred to as a typical flexicurity country, is less prominent (i.e. average) in this study, which can possibly be explained by the low rate of dismissal protection. Portugal shows the lowest level of flexicurity, followed by Czech Republic and the United Kingdom. The United Kingdom followed by Spain also displays the lowest levels of 'all security'. Sweden and Italy rank number one and two when it comes to the highest level of 'norm security' (i.e. the security for 'normal' permanently employed, full-time employees). Spain and the United Kingdom show the lowest levels of norm security. In Portugal, Poland and Italy the atypically employed have the least security in relation to the normally employed.

7.6.2 EES Indicators

The European Employment Strategy (EES) has developed indicators to assess flexibility and security in the Member States. Three indicators are particularly

63 Ibid.

64 A.S. Tangian, *Defining the Flexicurity Index in Application to European Countries*, Düsseldorf, WSI/Hans Böckler Stiftung, 2004.

65 Ibid. p. 12.

relevant to our analysis.[66]

The first indicator (key indicator 4 within the EES) pertains to the number of transitions between non-employment and employment and within employment by type of contract during one year. Here Eurostat uses the ECHP data as its source. The figures show that Luxembourg, Belgium and Portugal recorded the highest number of people employed in 2000 and still employed in 2001 (respectively 96 per cent, 95 per cent and 95 per cent against the EU-15 average of 93 per cent). Spain and Ireland rank last (91 per cent).

Austria, Germany and Spain have the highest proportion of unemployed persons in paid work after one year (53 per cent, 52 per cent and 52 per cent against the EU-15 average of 41 per cent).

With respect to the transition of inactive persons into paid employment, Denmark is the absolute forerunner (twenty-four per cent against the EU-15 average of 14 per cent) and Greece and Italy perform worst (seven per cent).

The second indicator (key indicator 15 within the EES), based on Labour Force Survey data, relates to the diversity of contractual and working arrangements including the total numbers of employees in part-time and/or fixed-term contracts plus the total of self-employed as a percentage of persons in employment. This indicator also takes into account the reasons reported by workers for engaging in certain working arrangements.

The Netherlands appears to have the highest proportion of part-time, fixed-term and self-employed workers (51 per cent, against the EU-25 average of 37.3 per cent), mainly due to the very high part-time work rates (35.7 per cent, against the EU-25 average of 14.2 per cent. Part-time work is no longer considered atypical work in this country). Spain ranks second (44.8 per cent), mainly due to the high rate for fixed-term work (25.9 per cent against the EU-25 average of 9.3 per cent). Interestingly, the Netherlands also has the highest number of persons with a part-time job who did not want a full-time job (27.5 per cent), whereas in France a relatively high share of workers have a part-time job because they could not find a full-time job (3.5 per cent). Fixed-term workers in Spain, however, most often state that they could not find a permanent job (17.5 per cent). In Slovenia fixed-term workers most often indicate that they did not want a permanent job (4.6 per cent).

The third indicator relates to transitions by type of contract, based on ECHP data (key indicator 16) – not including the new Member States – taking into account transitions between non-employment and employment and within employment by type of contract between 2000 and 2001.

France and Luxembourg have the largest proportion of workers with a permanent contract that still have a permanent contract one year later (ninety-four per cent, against the EU-15 average of ninety per cent). Spain (eighty-seven per cent),

---

66 The figures used here are taken from the First Draft of the Indicators for monitoring the Employment Guidelines 2004/2005 Compendium.

Germany and Ireland (both eighty-eight per cent) have the lowest proportion of workers that still have a permanent contract after one year.

The transition from fixed-time work to permanent work develops most smoothly in Luxembourg (sixty-two per cent of persons against the EU-15 average of thirty-two per cent), Portugal (forty-nine per cent) and the UK (forty-seven per cent).

Finally, the transition from non-employed to permanently employed occurs relatively easy in the Netherlands (fourteen per cent of persons, against the EU-15 average of eight per cent), the UK (thirteen per cent) and Denmark (twelve per cent).

7.7 CONCLUSION AND RECOMMENDATIONS

The starting point of this paper was to examine modes, combinations and equilibriums of flexibility and security in different national employment systems. We assumed that flexibility and security in the labour market are not merely opposites but that a balance between these widely acknowledged goals should, and in fact can, be established. We therefore presented country examples relating to three important domains of numerical flexibilisation strategies: hiring and firing, temporary agency work and part-time work. The selected examples show that high levels of flexibility in these areas can go hand in hand with either high or low levels of security. In order to draw lessons from this comparison the following questions have to be raised:

- Why do the countries examined have high levels of flexibility in the domains scrutinised?
- Why have some countries also developed high levels of security in the areas studied?
- What are the consequences of having or not having enhanced security?

Firstly, it seems fair to say that every country studied has developed its own distinct and perhaps favoured mode of numerical flexibilisation. None of the countries put the same emphasis on all three modes of flexibilisation, a finding confirmed by Section 7.4. In the Netherlands the prominence of part-time work and temporary agency work exists next to (if not caused by) a fairly strict system of dismissal protection. In Spain dismissal protection is also strict when it comes to the protection of core employee employment. Flexibility is sought and found by employers by using temporary (agency) workers, both in full-time and part-time positions. In Denmark, however, part-time work and temporary agency work rates are not very significant, perhaps due to the relative ease of hiring and firing. In the United States the growth of temporary agency work has coincided with the decreased importance (although still relevant) of the employment-at-will doctrine, hinting at a possible connection between the strictness of employment protection and the use of flexible staffing arrangements. Put differently, we notice here that flexibilisation strategies are tending to depend on the broader institutional and legal context, as well on the historical path a country has been following (in accordance with the concept of path dependency). In its further policy-making and legislative processes, Turkey will have to consider its particular context and historical path while avoiding a deterministic view.

Secondly, the security measures that some countries (in our sample, Denmark and the Netherlands) have introduced in addition to or in combination with flexibilisation are very interesting. In Denmark no additional security has been introduced *within* hiring and firing (which appears to be quite difficult to do), but workers benefit from high levels of income and reintegration policies if they have been fired. The Danish social security and activation/reintegration systems not only provide a safety net but also a springboard for workers who have temporarily lost employment. Hiring and firing flexibility and high levels of social security, plus fast and successful reintegration strategies form a 'golden triangle' where all elements are interwoven. The main flexibility-security nexus consists of numerical flexibility and high levels of social security (employment benefits). Altering or removing one of these elements will automatically lead to the loss of the other.

The Dutch story is different. In the Netherlands temporary work and part-time work rates have increased to the extent that they have become typical rather than atypical forms of employment, a position facilitated by government intervention. So many workers have adopted these types of employment on largely voluntary basis (notably in the case of part-time work), that a process of 'normalisation' has been initiated which has included introducing more security for this new workforce. The introduction of such security (employment security, social security) has contributed in turn to the further growth of both types of employment. A crucial difference between the Netherlands and Denmark on the one hand and Spain and the United States on the other can be observed in terms of labour market effects. While employment-at-will in the United States and part-time work in Spain may have had benign effects on employment growth, the risks of a segmented or even bifurcated labour market have also materialised to a significant extent. These negative effects have not occurred in Denmark and the Netherlands: on the contrary, the effects have been counteracted by the extra security that was inserted into the system. The above-average labour market performance of these two countries, as Section 7.4 shows, may be traced back to the sustainable balance achieved between flexibility and security.

The political and social feasibility of labour market and work organisation reform that take both flexibility and security into account depends on the extent to which new measures are perceived as serving the interests of the most prominent parties involved. Consequently, countries, sectors and companies that lack a tradition of and platform for coordination, consultation and negotiation seem to be at a disadvantage when it comes to producing well-balanced flexibility-security trade-offs.[67]

As our examples suggest, these trade-offs, or at least the possibility of them, seem to correlate with corporatist systems or other traditions of social dialogue, social partnership, consultation and coordination and require a climate and a degree of mutual trust. Employers must be willing to acknowledge that flexibility can adequately be attained (notably in a long-term perspective) within a context that provides reasonable levels of security to workers, while workers and their representatives must be willing to redefine security to a certain extent, such as in the form of transitional employment and employment security rather than job security or as a form of risk management.[68] Trust is a major factor here. If levels of trust are low or absent, either among the social partners or towards the government, flexicurity strategies can expect to meet with strong opposition and mistrust. An illustration of this was the reaction of trade unions and employer organisations to the European Commission's 1997 Green Paper, which promoted the idea of social partnership and balancing flexibility and security. Whereas in countries such as Finland the response from the social partners was positive, the French and German trade unions were very negative about the views included in the Green Paper, arguing that the idea of partnership represented a threat to the independence of unions and a denial of the importance of workers' rights, notably at the enterprise level.[69]

It appears likely that a high degree of negotiated flexibility and broad negotiation agendas have contributed to the Netherlands and Denmark achieving a successful balance between flexibility and security.[70] Adding employer flexibilisation strategies to the bargaining agenda and discussing them in an integrated manner along with security for employees has resulted in an increase in the acceptance of flexibilisation among employees. This has encouraged 'positive coordination', 'integrative bargaining', 'positive-sum-games' and 'negotiated flexibility', enabling mutual gains to be achieved through a more optimal way of dealing with the double requirement

67 D. Foden, 'The Role of the Social Partners in the European Employment Strategy', *Transfer* 5(4) (1999), pp. 522–541; D. Fouarge, *Minimum Protection and Poverty in Europe*, Thela Thesis, Amsterdam, 2002.

68 G. Schmid, 'Transitional Labour Markets and the European Social Model: towards a New Employment Compact', in G. Schmid and B. Grazier, *The Dynamics of Full Employment: Social Integration through Transitional Labour Markets*, Edward Elgar, Cheltenham, 2002; T. Wilthagen and R. Rogowski, 'Legal Regulation of Transitional Labour Markets. The Dynamics of Full Employment: Social Integration through Transitional Labour Markets', in G. Schmid and B. Grazier, *The Dynamics of Full Employment: Social Integration through Transitional Labour Markets*, Edward Elgar, Cheltenham, 2002, pp. 264–289.

69 A. Korver, *Rekindling Adaptability*, EFSQ, Amsterdam, 2001.

70 A. Anxo and J. O'Reilly, 'Working-Time Regimes and Transitions in Comparative Perspective', in J. O'Reilly, I. Cebrián and M. Lallement, *Working-Time Change*, Edward Elgar, Cheltenham, 2002, pp. 61–90.

of flexibility and security. Again, mutual trust, based on an understanding of mutual interests, is crucial.

The Dutch and Danish cases also suggest that the decentralisation of labour market policy has a beneficial effect on the introduction of flexicurity. Decentralisation has been pursued *under central* control in both Denmark and the Netherlands. As a result of this, parties involved in negotiating collective agreements, local organisations, companies and individual employers and employees have been given freedom to create tailor-made solutions with regard to flexibility and security needs. Furthermore, this process has been accompanied in both countries by strong economic performance, which provides a positive context for drawing up new rules on flexibility and security. One specific requirement appears to be that decentralisation be coupled with strong central coordination. The literature increasingly refers to the simultaneous occurrence of decentralisation and increasing – although perhaps more benign – central coordination.[71]

The new Turkish Labour Act has sought to enhance worker security by, for example, making it harder for employers to make and renew temporary contracts and by making layoff procedures costly and time-consuming. Measures to increase labour market flexibility have also been introduced with the new law. However, the actual implementation of this flexibility in collective agreements is a complicated matter. Several flexibility arrangements need to be agreed to by both employer and employee.[72] Unions have blocked the incorporation of flexibility in collective agreements as they view enhanced security measures for workers as a *sine qua non* for flexibility legislation. In this paper we have argued that successful and sustainable combinations of flexibility and security strategies are dependent on broad support from social partners. The Turkish government, unions and employer associations need to realise that social dialogue is a key instrument for simultaneously promoting the issue of worker security and labour market flexibility. Without support from all Turkish labour market actors for flexibility *and* security measures it will not be possible to achieve an appropriate equilibrium between flexibility and security.

71 L. Léonard, 'Industrial Relations and the Regulation of Employment in Europe', *European Journal of Industrial Relations* 7 (2001), pp. 27–47; K. Sisson and P. Marginson, 'Coordinated Bargaining: a Process for Our Times?', *British Journal of Industrial Relations* 40(2) (2002), pp. 197–220.

72 See, for instance, arts 14 and 63(2).

8. CONCLUSIONS

Nurhan Süral and Frans Pennings

8.1 INTRODUCTION

In Turkey, new debates on employment creation through flexibility, good corporate governance, corporate social responsibility and alternative dispute resolution are all having an impact on the classical model of labour legislation, which was primarily designed to protect the weaker party. As a result, labour legislation which, in Turkey as in EU countries, gave workers within the formal labour market a high degree of protection, is undergoing changes which may lead to greater uncertainty for those traditional workers. On the other hand these developments may lead to increased employment – very important in view of the high unemployment figures – and may also provide new opportunities for those confined to the informal labour market.

For this reason it was important to investigate Turkish labour law, the operation of the labour market and the position of actors within the labour market in order to see whether flexibility could be increased while maintaining sufficient security for workers and upholding the basic protection of labour law. In this chapter we will firstly summarise the flexibility debate and the issues that have affected it and then summarise our basic recommendations.

8.2 THE ISSUES SURROUNDING THE FLEXIBILITY DEBATE

The Turkish labour market was deregulated during the 1990s, a period during which a series of discussions and debates on this issue took place. Turkish policy makers claimed that deregulation would increase employment, particularly through a more flexible organisation of work. Stagnant economic conditions, worsened by the 2001 economic crisis, and the resulting high unemployment, led the authorities to consider the creation of dynamic and flexible labour markets. Increasing flexibility of the labour market by removing existing rigidities was particularly seen as a remedy for unemployment. It was expected that greater flexibility would:

- Create employment
- Increase enterprise adaptability

Pennings, *Flexibilisation and Modernisation of the Turkish Labour Market*, 183–188

– Provide better social inclusion for the unemployed, particularly women and young first entrants
– Combat undeclared work.

This led, among other things, to the Labour Act of 2003. A lot was expected of this Act, though flexibilisation remained a very delicate issue. Not only were the initial proposals relating to flexibility downgraded in the final version due to trade union opposition, but after the law was adopted little use was made of several of the newly introduced provisions.

The background to this discussion is Turkey's application for EU Membership. Talks between the EU and Turkey started on 3 October 2005, but were preceded by a long period of preparations aimed at adjusting Turkish law to the *acquis*. For the purposes of screening and the subsequent negotiations, the *acquis* is divided into a number of chapters, each covering a specific policy area. Social policy and employment, including non-discrimination and equal opportunities for women and men, is the topic of the nineteenth chapter in the preliminary indicative list of chapter headings.

The incorporation and implementation of Community legislation represents a key challenge for Turkey. The screening process during which Turkey's legislation will be evaluated in terms of compatibility with the Community rules started on 20 October 2005. This evaluation will constitute the basis for negotiations.

As outlined in Chapter 5, the *acquis* includes flexible work instruments. We noted in this chapter that Turkish labour law is generally in line with the EU instruments.

Legislative framework

The main findings of this comparative analysis of the legislative framework are:

1. *Rigidities*. Most of the existing rigidities were removed. Flexitime and flexible modalities of employment were regulated in Turkey's 2003 Labour Act, though some rigidities remain and hinder effective implementation.
   - *Temporary work*. The use of temporary workers has been limited to groups of enterprises and company conglomerations. Temporary work has not been established as a three-way relationship. Though private employment offices exist, agencies for temporary workers cannot be established. With better regulation, temporary work could have formed an important stepping stone to more permanent employment.
   - *Fixed-term work*. An objective cause seems to be required for the first fixed-term labour contract and a substantial reason justifying its renewal.

The law does not allow a great deal of freedom in respect of this type of contract.

- *Part-time and on-call work.* The minimum wage is the minimum amount of earnings subjected to contributions. Given the high level of contributions due, where a part-time worker or an on-call worker makes less than the minimum wage on a *pro rata* basis, employment of part-timers and on-call workers becomes relatively expensive for the employer. Moreover, where the part-timer or the on-call worker is engaged in one job, it may be difficult for the worker to build entitlement to long-term insurance benefits, particularly to old-age pensions. Consequently, both parties may prefer to operate in the informal market.
- *Flexitime.* Flexitime practices require mutual agreement. Where labour is unwilling, management will have no recourse to flexitime.
- *Contract termination.* Excessive protection of employees and the legal intricacies involved may have adverse effects on employment. Despite this, job security provisions have not been relaxed: traditional patterns of central control of dismissals continue.

2. *No strong incentives.* Atypical work is not really popular with employees. The principal concern of employees is job security rather than short-term financial gain. Given the expenses associated with some types of flexible contracts (see the various sections on part-time and on-call work *supra*) employers are discouraged to make use of atypical contracts.
3. *Revenue losses for public bodies.* The general practice of undeclared and under-declared work has implications for social security and tax revenue as well as the social rights and working conditions of employees.
4. *Vulnerability to blockage.* Implementation of the relevant provisions often depends on approval by the trade unions or employees. This makes it quite simple to block the implementation of the new rules.

Interplay of other factors within the labour market

It is important that we explore the actual implementation of legislation. If we find, for example, that part-time work is legally permitted, but in practice discouraged, we cannot say that the requirements of the *acquis* have been met.

We must remember that flexibility is not an end in itself. Its purpose is to increase employment and reduce unfair competition from the informal labour market. As the latter is a major employer of women, increasing flexibility in the formal labour market should also help improve the protection of female workers. Consequently, the legislation must be examined to see whether it has been successfully implemented and if not, the reasons for lack of success identified and investigated, otherwise the legislation will fail to achieve its aims.

In this book we have not restricted ourselves to written law but have also studied traditions and labour market actors, as they will either stimulate the implementation of the regulatory framework or hinder its adoption, reducing the whole flexibility process to a rhetorical exercise. The role of the social partners in the modernisation of work is therefore both crucial and decisive. Chapter 4 addresses these issues.

The Turkish labour market and the social partners have a relatively long tradition of serious rivalry. Previous labour legislation seems to be the basis of this rivalry: since the unions operated locally the labour market was highly diverse. Instead of allowing this problem to resolve itself – as has happened in other countries – the State intervened with legislation. The effect of this legislation was to impose limits of a unique nature on the collective bargaining powers of unions and a failure to reduce rivalry. This has in turn led to the lack of the mutual trust and cooperation necessary to find a new equilibrium between flexibility and security.

National traditions and national conceptions of social partnership have affected the successful implementation of the flexibility concept and may hinder innovative legislation. How industrial relations is organised is a key determinant of success in this area. We have identified a number of problems in this area:

1. *The State's paternalist attitude*. Traditionally, the State has been the main employer and has guaranteed life-long employment. This has meant that an attitude hostile to flexibility has developed over time.

2. *The roles assigned to legislation and the limits of collective bargaining*. Trade unions and employers' associations have traditionally relied on the government to legislate to resolve industrial relation problems rather than trying to reach their objectives by improving the system of collective bargaining in place. Consequently Turkish labour legislation covers a broad spectrum of issues which in other countries are usually left to the social partners to address through social dialogue. As a result, excessive regulation has reduced the room for collective bargaining.

3. *Partnership weaknesses*. The fragmentation of labour has resulted in polarisation and competition between the trade unions. As a result a compromise by any union is regarded as a sign of weakness and used as a weapon of attack by the competing unions. Once an intransigent stand is adopted (as has happened with flexibility), any discussion of issues tends to be on an emotional basis with slogans overriding facts and a reduced possibility of developing new initiatives. Distributive bargaining is prevalent; integrative bargaining is unknown.

4. *Substantial differences in perspectives and approaches*. The different perspectives and approaches of the social partners towards the issue of flexibility are adversely affecting the implementation of flexibility rules. Increasing the flexibility of the labour market by removing existing rigidities is regarded by the trade unions as solely beneficial to the employers. The unions have blocked flexibility practices, obdurately defending existing levels of protection without devising alternative solutions for generating employment. Employers, on the other hand, have continued to press for flexibility. Bridging the gap seems difficult, especially in light of the behaviour of the social partners.

Alongside our study of the social partners we also examined the role of the government and public organisations (as described in Chapter 3) with a view to better understanding the problems of implementing the flexibility rules. Although it can be said that in general these organisations have tried to supervise the implementation of rules and to maintain the law, we have identified room for improvement. The limited inspection capacity of public organisations has helped to perpetuate the existence of a large informal market.

The final main aspect discussed is the role of social security in assisting flexible workers and enabling those already within the formal labour market to accept greater flexibility. Moreover, the importance of the link between flexibility and security – flexicurity – has been stressed (see Chapter 7). In general, it appears that despite providing comprehensive protection to several groups within the formal labour market, the Turkish social security system has excluded others, including flexible workers. We investigated the reasons for this and the alternative options that are available. The social security system is an important aspect of the modernisation process, as there are tensions between this system and major elements of the *acquis*, such as the promotion of work, equal treatment, sustainability and the prevention of social exclusion.

8.3 THE MAIN RECOMMENDATIONS

As we have seen above, there are several reasons for encouraging further modernisation of the Turkish labour market. Modernisation is an ongoing process and several important problems still remain, including those associated with the informal labour market, unemployment and the unequal division of wealth.

Our main recommendation concerns redefinition of the roles of the key labour market factors. National efforts to increase flexibilisation in the formal labour market can be made more effective if all the stakeholders are involved.

The Government must set out what it thinks needs to be done to improve the functioning of the labour market and to ensure compliance with EU law and practice. It should also remove those impediments affecting the efficient functioning of the social partners in areas such as collective bargaining, social dialogue and conflict resolution. The Government and relevant public organisations must also reaffirm their commitment to reducing the informal labour market and promoting the protection of flexible work. This will require improved training and an increase in the number of inspectors available.

To bring about greater consensual adaptation to change, social partnership needs to improve. In this respect the strategy of the win-win situation, as discussed in Chapter 4, is important. To implement such a strategy the social partners must reconsider their attitude to the issues discussed in this book. It is important to find the right mix between economic and social concerns as there is no 'one size fits all' model.

A final recommendation concerns social security. The social security system must encourage the taking on of work within the formal labour market while also protecting flexible workers. This will require a major reorganisation of the system, involving creativity on the part of all the relevant stakeholders.

8.4 FINAL CONCLUSIONS

Our analysis has identified major problems in the current situation, problems which must be addressed. We have developed a number of key recommendations in response. However, it is important to recognise that reformation of the labour market is an ongoing process. While compliance with the EU *acquis* is providing an important stimulus to reform, the Turkish Government must also continue to modernise the labour market by tackling objectives such as increasing employment, fighting social exclusion, improving equality and creating a better division of wealth. This will bring the Turkish situation in line with EU Member States and will create a rationale for change acceptable to all the key stakeholders.

BIBLIOGRAPHY

Abraham 1990

Abraham K.G., 'Introduction', in: K.G. Abraham and R.B. McKersie (eds), *New Developments in the Labor Market: Toward a New Institutional Paradigm*, MIT Press, Cambridge, 1990.

Alpagut 2004

Alpagut G., 'Belirli Süreli İş Sözleşmesi', *Mercek*, Ocak 2004.

Anxo and O'Reilly 2000

Anxo D., and J. O'Reilly, 'Working-Time Regimes and Transitions in Comparative Perspective', in: J. O'Reilly, I. Cebrián and M. Lallement, *Working-Time Changes*, Edward Elgar, Cheltenham, UK, 2000.

Arbeidsinspectie 1999

Arbeidsinspectie, *Voorjaarsrapportage CAO-afspraken 1999*, Ministry of Social Affairs and Employment/Labour Inspectorate, The Hague, 1999.

Autor 2000

Autor D.H., 'Outsourcing at Will: Unjust Dismissal Doctrine and the Growth of Temporary Help Employment', Working paper no. 7557. National Bureau of Economic Research, Cambridge, Mass, 2000.

Barker and Christensen 1998

Barker K. and K. Christensen (eds.), *Contingent Work: American Employment Relations in Transition*, Ithaca, Cornell University Press, New York, 1998.

Barnard 2000

Barnard C., *EC Employment Law*, Oxford, 2000.

Benner 2002

Benner C., *Work in the New Economy: Flexible Labor Markets in Silicon Valley*. Blackwell Publishers Ltd, Oxford, 2002.

Blank and Freeman 1994

Blank R.M. and R.B. Freeman, 'Evaluating the Connection Between Social Protection and Economic Flexibility', in: R. M. Blank (ed.), *Social*

Protection versus Economic Flexibility: Is There a Trade-off? University of Chicago Press, Chicago and London, 1994.

Block 1992

Block R.N., 'The Legal and Institutional Framework for Employment Security in the United States: an Overview', in: K. Koshiro (ed.), *Employment Security and Labor Market Flexibility: An International Perspective*. Wayne State University Press, Detroit, 1992.

Bridges 1994

Bridges W., *Job Shift: How to Prosper in a Workplace without Jobs*, Addison-Wesley Publishing Company, Reading, Mass.,1994.

Çelik 2004

Çelik N., *İş Hukuku Dersleri*, revised 16th edition, Beta, 2004.

Clauwaert 1999

Clauwaert S. (ed.), *ETUI Legal Survey on Temporary Agency Work*, 4 October 1999, Brussels.

Commission on the Future of Worker-Management Relations (Dunlop Commission) 1994

Commission on the Future of Worker-Management Relations (Dunlop Commission). *Fact Finding Report*, Department of Labor and Department of Commerce, Washington, D.C., 1994.

Dereli 2005

Dereli T., 'Turkey', *International Encyclopaedia of Labour Law*, Kluwer Law International, The Hague, 2005.

Duran and Sugur 2005

Duran B. and S. Sugur, 'Islamism, Trade Unionism and Civil Society: The Case of Hak-Iş Labour Confederation in Turkey', *Middle Eastern Studies*, Vol. 41 (2005).

Estevao and Lach 1999

Estevao M.M. and S. Lach. *The Evolution of the Demand for Temporary Help Supply Employment in the United States*, NBER, New York, 1999.

Eurofoundation 2004

Eurofoundation. *Part-Time Work in Europe*, European Foundation for the Improvement of Living and Working Conditions, Dublin, 2004.

European Commission

European Commission, *Report of the European Commission's Services on the Implementation of Council Directive 97/81/EC of 17 December 1997 concerning the Framework Agreement on Part-Time Work Concluded by UNICE, CEEP and the ETUC*, Brussels.

European Commission
European Commission, *Report on the Implementation of Directive 91/383/EEC Supplementing the Measures to Encourage Improvements in the Safety and Health at Work of Workers with a Fixed-Duration Employment Relationship or a Temporary Employment Relationship*, Brussels, *s.d.*, 34 p.

European Commission
European Commission, *State of Implementation of Council Directive 93/104/EC of 23 November 1993, concerning Certain Aspects of the Organisation of Working Time*, Brussels, 1 COM (2000) 787 final, December 2000.

Farber 1995
Farber H.S., 'Are Lifetime Jobs Disappearing? Job Duration in the United States: 1973–1993', Working paper no. 5014. National Bureau of Economic Research, Cambridge, Mass., 1995.

Farber 1997
Farber H.S., 'Trends in Long-Term Employment in the United States', *1979–96*, Working paper no. 384. Princeton University, Princeton, N.J., 1997.

Foden 1999
Foden D., 'The Role of the Social Partners in the European Employment Strategy, *Transfer* 5(4) (1999).

Fouarge 1998
Fouarge D., *Minimum Protection and Poverty in Europe*, Thela Thesis, Amsterdam, 2002.

Freeman 1998
Freeman R.B., 'War of the Models: Which Labour Market Institutions for the 21st Century?', *Labour Economics* 5(1) (1998).

Freemand and Rogers 1992
Freeman R.B. and J. Rogers, W*hat Workers Want*, Cornell University Press, Ithaca, NY 1999.

Golden and Appelbaum 1992
Golden L. and E. Appelbaum, 'What Was Driving the 1982-88 Boom in Temporary Employment?', *American Journal of Economics and Sociology 51*(4), (1992).

Gould 1993

Gould W.B., *A Primer on American Labor Law*, MIT Press, Cambridge, Mass./London, 1993.

High Level Group 2004

High Level Group, *Facing the Challenge: The Lisbon Strategy for Growth and Employment*, Luxembourg, Office for Official Publications of the European Communities. Brussels, 2004.

Houseman, Kalleberg and Erickcek 2001

Houseman S.N., A.L. Kalleberg, and G.A. Erickcek, 'The Role of Temporary Help Employment in Tight Labor Markets', Working paper no. 01-73. W.E. Upjohn Institute for Employment Research, Kalamazoo, Mich., 2001.

Jacobs 1999

Jacobs A., 'The Netherlands', in: R. Blanpain and M. Biagi, (eds.), *Private Employment Agencies: The Impact of ILO Convention 181*, Kluwer Law International, The Hague etc., 1999.

Jacobs and Plessen 1992

Jacobs A.T.J.M. and W. Plessen, 'Deregulering in het arbeidsrecht', *SEW* 40(2) (1992).

Jacoby 1982

Jacoby S., 'The Duration of Indefinite Employment Contracts in the United States and England: A Historical Analysis', *Comparative Labor Law* 5(1) (1982).

Kalleberg 1997

Kalleberg A., *Non-Standard Work, Substandard Jobs: Flexible Arrangements in the US*, Economic Policy Institute, Washington, D.C. 1997.

Katz and Ziderman 1990

Katz E. and A. Ziderman, 'Investment in General Training: the Role of Information and Labour Mobility', *The Economic Journal* 100 (December 1990).

Katz and Krueger 1999

Katz L.F. and A.B. Krueger, 'The High-Pressure U.S. Labor Market of the 1990s', Working paper no. 416. Princeton University, Industrial Relations Section, Princeton, N.J., 1999.

Klaver, de, Klein Hesselink, Miedema and Schlangen

de Klaver P.M., D.J. Klein Hesselink, E.P. Miedema and C. Schlangen, *Ervaringen met en effecten van de Wet flexibiliteit en zekerheid: tweede meting 2000*, Ministry of Social Affairs and Employment, The Hague, 2000.

Korver 2001
Korver A., *Rekindling Adaptability*, EFSQ, Amsterdam, 2001.

Krueger 1991
Krueger A.B., 'The Evolution of Unjust-Dismissal Legislation in the United States', *Industrial and Labor Relations Review* 44(4) (1991).

Lee 1996
Lee D.R., 'Why Is Flexible Employment Increasing?', *Journal of Labor Research* 17(4) (1996).

Lenz 2000
Lenz E.A., *The Staffing Services Industry: Myth and Reality*, American Staffing Association, Alexandria, Virg., 2000.

Léonard 2001
Léonard E., 'Industrial Relations and the Regulation of Employment in Europe', *European Journal of Industrial Relations* 7(1) (2001).

Levine 1998
Levine D.I., *Working in the Twenty-First Century: Policies for Economic Growth through Training, Opportunity, and Education*, M.E. Sharpe, Armonk, N.Y., 1998.

Lips 1998
Lips B., 'Temps and the Labor Market: Why Unions Fear Staffing Companies', *Regulation Spring* (1998).

Madsen 2004
Madsen P.K, 'The Danish Model of 'Flexicurity': Experiences and Lessons', *Transfer* 10(2) (2004).

Ministerie van Sociale Zaken en Werkgelegenheid 1995
Ministerie van Sociale Zaken en Werkgelegenheid, *Flexibiliteit en zekerheid*, Sdu, the Hague, 1995.

Ministerie van Sociale Zaken en Werkgelegenheid 1997
Ministerie van Sociale Zaken en Werkgelegenheid. *Part-Time Work in the Netherlands*, The Hague, 1997.

Muhl 2001
Muhl C. J., 'The Employment-at-Will Doctrine: Three Major Exceptions', *Monthly Labor Review* 124(1) (2001).

Murray 1999

Murray J., 'Social Justice for Women? The ILO's Convention on Part-Time Work', *CELRL* Working Paper No. 15, 1999.

Murray 1999

Murray J., 'Normalising Temporary Work. The Proposed Directive on Fixed-Term Work', *ILJ* (1999).

NEI 2001

NEI, *Instroom uitzendkrachten 2000*, Rotterdam, 2001

Neumark 2000

Neumark D., 'Changes in Job Stability and Job Security: a Collective Effort to Untangle, Reconcile and Interpret the Evidence', Working paper 7472. National Bureau of Economic Research, Cambridge, Mass., 2000.

OECD 2004

OECD, *OECD Economic Surveys: Turkey*, Paris, 2004.

Ozaki 1999

Ozaki M. (ed.), *Negotiating Flexibility: the Role of Social Partners and the State*, International Labour Office, Geneva, 1999.

Plessen 2002

Plessen W.G.M., 'Drie jaar Flex en zeker, goede regulering of goede economie?', *Sociaal Maandblad Arbeid* (5) (2002).

Polivka 1996

Polivka A.E., 'Are Temporary Help Agency Workers Substitutes for Direct Hire Temps? Searching for an Alternative Explanation of Growth in the Temporary Help Industry', paper presented at the Society of Labor Economists Conference, Chicago, May 3–4, 1996.

Rifkin 1996

Rifkin J., *The End of Work: the Decline of the Global Labor Force and the Dawn of the Post-Market Era*, G.P. Putnam's Sons, New York, 1996.

Schmid 2002

Schmid G., 'Transitional Labour Markets and the European Social Model: towards a New Employment Compact', in: G. Schmid and B. Gazier. Cheltenham, *The Dynamics of Full Employment: Social Integration through Transitional Labour Markets*, Edward Elgar, Cheltenham, 2002.

Sciarra, Davies and Freedland

Sciarra S., P.L. Davies and M. R. Freedland. *Employment Policy and the Regulation of Part-Time work in the European Union: a Comparative Analysis*, Cambridge University Press, New York, 2004.

SCP 2000

De kunst van het combineren, SCP, The Hague, 2000.

Sisson and Marginson

Sisson K. and P. Marginson, 'Coordinated Bargaining: a Process for our Times?', *British Journal of Industrial Relations* 40(2) (2002).

Storrie 2002

Storrie D., *Temporary Agency Work in the European Union*, European Foundation for the Improvement of Living and Working Conditions, Dublin, 2002.

Streeck 1988

Streeck W., 'Comment on "Rigidities in the Labour Market"', *Government and Opposition* 23(4) (1988).

Süral 2005a

Süral A.N., 'Employment Termination and Job Security under New Turkish Labour Act', *Middle Eastern Studies*, Vol. 41 (2005).

Süral 2005b

Süral A.N., 'Reorganisation of Working Time and Modalities of Employment under the New Turkish Labour Act', *Middle Eastern Studies*, Vol. 41 (2005).

Tangian 2004

Tangian A.S., *Defining the Flexicurity Index in Application to European Countries*, Düsseldorf, WSI/Hans Böckler Stiftung, 2004.

Valdés Dal-Ré 2004

Valdés Dal-Ré F., 'The Difficulty of Reconciling Flexibility and Security in Spain: the Paradigmatic Case of Part-Time Work', *Transfer* 10(2) (2004).

Van den Toren, Evers and. Commissaris 2002

Van den Toren J.P., G.H.M. Evers and E. J. Commissaris, *Flexibiliteit en zekerheid: effecten en doeltreffendheid van de Wet flexibiliteit en zekerheid -eindrapport*, Ministerie van Sociale Zaken en Werkgelegenheid, Den Haag, 2002.

Van der Heijden, 1998

Van der Heijden P.F., 'The Flexibilisation of Working Life in the Netherlands', in: *Contribution to the 15th International Congress of Comparative Law*, Bristol, United Kingdom. 26 July–1 August, 1998.

Verhulp 1998

Verhulp E., 'De uitzendkracht in het Flex(s)t(r)ijdperk', *Sociaal Recht* 13(11) (1998).

Visser 2002

Visser J., 'The First Part-Time Economy in the World: a Model to be Followed?', *Journal of European Social Policy* 12(1) (2002).

Visser and Van Rij 1999

Visser J. and C. van Rij, *Vakbeweging en Flexibiliteit*, Welboom, Amsterdam, 1999.

Visser, Wilthagen, Beltzer and Koot-van der Putte 2004

Visser J., T. Wilthagen, R. Beltzer and E. Koot-van der Putte, 'The Netherlands: from Atypicality to Typicality', in: S. Sciarra, P. Davies, and M. Freedland. Cambridge University Press, Cambridge, 2004.

Wilthagen 1998

Wilthagen T., 'Flexicurity: A New Paradigm for Labour Market Policy Reform?' Discussion paper FS I 98-202, Social Science Research Center, Berlin, 1998.

Wilthagen 2002

Wilthagen T., 'The Flexibility-Security Nexus: New Approaches to Regulating Employment and Labour Markets', in: *British Journal of Industrial Relations Conference "The Politics of Employment Relations"*, Windsor, UK 2002.

Wilthagen and Tros 2004

Wilthagen T. and F. Tros, 'The Concept of "Flexicurity": a New Approach to Regulating Employment and Labour Markets', *Transfer* 10(2), (2004).

Wilthagen and Rogowski 2002

Wilthagen T. and R. Rogowski, 'Legal Regulation of Transitional Labour Markets', in: G. Schmid and B. Gazier, *The Dynamics of Full Employment: Social Integration through Transitional Labour Markets*, Cheltenham and Northampton, 2002.

INDEX